W9-BIO-040

Tommy guns at the ready, British Commandos take cover on a hill of rubble, the result of RAF bombing, after leading the way into the German city of Wesel in March 1945.

THE COMMANDOS

Other Publications:

PLANET EARTH
COLLECTOR'S LIBRARY OF THE CIVIL WAR
LIBRARY OF HEALTH
CLASSICS OF THE OLD WEST
THE EPIC OF FLIGHT
THE GOOD COOK
THE SEAFARERS
THE ENCYCLOPEDIA OF COLLECTIBLES
THE GREAT CITIES
HOME REPAIR AND IMPROVEMENT
THE WORLD'S WILD PLACES
THE TIME-LIFE LIBRARY OF BOATING
HUMAN BEHAVIOR
THE ART OF SEWING
THE OLD WEST
THE EMERGENCE OF MAN
THE AMERICAN WILDERNESS
THE TIME-LIFE ENCYCLOPEDIA OF GARDENING
LIFE LIBRARY OF PHOTOGRAPHY
THIS FABULOUS CENTURY
FOODS OF THE WORLD
TIME-LIFE LIBRARY OF AMERICA
TIME-LIFE LIBRARY OF ART
GREAT AGES OF MAN
LIFE SCIENCE LIBRARY
THE LIFE HISTORY OF THE UNITED STATES
TIME READING PROGRAM
LIFE NATURE LIBRARY
LIFE WORLD LIBRARY
FAMILY LIBRARY:
  HOW THINGS WORK IN YOUR HOME
  THE TIME-LIFE BOOK OF THE FAMILY CAR
  THE TIME-LIFE FAMILY LEGAL GUIDE
  THE TIME-LIFE BOOK OF FAMILY FINANCE

This volume is one of a series that chronicles in full the events of the Second World War. Previous books in the series include:

Prelude to War
Blitzkrieg
The Battle of Britain
The Rising Sun
The Battle of the Atlantic
Russia Besieged
The War in the Desert
The Home Front: U.S.A.
China-Burma-India
Island Fighting
The Italian Campaign
Partisans and Guerrillas
The Second Front
Liberation
Return to the Philippines
The Air War in Europe
The Resistance
The Battle of the Bulge
The Road to Tokyo
Red Army Resurgent
The Nazis
Across the Rhine
War under the Pacific
War in the Outposts
The Soviet Juggernaut
Japan at War
The Mediterranean
Battles for Scandinavia
The Secret War
Prisoners of War

WORLD WAR II · TIME-LIFE BOOKS · ALEXANDRIA, VIRGINIA

BY RUSSELL MILLER

AND THE EDITORS OF TIME-LIFE BOOKS

THE COMMANDOS

WORLD WAR II

Editor: Thomas H. Flaherty Jr.
Editorial Staff for *The Commandos*
Senior Editors: Anne Horan, Henry Woodhead
Designer: Herbert H. Quarmby
Chief Researcher: Philip Brandt George
Picture Editor: Clara Nicolai
Text Editor: Richard Murphy
Writers: Patricia C. Bangs, Donald Davison Cantlay, Richard D. Kovar, Brooke Stoddard
Researchers: Harris J. Andrews III, Loretta Y. Britten, Reginald H. Dickerson, Margaret Gray, Molly McGhee, Alfreda Robertson, Jayne T. Wise
Copy Coordinators: Ann Bartunek, Allan Fallow, Elizabeth Graham, Barbara F. Quarmby
Art Assistant: Mikio Togashi
Picture Coordinator: Betty Hughes Weatherley
Editorial Assistant: Constance Strawbridge

Special Contributor
Virginia Baker (translations)

Editorial Operations
Design: Arnold C. Holeywell (assistant director); Anne B. Landry (art coordinator); James J. Cox (quality control)
Research: Jane Edwin (assistant director), Louise D. Forstall
Copy Room: Susan Galloway Goldberg (director), Celia Beattie
Production: Feliciano Madrid (director), Gordon E. Buck, Peter Inchautequiz

Correspondents: Elisabeth Kraemer (Bonn); Margot Hapgood, Dorothy Bacon (London); Susan Jonas, Lucy T. Voulgaris (New York); Maria Vincenza Aloisi, Josephine du Brusle (Paris); Ann Natanson (Rome). Valuable assistance was also provided by: Janny Hovinga, Wibo van de Linde (Amsterdam); Bob Gilmore (Auckland); Helga Kohl (Bonn); Brigid Grauman (Brussels); Bing Wong (Hong Kong); Caroline Alcock, Pippa Pridham (London); John Dunn, Ernie Shirley (Melbourne); Christina Lieberman, Cornelis Verwaal (New York); Dag Christensen (Oslo); John Scott, Peter Ward (Ottawa); M. T. Hirschkoff (Paris); Eva Stichova (Prague); Bianca Gabbrielli, Mimi Murphy, Ann Wise (Rome); S. Chang (Tokyo); Traudl Lessing, Annelise Shulz (Vienna).

The Author: RUSSELL MILLER is a British journalist and freelance writer who contributes regularly to *The Sunday Times* of London. A former British Army officer, he is the author of another book in the Time-Life Books World War II series, *The Resistance,* and of *The East Indiamen* in The Seafarers series.

The Consultants: COLONEL JOHN R. ELTING, USA (Ret.), has written a number of military histories, among them *The Battle of Bunker's Hill, The Battles of Saratoga, Military History and Atlas of the Napoleonic Wars,* and—for the Time-Life Books World War II series—*Battles for Scandinavia.* He taught at the United States Military Academy at West Point and served there as associate editor of *The West Point Atlas of American Wars.*

BRIGADIER PETER YOUNG is a British military historian who commanded the British Army's No. 3 Commando and later the 1st Commando Brigade during World War II. He saw action in some of the major Commando operations of the War, including the raids on Guernsey in 1940, Lofoten and Vagsoy in 1941, Dieppe in 1942, the landings in Sicily and Italy in 1943, Normandy in 1944, and the Arakan in 1944 and 1945, and was awarded the Distinguished Service Order and the Military Cross. He is the author of *Bedouin Command, Commando* and *Storm from the Sea* as well as many other books about Commandos.

Library of Congress Cataloguing in Publication Data

Miller, Russell.
The commandos.

(World War II; v. 31)
Bibliography: p.
Includes index.
1. World War, 1939-1945—Commando operations.
I. Time-Life Books. II. Title. III. Series.
D794.5.M54 940.54'12'41 81-13600
ISBN 0-8094-3401-6
ISBN 0-8094-3400-8 (lib. bdg.)
ISBN 0-8094-3399-0 (retail ed.)

For information about any Time-Life book, please write:

Reader Information
Time-Life Books
541 North Fairbanks Court
Chicago, Illinois 60611

Second printing. Revised 1983. Printed in U.S.A.
Published simultaneously in Canada.
School and library distribution by Silver Burdett Company, Morristown, New Jersey.

CHAPTERS

PICTURE ESSAYS

THE STORMING OF EBEN EMAEL

Heading for Fort Eben Emael, the stronghold guarding the eastern frontier of Belgium, German sappers paddle across the Albert Canal in May of 1940.

A BELGIAN FORTRESS OVERCOME BY STEALTH

In 1940, when Adolf Hitler's war machine menaced France and England, both nations hoped that Belgium's Fort Eben Emael—a formidable redoubt on a promontory above the Albert Canal, 15 miles west of the German border—would check a German thrust to the southwest. The fort bristled with two 120mm and sixteen 75mm guns housed in steel-reinforced concrete bunkers, built to withstand the most powerful artillery. Aboveground, the wedge-shaped fort was protected on one side by a rocky cliff that dropped 130 feet straight down to the canal. The other two sides were fringed with minefields, machine guns, barbed-wire entanglements and a moat. Below ground were five miles of tunnels that linked one gun to another and gave cover to the fort's 780 defenders. By the standards of conventional warfare, Eben Emael seemed impregnable.

But before dawn on May 10, 1940, nine gliders swooped over the fort's outer defenses and landed on its grassy roof. The Belgians stared in disbelief as 70 German troopers disembarked and, in 20 minutes, captured 14 of the fort's 18 guns. At the same time other glider groups landed near three bridges that Eben Emael's guns defended, seizing two of the bridges intact. The Belgians at the fort fled below ground to try to defend themselves from within. Only there, and at one bridge, did the Germans meet protracted resistance.

When Fort Eben Emael fell, the main invasion route across Belgium to France lay unobstructed, and the Wehrmacht traveled that way to complete its conquest within the month. For the Allies as well as the Axis, the raid had another significance: It showed that, with special training, stealth and surprise, a diminutive force could overcome one far larger—and pave the way for a major military undertaking. The term "commando" had not yet entered the lexicon of World War II, but the German raiders foreshadowed the techniques in which commandos would specialize, operating both independently and within major campaigns. How the German raiders accomplished their exploit is shown on the following pages in on-the-scene pictures and in clips from a subsequent German film re-creating the raid.

Atop limestone cliffs, Fort Eben Emael overlooks the Albert Canal. The trails connect gun emplacements, which were also linked underground.

Preceded by a flamethrower, German raiders approach a concrete bunker at Fort Eben Emael. Gliders deposited the men within 20 yards of their targets.

Training for the assault on Eben Emael, attack gliders and a tow plane soar over German farmland. Once in sight of their targets, the gliders were released.

REALISTIC TRAINING ON MOCK TARGETS

One key to the success of the German coup at Fort Eben Emael was the prolonged and rigorous training that preceded the raid. The troops were recruited in November 1939 from among elite parachutists, skilled sappers (demolition specialists) and champion glider sportsmen. For six months they received extraordinarily realistic training.

The raiders practiced on a mock fort that exactly matched the specifications of the real Eban Emael. By lucky coincidence, German subcontractors had been imported to Belgium between 1932 and 1935 to build the fort and had taken its plans home to Germany with them. Moreover, unlike most soldiers of the day, the men training for Eben Emael used real gun emplacements—those along the silenced border of Czechoslovakia.

The training combined attention to detail with calculated flexibility. The men were divided into squads, each with an assigned target. But they also studied targets not their own so that they could back up one another in an emergency. Even the glider pilots learned to fight; once they had landed, they were expected to join their passengers in the assault.

A German soldier makes ready to leap from his glider during a simulation of the planned attack.

An assault team charges past a barbed-wire entanglement. Drill reduced to seconds the time that men needed to spring out of the gliders and into action.

Destroyed by its Belgian defenders, the bridge that crossed to the fort from the village of Kanne slumps into the Albert Canal.

Bypassing the blown-up bridge, German troops lug a rubber boat through Kanne to the Albert Canal. The villagers were so stunned they put up little resistance.

A CANAL CROSSING UNDER FIRE

Against the possibility of a conventional overland approach, the Belgians had laid charges to blow up the three Albert Canal bridges covered by the fort's guns. At two of the bridges the German glidermen took advantage of the shock produced by their unorthodox mode of arrival; they quickly defused the explosives and captured the bridges intact.

However, the third bridge—at Kanne, about a mile northwest of the fort—was set in rough terrain, so the gliders were forced to land some distance from their objective. In the time the Germans spent reaching the bridge, its Belgian defenders ignited a fuse hidden in a nearby road marker and blew up the bridge. When the Germans tried to cross the canal—some working their way single file across the collapsed superstructure of the bridge—a seven-man squad in a bunker at the bridge and other Belgians along the banks of the canal turned their guns on the raiders. The Germans struggled for 10 hours before they were able to overcome the Belgian resistance, seize the bunker and secure the village of Kanne, which lay astride the canal. Now only the fort—already crippled—remained to be cleared.

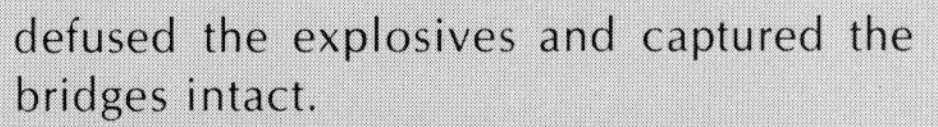

Stroking through the smoke of Belgian artillery, German troops negotiate the Albert Canal by dinghy.

Their mission accomplished, two German attack gliders rest on the grassy roof of Fort Eben Emael. Barbed wire had been wrapped around the gliders' skids to bring them to a quick stop on landing.

Carrying an explosive on a long pole, a German sapper (top) sneaks across a Belgian bunker at the western approach to Fort Eban Emael. At bottom, the charge explodes after being lowered into a gun embrasure.

In this German re-creation of the assault, a white smoke screen rises above the cliff as reinforcing German troops approach the northern tip of the fort by dinghy.

BEATING BACK A COUNTERATTACK

As the first day of fighting wore on at Fort Eben Emael, the Belgians recovered sufficiently from their surprise to threaten a breakout from the underground passageways into which they had withdrawn, and to challenge the German raiders who occupied the surface of the fort.

But the Germans beat back the Belgian counterattack, and—joined by reinforcements of 50 men early the next morning—terrorized the Belgians by dropping explosives at random down the steep stairways that led from the guns on top to the tunnels below. They also made forays into some of the tunnels, firing deafening, demoralizing volleys down the long passageways.

The Belgians were subdued by the raiders everywhere in the fort except at one western gun emplacement, which overlooked the blown-up bridge from Kanne. The raiders assailed this final bunker with a flamethrower and exploded a charge against the embrasure. That silenced both the gun and its defenders, opening the way for the Germans to enter the interior of Fort Eben Emael unopposed.

Carrying the white flag of surrender, a Belgian soldier emerges from the fort on May 11, 1940.

TAKING OVER A BATTERED PRIZE

By midmorning on the second day of the assault, nearly a full battalion of Germans ranged practically at will over the grounds and around the walls of Fort Eben Emael. The darkened tunnels under the fort were strewn with dead and wounded. The survivors were so demoralized that many were clamoring for an end to the struggle; even when the commander agreed to surrender, he could not round up all his men. One Belgian officer was discovered ignominiously hiding under a bed.

Shortly after noon on the second day, the Belgians surrendered. The only task that remained for the Germans was to search the fort and tally the haul, which included the 18 big guns. Afterward, the attackers collected their gear and headed for a local inn to relax before boarding trucks to return to Germany.

German soldiers survey the grounds near a blasted gun emplacement. After the battle, the Germans turned the fort into a machine shop and a barracks.

Fresh German troops stand about indifferently as wounded Belgians lie on the grass awaiting medical attention. The defenders lost 25 dead, 59 wounded.

Tired and dirty but flushed with success, the Germans enjoy a breather back at their barracks in Germany. Regular troops had replaced them to hold the fort.

Adolf Hitler stands with the officers who led the raid on Eben Emael after personally awarding each of them the Knight's Cross, Germany's highest combat decoration. At a separate ceremony, enlisted men were given the Iron Cross. In addition to receiving medals, all officers and men were promoted one grade in rank. Within weeks of the exploit, the unit that had trained so long for the brief assault was disbanded and its members were scattered throughout the Wehrmacht.

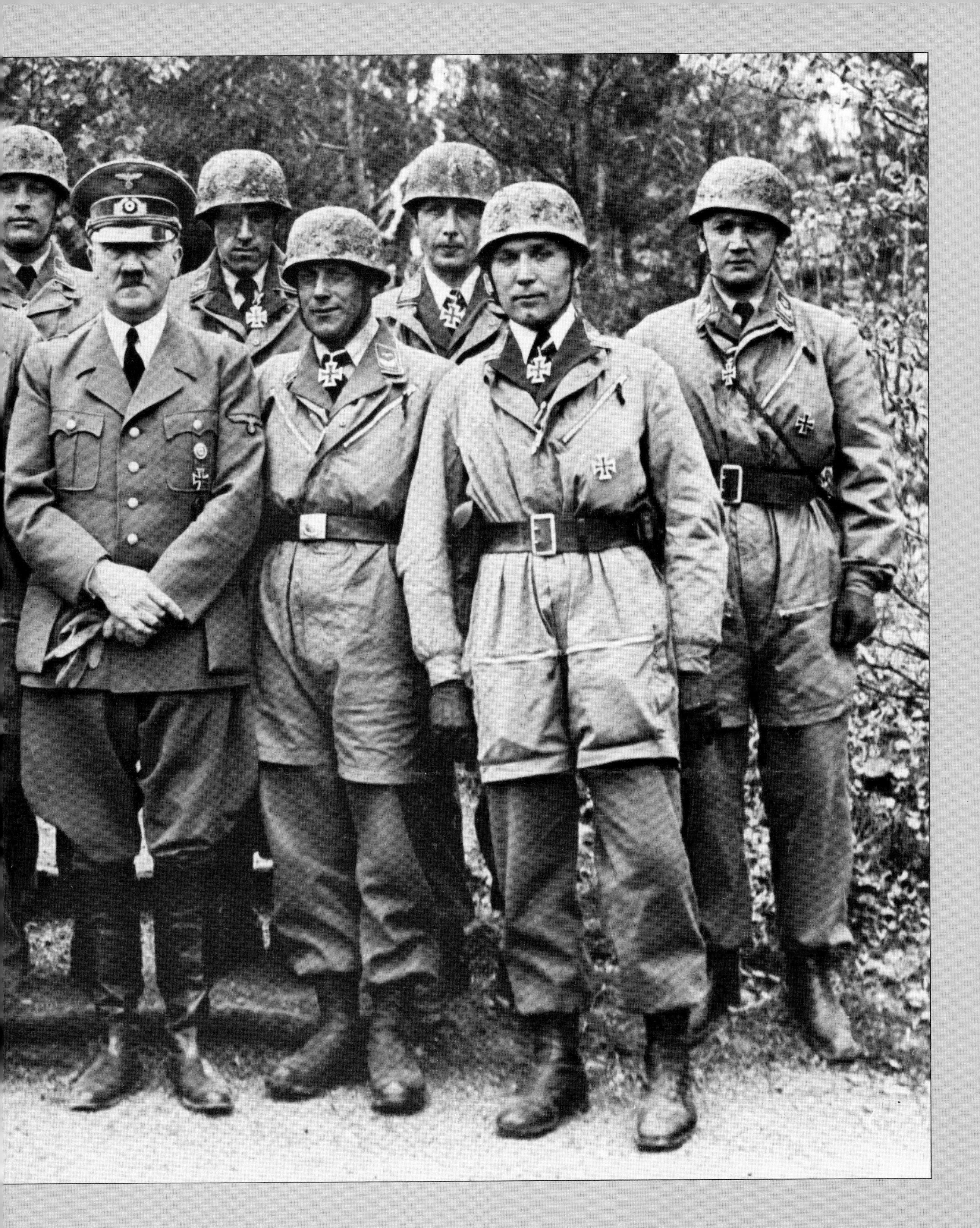

1

Responding to a call for a "reign of terror"
Volunteers aplenty for perilous duty
Early blunders on the French coast
A demoralizing lull for men of action
Easy triumph in the Lofotens
A dashing new leader for the Commandos
The raiders' "good, clean battle" at Vagsoy
The birth of the U.S. Rangers
The high price of success at Saint-Nazaire

A NEW BREED OF SOLDIER

On the afternoon of Tuesday, June 4, 1940, Prime Minister Winston Churchill announced to a hushed House of Commons that the remnants of the British Army had been withdrawn from the beaches of Dunkirk "out of the jaws of death and shame." After retreating to the French port on the English Channel, the British forces had narrowly escaped annihilation at the hands of the victorious German Wehrmacht, which was concluding its devastating blitzkrieg of Western Europe. Now France was crushed, and Great Britain stood alone against the formidable German armies. The future was grim.

That evening, as Lieut. Colonel Dudley Clarke, a staff officer at the War Office in Whitehall, walked slowly home through the gathering dusk, he wondered—as people everywhere were wondering that night—what lay in store for Britain. Clarke was an officer with some 20 years' service and a deep interest in military history. And as he strolled, he tried to analyze what other nations had done in the past when their armies were driven from the field.

In the Peninsular War of 1808-1814, he remembered, Spaniards responded to the French aggressors by staging hit-and-run raids behind enemy lines with small bands of lightly armed irregular soldiers referred to as guerrillas. Ninety years later, when Britain invaded the Transvaal in South Africa, marauding bands of the Dutch settlers called Boers fought back with similar raids. In British-occupied Palestine in 1936, Clarke himself had witnessed how a handful of ill-armed Arabs, attacking by surprise and maneuvering superbly, had tied down more than an entire corps of regular British Army troops.

Surely, Clarke thought, Britain might learn from the tactics of Spaniard, Boer and Arab. Before he went to bed that night, he sat down at a desk in his study with a sheet of paper before him. In neat script, he outlined a plan for a new kind of British force cast in the mold of history's guerrilla movements. For want of a better name, he used the one adopted by the Boers. They had called their troops "commandos," from an Afrikaans word meaning military units.

At the War Office next day, Clarke's superior—Sir John Dill, chief of the Imperial General Staff—spoke of the urgency of rekindling the Army's offensive spirit. Clarke produced his one-page outline, and Dill took to the idea as soon as he read it. He promptly passed Clarke's outline on to the Prime Minister. Churchill had been thinking along the same lines; he liked Clarke's idea so well that one day later the War Cabinet received a memorandum from him. "Enterprises must be prepared with specially trained troops of the hunter class who can develop a reign of terror down the enemy coast," Churchill wrote. "I look to the Joint Chiefs of Staff to propose measures for a ceaseless offensive against the whole German-occupied coastline, leaving a trail of German corpses behind."

Shortly before lunch that day, Sir John Dill asked Clarke to come into his office and told him: "Your commando scheme is approved, and I want you to get it going at once. Try to get a raid across the Channel mounted at the earliest possible moment."

Thus was born a breed of fighting men that combined the tactics, independence and resourcefulness of the guerrilla with the training and discipline of the professional soldier. The mixture was destined to produce a military elite: the commandos. Their first task was to steal from the sea to strike, swift and hard, at the bastions of Hitler's Fortress Europe. In "butcher-and-bolt" raids along the entire coast of occupied Europe, they killed, captured and destroyed. Gradually, as they acquired special skills that enabled them to graduate from mere hit-and-run raids on coastal outposts, the commandos branched out to extensive operations deep behind enemy lines. In the sand wastes of the North African desert, commando-like units adapted centuries-old Arab survival tactics and dwelt for weeks at a time in the heart of German-held territory. Elsewhere, waterborne commandos mastered the tricks of rough-water canoeing to penetrate alien waterways and sabotage Axis shipping.

Although neither Clarke nor anyone else in England knew it at the time he conceived the idea for the British Commandos, the Germans had independently developed much the same sort of group for a raid on the Belgian fort of Eben Emael *(pages 6-19)*. The Germans disbanded that group when its mission was completed, but later, on the Eastern Front, they would create a more permanent force, called the Brandenburgers after the town in which they trained. Speaking fluent Russian and wearing Red Army uniforms, the Brandenburgers operated entirely behind Soviet lines to frustrate and confound their enemy.

In the West, the example of the British Commandos spawned a host of similar outfits with names of their own, the U.S. Rangers and the Australian Independent Companies among them. And as the momentum of the War gradually shifted in the Allies' favor, the role that these groups played was further expanded to suit Allied strategy. They were called upon to organize and train burgeoning civilian resistance groups in Europe, and later to work with conventional troops in staging major offensives—with the commando groups always in the vanguard of the assault.

No matter what their nationality or allegiance, units of commando-style troops the world over were employed for the most hazardous of the War's tasks. Almost always their members were volunteers. They were romantic, independent, often fanatical, sometimes eccentric, occasionally suicidal. They all knew beforehand that their capture might mean death by firing squad. Facing that ultimate possibility required two exceptional characteristics: outstanding courage and an unquenchable lust for war.

Dudley Clarke took seriously his order to "get going"; the first British Commando raid was launched in scarcely three weeks. On the night of June 24, four Royal Air Force air-sea rescue boats throbbed across the English Channel toward the coast of France. On board were 115 hastily chosen volunteer soldiers, all of them busily blacking their faces for camouflage. They used make-up that had been supplied by a London theatrical costumier; they found this amusing, and as they applied the blacking they cracked minstrel jokes. Their plan was to land at four points along the French coast south of Boulogne to test the German defenses and take some prisoners.

The timing was propitious. The armistice between Germany and defeated France was due to take effect the following morning. A Commando strike would show the Germans that, notwithstanding the fall of France, Great Britain intended to fight on.

But as a prelude to the offensive demanded by the Prime Minister, the raid was hardly promising. One landing party splashed ashore, blundered around a desolate area of sand dunes in the dark for a while, discovered nothing, encountered no one and duly reembarked. Another boat found that a German seaplane anchorage was straddling its intended landing site, and none of the soldiers on board managed to make it to shore. A third group landed near the town of Le Touquet, surprised two German sentries and killed both of them. But not one of the fledgling Commandos thought to search the bodies, as they had been trained to do, for documents that might have yielded valuable military information. They did not even bother to find out what the sentries were guarding.

The fourth boat, with Clarke on board as an observer, had a faulty compass and very nearly steered straight into German hands. "Suddenly, without the slightest warning," Clarke later wrote, "a searchlight flashed out in the darkness right ahead." They had almost blundered into Boulogne harbor. Hastily they turned back out to sea and resumed the search for their landing site.

When at last they located the right beach, the Commandos slipped over the side and waded ashore. They found nothing but sand dunes. Then, just as they were preparing to reembark, a German patrol appeared on bicycles at the far end of the beach. Major Ronnie Tod was carrying one of the 20 Tommy guns the Commandos had been issued for the raid. Unfortunately, he had a defective weapon: As he cocked it, the magazine fell off and clattered onto the stony beach. The Germans immediately opened fire. "It is doubtful if they had much to aim at in the darkness," Clarke reported, "but they must have directed it all at the shadow of the boat, for the bullets started to fly around us. Suddenly something caught me a violent blow on the side of the head and sent me headlong to the deck. A moment or two must have passed before I struggled to my feet again, for by then someone was shouting that the Germans were making off."

Clarke had been nicked by a stray bullet that almost severed his ear. No one else was hit, and all of the Commandos got safely back into the boat before German reinforcements arrived on the scene.

The four air-sea rescue boats straggled back across the Channel independently. One of them was refused entry to Folkestone harbor until the identity of its occupants could be established. While the men drifted off the harbor boom, they drank the rum that such boats carried for reviving airmen plucked from chill waters. As a result, many of them were distinctly unsteady on their feet when they were at last allowed ashore. As a final indignity, they were arrested by the military police on suspicion of being deserters. It was not, perhaps, the heroes' welcome they were expecting.

After that debacle, the War Office recognized that special recruiting, training and equipment would be necessary if Churchill's call for a "reign of terror down the enemy coast" was ever to be fulfilled. Circulars were sent to all military commands inviting volunteers for hazardous duty of an undefined nature. Potential recruits were warned they would have to become accustomed to "longer hours, more work and less rest than the regular members of His Majesty's Forces and must also become expert in all military uses of scouting—ability to stalk, to move across any type of country by day or night, silently and unseen, and to live 'off the country' for a considerable period."

The fact is that the qualifications Clarke was looking for were not limited to those listed in the circular. He was seeking men, he wrote, with "a dash of Elizabethan pirate, the Chicago gangster and the frontier tribesman, allied to a professional efficiency and standard of discipline of the best regular soldier."

From Scotland and southern England, Commandos raided the German-occupied coasts of Norway and France between June 1940 and March 1942. Their Norwegian targets were fish-oil factories and Army outposts in the Lofoten Islands and Vagsoy. In France, Commandos struck at beach defenses near Boulogne, an airfield on the island of Guernsey, a radar station near Bruneval and docks in the port of Saint-Nazaire.

The response, from an army smarting after Dunkirk and eager for revenge, was overwhelming. As the applications poured in, a series of secret meetings was held at the London home of Constantia Rumbold, a diplomat's daughter who was helping Clarke as a voluntary worker. There Clarke and other War Office planners thrashed out the organization and role of the Commandos. To maintain security, all of the officers came to the Rumbold home in plain clothes and told the butler who answered the door that they were members of a charity committee.

From the beginning, Clarke was determined to dispense with conventional army rules and regulations. To instill independence and self-reliance, he proposed that Commandos not be provided with barracks or mess-hall rations. Instead, he suggested that each man be given an allowance from the day he joined; thereafter he would be responsible for his own food and lodging. To the surprise of everyone, the War Office agreed. For officers the allotment might be as high as 13 shillings and four pence—not bad money in 1940, when a decent room could be had for six shillings a day. The Commando could lodge as he chose; he might take a hotel room or he might seek other quarters. In the event, so many civilians proved eager to cooperate with the war effort that many a Commando got free room and board with a hospitable family that had a room to spare, then pocketed the full allowance. One Commando remembered, "I was solvent for the rest of the War."

None of Clarke's suggestions pleased the military traditionalists, and the commando concept was bitterly criticized by many officers, who complained that the formation of a so-called elite force would drain the best men from their units. This new organization, they argued, could do nothing that their own units could not.

The second Commando raid seemed to bear out the concerns of the military establishment. The purpose of the raid was to sabotage Le Bourg airfield at Guernsey, in the Channel Islands. The British hoped to prevent its use by the Luftwaffe as a forward fighter base during the German invasion of England that was expected at any moment.

Two destroyers, the *Scimitar* and the *Saladin,* were assigned to carry the raiding party of 32 officers and 107 enlisted men. On the night of July 14, in a choppy sea off the coast of Guernsey, the raiders scrambled down the sides of the destroyers into landing launches. The Commandos' troubles began immediately. Their launches had recently been electrically wired to throw magnetic mines off their trail—but the wiring had the unexpected effect of making the Commandos' compasses wildly inaccurate. As a result one boatload of men headed confidently for their designated beach and found themselves facing the cliffs of Sark, an island seven miles east of Guernsey. Another launch had to turn back because of engine trouble.

Eventually 40 men, under the command of then Lieut. Colonel John Durnford-Slater, made it to shore—but only with difficulty. "I jumped in, armpit-deep," Durnford-Slater later recalled. "A wave hit me on the back of the neck and caused me to trip over a rock. All around me officers and men were scrambling for balance, falling, coming up and coughing salt water. I doubt if there was a dry weapon amongst us. Once on shore, we loosened the straps of our battle dress to let the sea pour out."

After they pulled themselves together, the bedraggled Commandos squelched up a long flight of concrete steps to

Brigadier John Durnford-Slater, leader of several early Commando raids, reflects the quiet self-assurance that carried Commandos through their daring work. "It is the greatest job in the Army," said a fellow officer, adding, "It's revolutionary."

the clifftop and headed for the airfield. They found it completely deserted and clearly unused. The nearby barracks, where they expected to find German troops billeted, was empty. Disconcerted, the Commandos combed the Jerbourg peninsula on the southeast corner of the island; they found nothing. By the time they got back to the beach, the rising swell and the crashing surf had forced their launch to withdraw from the shore. The luckless raiders tried to get out to the launch in a dinghy, but it capsized after only a few trips and smashed to pieces on the rocks. The remaining Commandos had to swim to the launch.

Durnford-Slater was under no illusions about the adventure. "The raid was a ridiculous, almost comic, failure. We had captured no prisoners. We had done no serious damage. We had caused no casualties to the enemy. We had cut through three telegraph cables: A youth in his teens could have done the same. On the credit side, we gained a little experience and learned some of the things not to do."

Despite the comic-opera aspect of those first two raids, Churchill's enthusiasm for the Commandos persisted. On July 17, 1940, Fleet Admiral Sir Roger Keyes was appointed Director of Combined Operations, a new organization established to direct all raiding missions and to coordinate them with Naval and Air Force operations. Keyes was a prickly, opinionated old warrior who had served in the Navy since his youth. He was also Member of Parliament for Portsmouth and had frequently criticized the conduct of the War. But he was extremely popular with the public, to whom he was known as the "hero of Zeebrugge" for a daring raid he had led on the German-held Belgian port of that name in 1918.

Keyes had ambitious plans for the Commandos: He intended to use them in large-scale operations that would gain for them the same kind of glory he had won at Zeebrugge. That was no easy goal, considering the shortage of arms and equipment, but he was optimistic that once his force was assembled, trained and ready to strike, the necessary hardware would be provided. But Keyes underestimated the resentment that the Commandos had provoked. Bureaucrats in the War Office had no intention of catering to this raffish, irregular and unconventional organization. Keyes fumed and thumped tables, but got nowhere.

At that point Churchill stepped in again. He wrote to Anthony Eden, the Secretary of State for War, on August 25. "I hear that the whole position of the Commandos is being questioned," he began. "I thought therefore I might write to let you know how strongly I feel. There will certainly be many opportunities for minor operations, all of which will depend on surprise landings of lightly equipped, nimble forces accustomed to work like packs of hounds instead of being moved about in the ponderous manner which is appropriate to regular formations. For every reason, therefore, we must develop the storm troop, or Commando, idea." In response to Churchill's appeal, Eden issued orders to accelerate the Commando program.

By October 1940, the volunteers, designated the Special Service Brigade, totaled some 2,000 men. As the brigade expanded, it was organized into units called Commandos, and numbered from one to 12. Each Commando was further divided into sections called troops; at full strength, each troop would comprise 50 men. As the War went on, the number of Commando units increased, and the sizes of individual units varied from a handful to more than 100.

The new Commandos threw themselves wholeheartedly into a crash training program of assault courses, speed marches and amphibious landing exercises in camps that were scattered throughout the Scottish Highlands. "Night and day we trained," recalled Peter Young of No. 3 Commando. Each troop would take turns rushing in and out of

Concealing their high hopes with dubious scowls, British Prime Minister Winston Churchill and Sir Roger Keyes, head of the Commandos, review an exercise on a Scottish hillside. Both championed the new hard-hitting special force, but they had trouble getting funds from the War Office.

the landing craft. "Before long," Young said, "30 men, fully armed, could clear one and double up the beach to cover in about 15 seconds."

"There was nothing to do but work," said Durnford-Slater. "We would start on the landing craft at 8 a.m. and follow on with drill, marching, shooting and long schemes on the hills. We also went in for obstacle courses and close combat, which included wrestling and work with knives and pistols, taught by two ex-Shanghai policemen. We learned methods of getting into houses, throwing grenades in front of us and shooting the Tommy guns. A normal day would end at dark, but at least three times a week the men were out at night."

The training was guaranteed to appeal to men of action; but of real action there was no sign. Keyes finally came up with two proposals to make use of his Commandos. The first plan was to seize the Azores; if Spain should fall to the Germans, thus barring the Mediterranean to Allied convoys bound for the Middle East, a base on the Azores would help ensure a safe route via the South Atlantic and the Cape of Good Hope. In high spirits five Commando units began intensive training at Inveraray, in Scotland. But after weeks of tense expectation, they were told that the attack had been indefinitely postponed.

The next plan was to seize Pantelleria, an island between Sicily and Tunisia, to afford the British another Mediterranean base. Keyes persuaded the Prime Minister to give him personal command of the Pantelleria operation, and he was thrilled by the prospect. Two thousand Commandos trained for the raid, and through part of December they were in daily expectation of leaving. But at the last moment the operation was canceled.

The disappointments began to affect morale. The men grumbled, and in the local pubs, drunkenness increased. Said Brigadier J. Charles Haydon, head of the Special Service Brigade, in a report at the time: "A great enthusiasm at the beginning has evaporated, or at least decreased, owing to the repeated postponements of expected events and enterprises. There is a growing irritation with life due partly to these postponements and partly to being harried from pillar to post, onto ships and off them, into billets and out of them, and so on. There is, in short, a sense of frustration."

At last, in February 1941, the commanding officers of Nos. 3 and 4 Commandos were summoned to a meeting at the Marine Hotel in the Scottish town of Troon and briefed on the Lofotens, a group of Norwegian coastal islands well inside the Arctic Circle. Factories in the Lofotens processed herring and cod oil into glycerine that Germany used for manufacturing munitions, and into vitamin A and B pills that supplied the Wehrmacht. The British War Office had decided to send the Commandos to blow the factories up. And this time there was no postponement.

At midnight on March 1, escorted by five destroyers, the raiding force sailed from Scapa Flow at the northern tip of Scotland in two cross-channel steamers, the *Queen Emma* and the *Princess Beatrix,* which had been converted into troop carriers. On board were 500 Commandos, a detachment of Royal Engineers and a platoon of 52 Norwegian volunteers. In the three days of the journey, many of the men suffered from seasickness as the steamers rolled and pitched in the stormy northern waters.

On the night of March 3, the navigation lights of the Lofotens were sighted. At 4 a.m. on March 4, in the pale gray light of dawn, the Commandos lowered their landing craft, loaded them and steered for the shores of the two islands where the factories stood. It was a frigid morning. One officer was bundled up in two undershirts, two pull-overs, a shirt and vest, a wool-lined coat, woolen pants, woolen socks and fur-lined boots, and still he complained about the cold temperature.

Though they saw no sign of enemy activity on the shore, the Commandos had every reason to expect that their landing would be opposed. "We approached the quay fully prepared for an ambush," said Peter Young, in command of No. 6 Troop. "It was a complete anticlimax when crowds of Norwegians of both sexes reached down for our weapons and hoisted us ashore." The reception was welcome nevertheless. The only opposition came from an armed German trawler, the *Krebbs,* which resolutely sailed out alone from the harbor to engage the destroyers. She was quickly set afire and sunk.

The Commandos took over the telegraph station and telephone exchange and began rounding up Germans (mostly merchant seamen) and Norwegian collaborators pointed out to them by the townspeople. The Royal Engineers,

QUICK-FIRING WEAPONS FOR MEN ON THE RUN

For the hit-and-run tactics in which they specialized, Commandos needed a gun that was lightweight, compact and capable of rapid fire. They got those features in the Tommy gun and the Sten *(below)*.

The Tommy gun was the brainchild of General John T. Thompson, who served as a U.S. Army ordnance officer in World War I. He wanted a weapon that could do what the machine gun could do—fire automatically, and thereby mow down a number of men in one burst, but also be portable and manageable by men acting independently on the move. In 1917 he invented such a weapon. It weighed only 12 pounds when loaded. He named his creation the Thompson submachine gun.

Thompson just missed having his gun adopted in World War I, so it languished for a decade—until the mid-1920s, when it was discovered by Chicago gangsters who were vying for the fortune to be had from peddling liquor in defiance of Prohibition. As the weapon gained notoriety in news stories about the gangsters, it became known as the Tommy gun.

Peacetime armies, with no pressing incentive to modernize, were slow to adopt the new gun. As late as 1940, when the first Commando unit was formed, the entire British Army owned only 40 Tommy guns. Each was handmade and, at $225 apiece, the price was steep.

Two engineers, Major Reginald V. Shepherd and Harold J. Turpin of the Royal

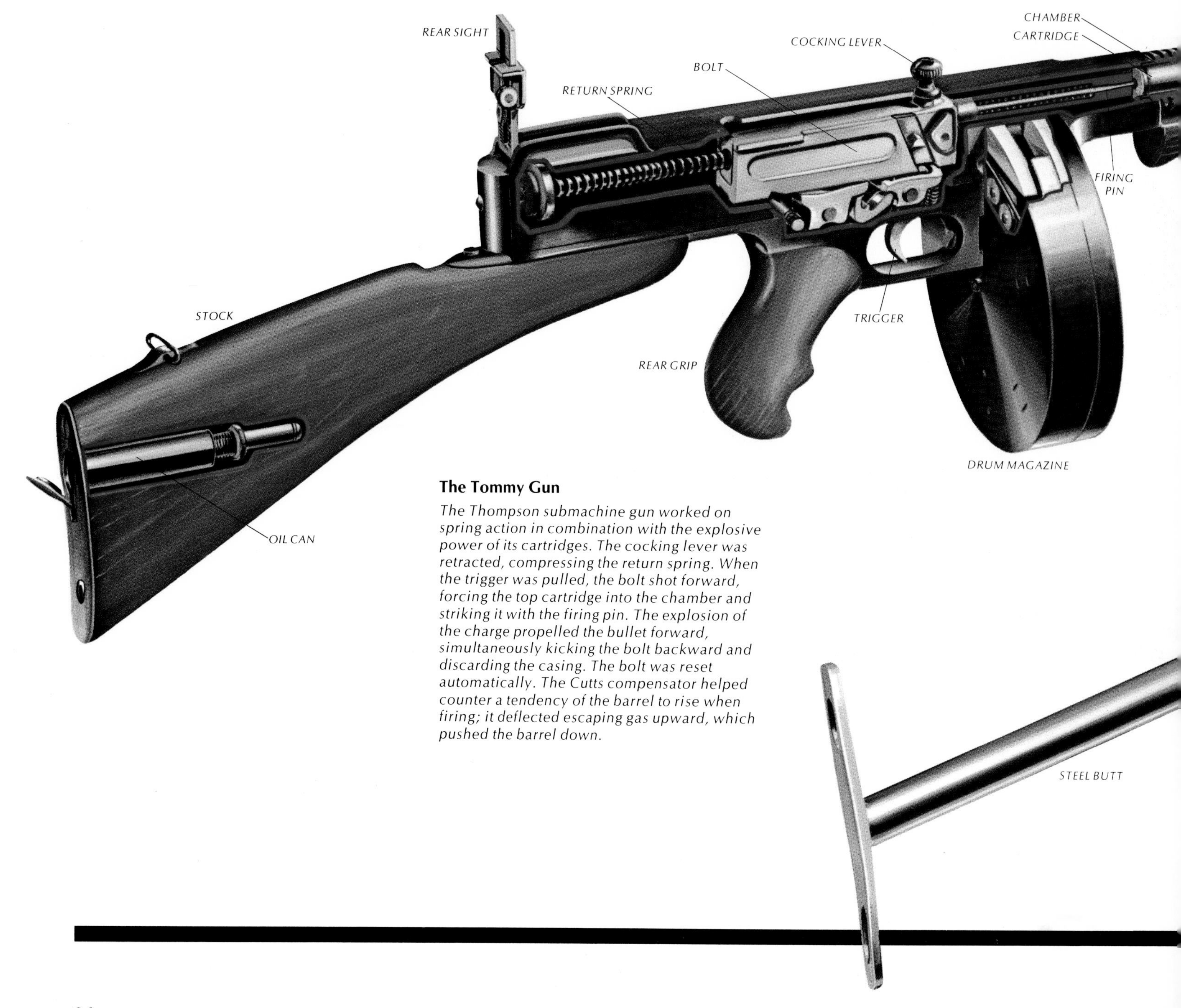

The Tommy Gun

The Thompson submachine gun worked on spring action in combination with the explosive power of its cartridges. The cocking lever was retracted, compressing the return spring. When the trigger was pulled, the bolt shot forward, forcing the top cartridge into the chamber and striking it with the firing pin. The explosion of the charge propelled the bullet forward, simultaneously kicking the bolt backward and discarding the casing. The bolt was reset automatically. The Cutts compensator helped counter a tendency of the barrel to rise when firing; it deflected escaping gas upward, which pushed the barrel down.

Small Arms Factory at Enfield, devised an alternative. Their version was shorter by three inches, lighter by four pounds and lacked such frills as a hideaway oil can. Not the least of its virtues was that it consisted of a mere 24 parts and could be mass-produced for less than $15. The gun came to be known as the Sten, an acronym that combined the initials of its inventors' last names with the first two letters of Enfield. Before long, British Commandos and their counterparts in the other forces were armed with Stens or with close imitations.

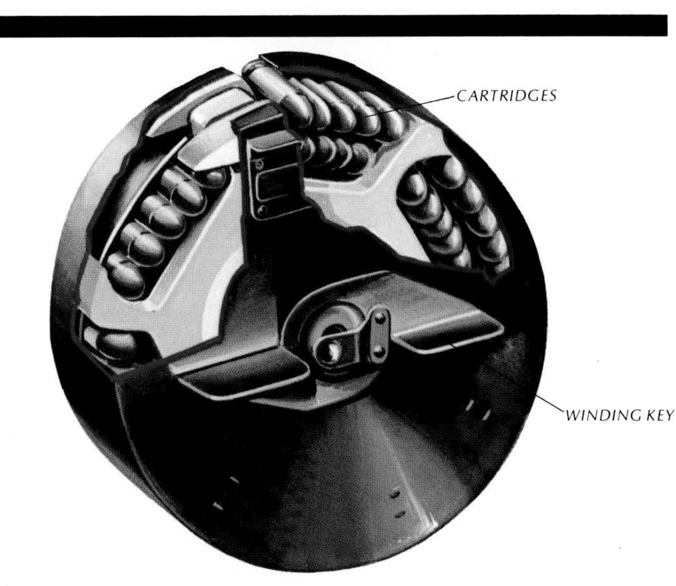

FRONT SIGHT
CUTTS COMPENSATOR
BARREL
FOREGRIP

The Drum Magazine

The magazine of the Thompson submachine gun contained a coiled spring that propelled up to 50 cartridges in a spiral to an opening at the top; then the bolt pushed the cartridges into the gun. When the magazine was empty it was replaced by a full one, and the spring was recoiled by means of the winding key.

BOX MAGAZINE
VENTILATION HOLES
FRONT SIGHT
CARTRIDGES
BARREL
RETURN SPRING
COCKING LEVER
BOLT
BARREL SLEEVE
REAR SIGHT
CHAMBER
EJECTION PORT
TRIGGER

The Sturdy Sten

The Sten gun operated in essentially the same way as the Thompson. The bolt pushed the cartridge into the chamber just below the front sight, and the firing pin struck the rear of the cartridge. After the powder exploded, the bolt compressed the return spring and the cartridge casing flew out through the ejection port. The firing action continued until the trigger was released or the cartridges were spent. The box magazine, which was less expensive to make than the drum type, fed 32 cartridges into the chamber. The barrel sleeve, which was perforated with ventilation holes for cooling the chamber area, served as a hand grip.

meanwhile, went methodically about their business. Ear-shattering explosions were followed by clouds of billowing black smoke as 18 fish-oil factories blew up, along with storage tanks containing 800,000 gallons of fuel oil. Five small merchant ships were destroyed by the resulting fire. At the telegraph station, Commando Lieutenant R. L. Wills sent off a telegram addressed to A. Hitler, Berlin: "You said in your last speech German troops would meet the English wherever they landed. Where are your troops?"

Soon after midday, the soldiers returned to their boats; as the landing craft moved out of the harbor, the townspeople—delighted by the raid though it had destroyed their chief source of livelihood—gathered on the quay and sang the Norwegian anthem. Some 314 of them, including eight women, had volunteered to return with the Commandos to Great Britain to join the Norwegian forces that had fled there in April 1940 rather than surrender to the Germans. Also on board were 216 German prisoners. The only injury the British had sustained during the entire raid was incurred by an officer who accidentally shot himself in the thigh with an automatic he carried in his pants pocket.

Peter Young, shown here as a colonel and wearing the Commando green beret, fought as a second lieutenant in the first Commando raid, on Guernsey in 1940, and took part in a score of later operations from Norway to Burma—more than any other Commando.

The raid had been an unalloyed success, but a crisis was brewing for Sir Roger Keyes. In April 1941 the Prime Minister approved plans for Commandos to occupy the Canary Islands to protect British convoys en route to the South Atlantic. However, weeks turned into months and there was no sign of the operation getting started. Every day Keyes became more resentful of what he viewed as needless procrastination by War Office bureaucrats.

In August, a demonstration landing exercise was scheduled at Scapa Flow for the edification of King George VI. The exercise was a fiasco. Communications failed, the beach became choked with equipment and the men exhibited precious little of their touted élan. The raid on the Canaries was indefinitely postponed.

By this time, relations between Keyes and the commanders of the Naval and military forces had deteriorated seriously; Keyes even began complaining that junior officers in the Admiralty were plotting against him. At the end of September, Keyes's title was changed from Director of Combined Operations to "Adviser"—a move calculated to enrage the gallant admiral. He declined the post, indignantly telling the Prime Minister that he could not accept "such a sweeping reduction in status."

Keyes, still a Member of Parliament, stood before the House of Commons and delivered a bitter farewell message in which he spoke of "having been frustrated in every worthwhile offensive action I have tried to undertake," and railed against "the negative power which controls the war machine in Whitehall. Great leaders of the past have always emphasized the value of time in war: Time is passing and so long as procrastination, the thief of time, is the key word of the war machine in Whitehall, we shall continue to lose one opportunity after another during the lifetime of opportunities."

Churchill's choice as a replacement for Keyes both surprised and delighted the Commandos: Captain Lord Louis Mountbatten *(pages 168-179)*. He was a man as likely as Keyes to arouse passions, but for different reasons. Rich, handsome, a cousin of the King, a fine polo player and a member of fashionable London society, Mountbatten was thought by some to be a playboy and dilettante. But to others he was a brave Naval officer and a gifted leader who almost invariably aroused the admiration of subordinates. He

From a quay in the Norwegian Lofoten Islands, three British Commandos watch as fish-oil storage tanks burn in March 1941. Factories in the Lofotens produced half of Norway's fish oil—and processed much of it into glycerine for the manufacture of German explosives.

also had the ability—and the contacts—to cut through red tape and get things done.

Captain Mountbatten had recently returned from the Mediterranean, where he had narrowly survived the sinking of his destroyer, the *Kelly*. Now, as Chief of Combined Operations, he was promoted to Acting Vice Admiral of the Royal Navy and given the honorary ranks of Lieutenant General in the Army and Air Marshal in the Royal Air Force. The new titles were more than mere glitter; they underscored the necessity of involving Great Britain's three military services as support forces for Commando operations on a large scale.

Interservice cooperation was put to the test in December in the first big Combined Operations raid of the War—at Vagsoy, an island off the Norwegian coast between the ports of Trondheim and Bergen. The purpose of the raid, like that of the attack on the Lofotens, was mainly economic—to destroy fish-oil factories and merchant shipping. But unlike the Lofotens, Vagsoy was heavily fortified with coastal batteries and German garrisons, and thus there was little possibility of an unopposed landing. The plan was for one group of Commandos to attack and hold the village of South Vagsoy long enough for another to blow up the factories. But first the coastal guns and antiaircraft batteries on Maloy, a tiny island protecting the channel between Vagsoy and the Norwegian mainland, had to be silenced.

An essential component of the operation was the close cooperation of both the Royal Navy and the Royal Air Force. As the Commandos were going in, Hampden bombers would attack nearby German-occupied airfields, and a cruiser and four destroyers would bombard German artillery positions on Vagsoy and Maloy. During the raid, Blenheims and Beaufighters were to provide cover. The raiding force was made up of 576 men from Nos. 2 and 3 Commandos along with engineers, medics and a Norwegian detachment. The date was set for December 26, 1941, when the Germans might be resting after Christmas festivities.

Mountbatten went to Scapa Flow to wish the raiders good luck. "This is my first experience in telling people what to do in an action without going in myself," he told the Commandos, "and I don't like it." He went on to say that when his destroyer had gone down off Crete a few months earlier the Germans had machine-gunned the survivors in the water. "There is absolutely no need to treat the Germans gently on my account," he said. "Good luck to you all."

At 9:15 p.m. on Christmas Eve, the raiding force left Scapa Flow aboard seven ships and plowed straight into the teeth of a gale blowing in from the Atlantic. Because of the storm, the raid was delayed for 24 hours. By the time the ships made landfall off Vagsoy in the early hours of December 27, the sea was calm.

Major Robert Henriques was on the bridge of the cruiser *Kenya* as the flotilla approached its target. "It was a very eerie sensation entering the fjord in absolute silence and very slowly," he remembered. "I wondered what was going to happen, for it seemed the ship had lost her proper element, that she was no longer a free ship at sea. Occasionally I saw a little hut with a light burning in it and I wondered whether the light would be suddenly switched off, which would mean the enemy had spotted us, or whether it would continue to burn as some Norwegian fisherman got out of bed, stretched himself and went off to his nets. Exactly one minute late, the landing craft were lowered and could just be seen through glasses, black beetles crawling in the shadow of the mountains up the black waters of the fjord."

A German lookout on the shore of the fjord a few miles south of Vagsoy was first to spot the approaching ships. He telephoned the Vagsoy garrison commander, but got no reply; the captain was shaving and his servant was too busy polishing the captain's boots to answer a ringing telephone. The lookout next telephoned the harbor captain's office at South Vagsoy and reported that seven blacked-out ships were entering the fjord. He was told not to worry: A small convoy was expected. When the lookout pointed out that the vessels did not look like merchant ships, he was accused of being drunk.

The lookout tried again. He gave a message—"Unidentified warships entering fjord"—to a signal orderly to transmit by blinker to the Naval signal station at Maloy. Immediately after receiving the message, the signaler inexplicably jumped into a rowboat to deliver it personally to the Naval headquarters at the Hagen Hotel in South Vagsoy. At the hotel, the signaler was asked if he had alerted the Maloy battery. "No, sir," he replied. "It is an Army battery and this is a Naval signal."

At that minute, 8:48 a.m., any doubts about the intentions of the unidentified ships were dispelled. The 6-inch guns of the *Kenya* opened up and a salvo of shells exploded in and around the battery on Maloy, where the German troops were gathered in a barracks room to hear a noncommissioned officer lecture on "How to behave in the presence of an officer." Two minutes later, the four destroyers joined in: Shells rained down at the rate of 50 a minute, destroying the barracks and three of the four coastal guns. Under cover of this storm of fire, the Commando group assigned to capture the island forged toward the shore in a landing craft. As soon as the Naval bombardment ended, the Hampdens droned in, dropping smoke bombs at low level, and in their wake the Commandos sprang ashore.

Despite this daunting prelude, the German garrison on Maloy put up courageous resistance as the Commandos, Tommy guns blazing, fanned out through the barracks. Captain Peter Young and a lance corporal named Harper literally bumped into two Germans as they turned one corner. The raiders sprang back behind cover, then jumped out again, shouting *"Hände hoch!"*—"Hands up!" "The nearest German snatched at my bayonet," Young recalled, "and instead of sticking it into him—which did not occur to me—I drew it back, fully expecting him to surrender. Instead, he turned and ran and as he did so I pulled the trigger, firing from the hip. I was slightly surprised to see him stagger and lean heavily against the wall of a hut. In the instant it took me to reload, Harper let fly with his Tommy gun and gave him a burst. As the second German took aim at me with his pistol from a doorway, Harper swung his gun on him and gave him the rest of the magazine." With one round-the-corner encounter after another, the Commandos took control of the island; by 9:20 a.m. it was in their hands.

On Vagsoy the fighting was harder. The Commandos ordered to take the town of South Vagsoy were unlucky from the start. One of the Hampdens overhead was hit by antiaircraft fire and dropped a 60-pound phosphorous smoke bomb prematurely—directly into a landing boat, killing or badly injuring half of the Commandos on board. When the boats reached the shore, the Commandos were immediately engaged by German troops.

Slowly the Germans retreated among the wood houses of the town as the Commandos, firing in short bursts and dashing from doorway to doorway, pressed forward through the snow-covered streets. German riflemen quickly took positions in doorways and windows and made every British move dangerous, particularly for officers in the vanguard of the assault. Captain Johnny Giles of No. 3 Troop, leading a wild charge through a big house in the town's main street, hurled grenades through every door. For a second, he paused in the back door while he decided his next move—and was shot dead by a sniper.

At the Ulvesund Hotel farther along the street the British lost two more officers. With a grenade in his hand, Captain Algy Forrester of No. 4 Troop led the assault. As the captain raced toward the front door, a burst of fire from inside the hotel knocked him off his feet and he fell forward onto the grenade, which exploded under him. Leading a second charge, Norwegian Captain Martin Linge was shot dead in the doorway.

At 10:20 a.m. the reserve troops that had been held on one of the ships were sent in to help counter the strong opposition in the center and north of town. They were soon joined by Captain Young and his troop, who had hurried over from Maloy, where the fighting had long since ended. "I knew things must be bad," recalled Young, "because when we arrived at South Vagsoy I heard someone say 'Good old 6 Troop.' Under normal circumstances, no one had a good word for us."

Young discovered that only one of the first two troops to reach the town still had an officer fit for action; as a result the attack had lost its momentum. The main street was virtually impassable: On one side of it was a steep, snow-covered mountain, and on the other side the icy waters of the fjord; the street itself was covered by German riflemen. Young decided to try to work through the warehouses along the waterfront. Ordering two men to cover him with Tommy-gun fire from the windows of a captured warehouse, Young advanced in a series of bold dashes, his men following. After failing in two attempts to storm a big warehouse that stretched almost from the edge of the fjord to the main street, Young set the building on fire. When the Germans who had been holding it stumbled out through the smoke, "they disdained their chance to surrender," reported Young laconically. The Commandos mowed them down with a hail of gunfire.

For more than two hours the fighting was savage. A German sailor emerged from a side street, threw a stick grenade at a Commando officer and then put up his hands to surrender. He was shot where he stood by a Commando sergeant. The officer dived into a doorway and escaped harm.

Building by building, the Commandos took control of most of the town. By midday, fighting in the streets of South Vagsoy was reduced to sporadic bursts of fire. Much of the town was in flames as the raiders began to withdraw down the main street. Houses were burning on both sides and timbers were crashing to the ground. On the way back to his headquarters, Durnford-Slater had a brief but gentlemanly exchange with one of the enemy. "I saw a handsome young German lying in the gutter, seriously wounded in the chest and obviously near death," Durnford-Slater recalled. "When he smiled at me and beckoned, I walked over and spoke to him. He could speak no English but indicated he wished to shake hands. We did. I think what he meant, and I agreed, was that it had been a good, clean battle."

While the Commandos were engaged in South Vagsoy, the Royal Navy was equally busy at sea. The *Kenya* fought a four-hour duel with a German battery on the island of Rugsundo, four miles southeast of Vagsoy, before silencing its guns. The destroyers sank nine merchant ships and won an unexpected prize when an armed German trawler, the *Föhn,* ran aground during the battle. After a brief fight with her crew, British sailors captured the *Föhn's* code books, which yielded a treasure for British intelligence: The books contained the radio call signal of every German vessel in Norway and France, along with challenges, countersigns and emergency signals.

By 3 p.m., as the Arctic night was closing in, all of the British troops were back on board their ships, along with 98 German prisoners and 71 Norwegian volunteers. The Commando demolition teams on Maloy had blown up every German installation. At Vagsoy all of the fish-oil factories, the radio station and the lighthouse had been demolished. Some 150 Germans were killed in the raid. The Commandos had lost 19 men and were bringing back 52 wounded.

The Vagsoy raid, Britain's initial effort to synchronize its three services in a full-scale assault, was a shining success: The fighter screen over the action and the Naval bombardment of the gun batteries had allowed the Commandos to get on with their job without interruption from air or sea.

The raid had proved, once and for all, that determined troops, backed up by warplanes and warships, could attack and overcome a staunchly defended enemy stronghold.

After the raid on Vagsoy, resistance to the Commandos subsided. On January 21, 1942, Mountbatten submitted to the chiefs of staff another plan, this time for a hit-and-run raid to snatch secret equipment from a German radar station in France. British intelligence was convinced that German scientists had developed a new form of radar that enabled the enemy to detect the bearing and altitude of approaching aircraft. A plane of the RAF's Photographic Reconnaissance Unit had located a suspicious new radar station near the French coastal village of Bruneval, between Le Havre and Étretat. British scientists desperately wanted a look at the equipment installed there so that they could devise countermeasures. When Mountbatten offered to get the equipment for them, they promptly accepted.

The radar station was situated on an isolated plateau atop 300-foot cliffs that dropped precipitously to the Channel. The only approach from the sea was a steep, narrow gully protected by machine-gun posts and pillboxes. Any force attempting to attack up that gully would almost certainly be annihilated. But behind the station were open fields, perfectly suited to a parachute landing. Mountbatten proposed to drop a company of paratroopers behind the station at night: They would attack instantly and then withdraw down the gully, assaulting the German shore defenses from the rear, and make their escape in waiting ships.

The training of parachutists from the newly formed 1st Airborne Division began at once; a detailed model constructed from aerial-reconnaissance photographs helped the men plan the timing for each phase of the operation. The assault force was made up of a company of the 2nd Parachute Battalion, under Major John D. Frost, along with a small party of engineers and an expert radio technician, Flight Sergeant E. W. F. Cox, who was to be responsible for removing the radar equipment. A night with a nearly full moon, February 27, was chosen for the raid.

For several nights before the attack, low-level air raids were staged over the Normandy coast so that the dozen Whitley bombers that were to transport the assault force would not receive undue attention. The diversionary tactic

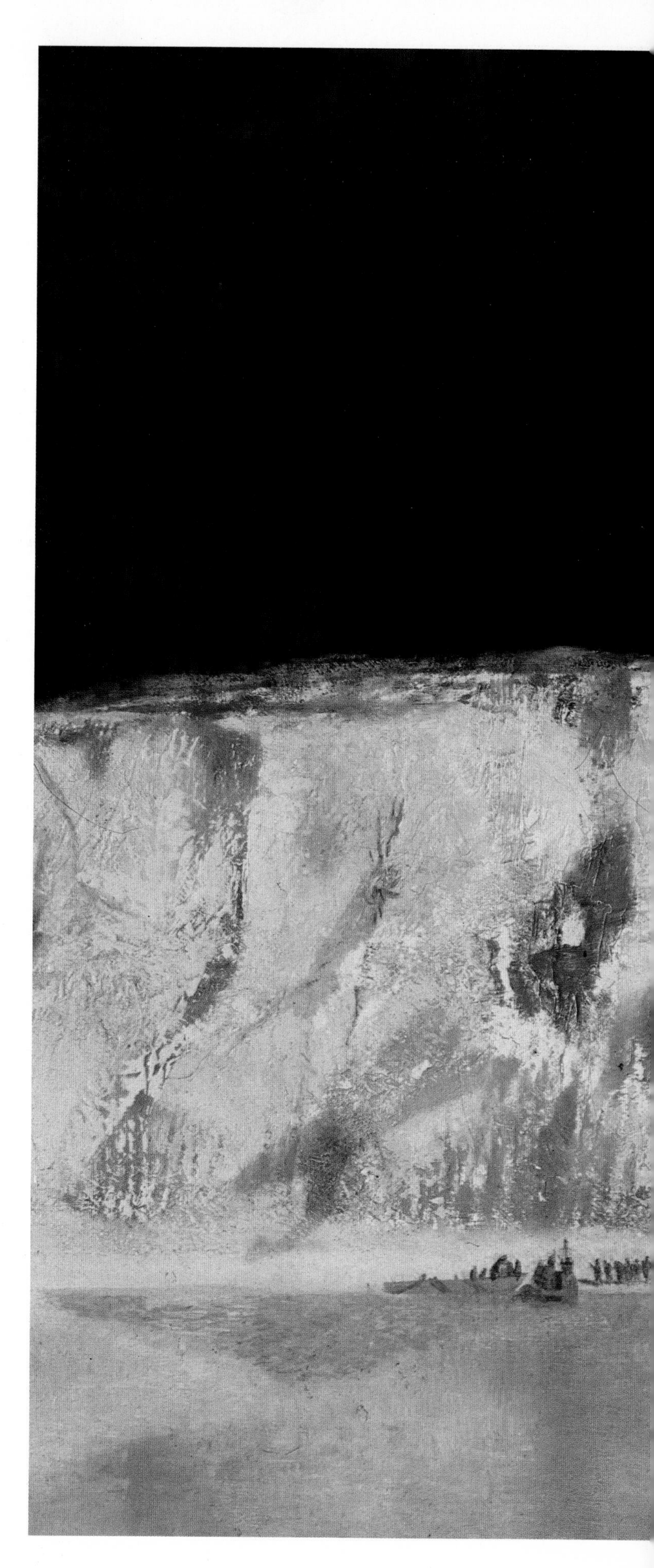

A contemporary painting by official War artist Richard Eurich shows special forces parachuting in for a raid on a German radar station at an isolated headland near Bruneval, France. A Royal Navy team waits offshore and on the beach to evacuate the paratroopers.

worked. About midnight on the 27th of February, 10 of the planes arrived over the drop zone without interference from German antiaircraft fire, and the parachutists began hurling themselves into the clear, cold night. Most of the men landed right on target. Only two planes were forced off course by enemy flak, and these aircraft dropped their parachutists about a mile away on the side of the gully across from the radar station.

Frost decided not to wait for these men to catch up, and ordered an immediate attack. Splitting into four teams, the parachutists raced across the moonlit fields. Frost's team was to storm the villa next to the radar station, where the majority of the German technicians were thought to be housed. Another team headed directly for the station, which sat in a shallow depression between the villa and the cliffs. A third team took up positions to defend against a possible attack by a German garrison known to be billeted in La Presbytère, a large farm to the north, while a fourth team went to clear the gully in preparation for the withdrawal.

By an extraordinary stroke of luck, only one German sentry was awake as the raiders approached the villa. By the time he had run to the barracks to wake the sergeant of the guard, the leading parachutists were on the doorstep. Frost's group burst into the villa and found only one man inside. The raiders killed him as he fumbled for a gun. Leaving a few men to hold the villa, Frost hurried on to the radar station, where he found that five of the six Germans inside had already been killed. The sixth was captured as he ran toward the cliff edge.

Heavy machine-gun fire opened up from the direction of the farm as Flight Sergeant Cox, apparently unperturbed by the hail of bullets ricocheting around him, began dismantling the radar equipment; it was still warm after tracking the aircraft in which the visitors had arrived. Two bullets hit parts of the equipment while it was actually in Cox's hands, but he calmly continued with his work. Engineers used crowbars to wrench the last components from their mountings, then the equipment was loaded onto a collapsible handcart that had been dropped with the raiders. Heaving and pushing the heavily laden cart as they went, the raiders began to withdraw across the fields toward the gully. Before the last man had departed, the radar station was blown up to make the Germans believe that the purpose of the raid had been sabotage.

The lights of German trucks could be seen coursing down a road toward La Presbytère as the parachutists hurried away. Time was now of the essence. If the gully had been cleared, the paratroopers would be able to make their escape. But the team assigned that job was undermanned and too weak to attack. Most of its members had been in the

British paratroopers search two Germans captured in the raid on the Bruneval radar station. The prisoner on the right, a Luftwaffe radar operator, was taken to England to help explain the German detection equipment; the prisoner on the left is an infantryman.

planes that were forced off course, and these parachutists were still struggling across country toward the gully. Fortunately, they arrived in the nick of time; despite their long and exhausting forced march, they joined their teammates in storming a pillbox overlooking the beach and clearing the last obstacle to the escape.

On the beach, Frost signaled out to sea with a flashlight. After an agonizing wait, he heard a voice in the dark call out: "Sir! The boats are coming in. God bless the ruddy Navy." First to go on board the landing craft was the radar equipment, followed by the paratroopers. Under intermittent fire from machine-gun posts along the cliffs—the German trucks had delivered men to the defenses—the ships headed out to sea.

The whole force, escorted by destroyers (and covered by Spitfires after dawn broke), arrived back in England at midmorning. The raiders had lost one man killed and seven missing; a further five were wounded. With the new German equipment in their hands, British scientists were able to devise countermeasures that were to save countless aircraft—and fliers—during the stormy years that lay ahead.

The success of the Vagsoy and Bruneval raids reflected the growing competence of the commandos and provided an inestimable morale boost for the Allies, who saw little else going right in the War. The latest commando exploits served to sweep away the controversy that had marked the force's inception; now even British Army traditionalists recognized its value, and a special school for Commandos was opened at Achnacarry, Scotland, where training was expanded and centralized *(pages 58-73)*.

The Commandos also impressed the Army of the United States, which had entered the War the previous December. One American admirer was Lucian K. Truscott Jr., then a brigadier general attached to Mountbatten's Combined Operations Headquarters. In the spring of 1942, after a close study of the training at Achnacarry, Truscott suggested to Brigadier General Dwight D. Eisenhower, then assistant chief of staff in charge of War operations, that the Americans follow the British lead and create a commando outfit of their own. His suggestion was quickly approved.

It fell to Truscott to choose a name for the new special force. Since the word "commando" belonged to the British, Truscott selected "Rangers" after the Colonial guerrillas who had fought the French and the Indians in the French and Indian War of 1755-1763.

A call for volunteers "not averse to dangerous action" from the U.S. 34th Infantry Division and 1st Armored Division, stationed in Northern Ireland, produced an overwhelming response. Nearly 500 candidates were selected, and the first U.S. Rangers arrived at Achnacarry on June 1, 1942, to begin training. To the undisguised surprise of some of the British instructors, the Yanks acquitted themselves with great credit.

The British Army Commandos had also picked up a home-grown rival: the Royal Marine Commandos. One of the original functions of the Marines had been to provide detachments for amphibious raids on enemy coastlines. After Dunkirk, however, they could not be spared for cross-Channel forays: As one of the few British fighting formations with knowledge of amphibious warfare, they had to be kept available for defense against an anticipated German invasion. Then, once the threat of invasion had abated, the Royal Marines found that their original role had been usurped by the Army Commandos.

As early as February 1942, the Marines had begun to emulate the Commandos. One call for Royal Marine volunteers for Commando training produced 6,000 men; they were organized in two units, Nos. 40 and 41 Royal Marine Commandos. Within the year, the entire Marine division would be retrained for service as Commandos. This transformation engendered a fierce rivalry between the Marine and Army Commandos, and that rivalry would last for the entire War.

Through the winter and spring of 1942 the Allies were rocked by one setback after another. In the North African deserts, the British Eighth Army was losing ground to a resurgent German Afrika Korps. In the Far East the Japanese were sweeping into Hong Kong and through Malaya to the great citadel of Singapore. In the Philippines, General Douglas MacArthur, commander of the U.S. forces in the Far East, was fighting a losing battle to hold the islands. And in the North Atlantic, German U-boats were exacting an awesome toll on Allied shipping.

In late January of 1942, the 45,000-ton German battleship *Tirpitz* was lurking in the deep waters of the German-occupied Norwegian fjords, giving every sign of preparing to sortie against Allied convoys in the Atlantic. If she did so, she could deprive both Britain and the Soviet Union of vital supplies. On January 25, Churchill noted in a memo to his Chiefs of Staff that no other target was as important as the *Tirpitz*. "The whole strategy of the war," he wrote, "turns at this period on this ship, which is holding four times the number of British capital ships paralysed, not to speak of two new American battleships retained in the Atlantic."

The *Tirpitz* could operate in the Atlantic only if she had a base of operations along the Atlantic coast of Europe. Such a haven was provided by the French port of Saint-Nazaire, where a huge dry dock had been built before the War to accommodate the liner *Normandie*. If the *Tirpitz* could be denied the use of this dock, the only one in France big enough, she was unlikely to venture out of North Sea waters.

The chance to stalemate the *Tirpitz* in Norway triggered the most daring and dangerous raid ever planned in Mountbatten's Combined Operations Headquarters. On the night of March 27, 1942, a flotilla of darkened vessels entered the estuary of the Loire River, heading for the Naval base at Saint-Nazaire. On board the leading vessel, Motor Gunboat 314, were the joint commanders of the operation, Lieut. Colonel Charles Newman of No. 2 Commando and Captain

Major General Lucian K. Truscott Jr., who founded the American Rangers, wears riding breeches—signifying his membership in the cavalry—as he observes exercises at the British Commando training center in Scotland.

American Rangers inspect mock graves at the Commandos' training grounds in Achnacarry, Scotland. The inscription on the tombstone at left cautions against walking in front of a fellow Commando's rifle.

Robert "Red" Ryder of the Royal Navy. Before the night was out, both would earn the Victoria Cross. Behind MGB-314 was an old American destroyer, the *Campbeltown,* with a force of 75 Commandos on board. The *Campbeltown's* funnels had been cut back to disguise her as a German *Möwe*-class destroyer, and her bow was packed with explosives. In the forthcoming drama, the *Campbeltown* was to play the leading role: Her assignment was to ram the steel gates of the *Normandie* dock and blow them to bits by means of a delayed explosion.

On either side of the destroyer, in columns along its port and starboard, were 16 mahogany-hulled motor boats carrying some 200 more Commandos. Because of the length of the proposed journey, each boat was carrying extra fuel in tanks lashed to its deck. The auxiliary fuel tanks made the wood boats extremely vulnerable in the event of an attack, but no other craft were available for the operation. The planners were hoping that the element of surprise would safeguard the men on board, but no one had any illusions about the risks. During planning, a senior Naval officer had warned Mountbatten: "We may lose every man." With a slight grimace, Mountbatten had agreed, but added, "If they do the job, we've got to accept that."

Shortly before midnight, the raiders heard the approach

of heavy aircraft, and the horizon in the east was silhouetted as swiveling fingers of searchlights illumined the sky. Colored tracers flickered up from the ground, and the distant thumps of antiaircraft batteries echoed through the night. British bombers were diverting attention from the vessels slipping quietly up the river. But the air raid did not last long. In order to save French lives, the pilots had been instructed not to attack unless they could clearly identify dockyard targets. When clouds drifted across the town, the raid came to a halt prematurely, and one after another the searchlights flickered out.

By 12:30 a.m. the flotilla had crossed the dangerous shoal waters across the mouth of the Loire. Twice the *Campbeltown* scraped the bottom; twice, with propellers churning, she pulled free. Luck seemed to be with the British. About two miles from the harbor they passed a lighthouse, which stood in midstream, without being detected. Both banks of the river were dark and quiet. To the men in the flotilla, it was disconcerting that they had got so far without being seen. Nothing now disturbed the quiet of the night except the throb of the vessels' engines; the Commandos talked in whispers.

At 1:22 a.m., just eight minutes from the moment the *Campbeltown* was due to hit the dock gates, every searchlight along both banks of the river was suddenly switched on. The entire force was revealed as if on a floodlit stage. The Germans hesitated. Two signal stations challenged and MGB-314 replied with a message in German—prepared with the German code books seized from the trawler off Vagsoy. A few bursts were fired from the shore battery, and both MGB-314 and the *Campbeltown* made the signal "ship being fired on by friendly forces." These delaying tactics won the raiders a precious four minutes as the *Campbeltown* increased her speed for the final run.

"Those few minutes seemed like a lifetime," remembered Colonel Newman. "Then, without warning, the whole bag of tricks was let loose. The noise was terrific. Tracers of every color poured into our fleet—*Campbeltown's* sides seemed to be alive with bursting shells. Every vessel answered with fire. Oerlikon, Bren, and mortar fire poured into the searchlight and gun positions."

At 1:34, the *Campbeltown,* with smoke billowing from her engine room, smashed into the gates of the *Normandie* dock. "There was a grinding crash," Ryder and Newman reported, "and the flash of some minor explosion in her forecastle as she came to rest. Flying timber, smoke, sparks and flames made it impossible to see very clearly, but when these had cleared away, there she was, firmly wedged in the center of the main gate."

Through the smoke and storm of gunfire, the Commando assault parties scrambled over the bows of the destroyer and down iron ladders to the quay, where they raced into the shadows of the dockyard; some of them were bent double from the weight of the explosives they carried on their backs. Many fell wounded before they could get off the *Campbeltown's* deck. When some of the iron ladders broke, men swarmed down by rope.

These first men ashore wasted no time. Newman had warned them all to be "quick in and quick out." One group dealt with guns surrounding the dock: They ran straight to their first objective, a light gun in a sandbagged pit not far from where they landed. A grenade thrown out from the pit as the men approached was neatly kicked back by one of the Commandos, and it burst among the German gunners. Leaving six Germans for dead, the Commandos swept on to a concrete bunker housing a 37mm gun, which they put out of action with grenades. By the time a third and a fourth gun were similarly destroyed, four of the 12 Commandos in the group had been wounded; nevertheless, the little band now held a perimeter against stiffening German opposition.

Demolition teams had been assigned to destroy the equipment at both ends of the dock: the pumps that raised and lowered the water level in Saint-Nazaire's locks, and the winding wheels that opened and closed the gates. One team, led by Lieutenant Stuart Chant, had to blow up the pumping equipment 40 feet below ground. Chant had been wounded in the leg and both arms by a shell while lying on the deck of the *Campbeltown* to brace himself for the impact as the ship hit the dock. Despite his injuries, he led his men down the long flight of steps into the pumping house, helped fix 150 pounds of explosive around the pumps, then limped painfully back up to ground level as the 90-second fuse burned away.

The pumping house exploded with a deafening roar that, for a moment, drowned the sounds of the furious battle being fought all around. This explosion was followed seconds later by another in the winding house that rendered the dock gates useless.

At the opposite end of the Saint-Nazaire dock, the Commandos ran into a hail of fire from machine guns and Oerlikons that were mounted on towers, and from ships in a nearby basin. The Commandos had been ordered to destroy the second set of pumping and winding houses and steel gates. In the face of murderous fire, one team of Commandos began to lay underwater charges against the dock gates while another team smashed its way with a sledgehammer into the pumping house. Bullets ricocheting off the gates eventually forced the first team back, but then Sergeant Frank Carr ran out alone onto the gates and set fire to the charges that had been laid. The partial charges did not destroy the gates, but they did cause serious damage. Immediately afterward, a pumping house exploded with a roar.

Meanwhile, Ryder and Newman had landed from their gunboat headquarters. Ryder hurried across the quay to ensure that the *Campbeltown* was securely wedged into the gates and that she had been satisfactorily scuttled. As he ran, he heard a series of explosions and in a moment saw that the old destroyer was sinking at the stern. On his way back to the gunboat, Ryder was almost blown off his feet as another pumping house exploded.

Newman, in high spirits at the apparent success of the raid so far, looked around and found a likely headquarters from which to direct the remainder of his operation. Reconnoitering for an entrance, he surprised a German sentry, who threw his hands up in terror despite the fact that the equally startled colonel blurted: "Sorry!" Recovering his composure, Newman questioned the sentry and found he had stumbled on the German headquarters.

Suddenly Newman and his men came under heavy fire from minesweepers and harbor-defense craft, which had begun firing from close range at the Commando groups flitting in and out of the shadows in the dockyard. German machine guns mounted on the roof of nearby submarine pens inflicted serious losses until a Commando sergeant, oblivious of the fire, set up a 2-inch mortar and silenced the machine guns with a continuous barrage of shells that were passed to him by a chain of hands, including Newman's. But with gunfire still coming from all directions, Newman moved to a new position in the cover of a shed near the quay. From there he could call in the demolition teams as they returned. He was still irrepressibly cheerful—the explosions from both ends of the *Normandie* dock had led him to believe that all was going well.

In fact, the operation was running into serious difficulties. The starboard column of six motor launches had been due to land 85 Commandos close to the *Normandie* dock, but fire from the shore was causing havoc. The first boat in the column, ML 192, was hit three times and set ablaze. With a four-foot hole in her side and the steering smashed, her skipper gave the order to abandon ship; only five of the 14 Commandos on board got ashore. One of them, Captain Michael Burn, attempted to carry out alone the task allotted to his team: He ran for three quarters of a mile through the enemy-occupied dockyard to the gun towers that his team

German officers interrogate Lieut. Commander Stephen Beattie, captain of the Campbelltown, taken prisoner during the Saint-Nazaire attack in March 1942. Two dozen captured Commandos so staunchly withstood questioning that a day later about 40 Germans were killed by a time bomb while they were investigating the ship in the harbor.

was supposed to attack, only to find that they were unoccupied and unarmed.

Both the second and third boats in the starboard column managed to land their troops, but the fire was so intense that the Commandos were forced to reembark. While maneuvering to make another landing attempt, both boats suffered several hits, caught fire and were abandoned. The fourth boat in the column was hit as she turned to land and blew up; most of those on board were killed. The fifth boat also came under such heavy fire that she was forced to withdraw before landing her troops. Only the sixth boat, ML 177, managed to get her men ashore—a team under Sergeant Major George Haines, whose task was to silence guns reported to be on the sea wall. Finding no guns there, Haines and his team made their way to the impromptu headquarters and reported to Newman.

With Haines's arrival, Newman recognized that, because only a handful of men in the starboard boat column had made it ashore, any further action to demolish the dock would be foolhardy. Instead, he decided to establish a fighting perimeter and withdraw his troops to the *Mole,* a landing ship about 50 yards downstream. The Commandos in the port column of motor launches had been ordered to land there and establish a bridgehead through which the whole force could escape.

To organize the withdrawal, Newman and another officer made their way through the warehouses lining the quay. Emerging from behind a line of railway trucks, they had their first glimpse of the river at the *Mole.* The hellish scene there brought them both up short. "Good heavens!" Newman exclaimed. "Surely those aren't ours!"

The river itself seemed to be on fire. Close by the *Mole* were the smoking hulks of several motor launches, still glowing red. In the center of the river more fires blazed, and a pall of black smoke curled upward in the beams of the searchlights that illuminated the nightmarish spectacle. "Well," said Newman, "there goes our transport."

The boats at the *Mole,* which were to provide the Commandos with their way home, had met disaster. One after another had been hit and ignited while attempting to land its troops. Ryder, back at his gunboat headquarters, had faced the realities of the situation. With the exception of the gunboat, all of the vessels still afloat were on fire and all were littered with dead and wounded. The *Mole* was in the firm control of the enemy, and fierce fighting elsewhere prevented any hope of rescuing the Commandos from the dock. Reluctantly, Ryder gave the order for the surviving vessels to withdraw.

Now Newman had to figure out what to do about his stranded soldiers. "I decided that transport home would not be forthcoming," he recalled, "and so I called a confab by a railway truck and decided to break inland with the idea of making for Spain."

Newman's force in the dockyard area now numbered about 100 men. Although most of them were wounded and all were exhausted, their spirits were high. Behind the cover of railroad cars, with small-arms fire rattling from all sides and smoke drifting across the dockyard, Newman issued his

Observing a form of military etiquette that did not last beyond the first years of the War, a German honor guard stands watch at the flag-draped bier of one British Commando killed in the raid on Saint-Nazaire, while captured Commandos parade by to pay respects to their fallen comrades. To end the mass burial, the Germans fired three rifle volleys in salute.

instructions. The Commandos were organized into groups of 20 and told to fight their way out of the docks and break into open country, where they could expect help from the local people. "The orders were received with grins," Newman recalled, "which reflected their delight at being able to continue the scrap."

Newman's own group moved out in good order, tore across a bridge leading out of the dockyards as bullets whined in the girders over their heads, and made their way into the town of Saint-Nazaire. "The sequence of events during the next half hour I cannot adequately describe," Newman remembered. "We seemed to be at one moment jumping over a wall into someone's back garden, then bursting through houses back into the road.

"I remember going head first through a window into somebody's kitchen—there to see breakfast laid out on a check tablecloth and thinking how odd it all was. The next moment we were dashing along a road when an armored car appeared spitting fire, but we were lucky to find a small alley to dodge into as it passed. Someone scored a good hit as a motorcycle and sidecar, full of Germans, came dashing across a square.

"By this time ammunition was running out. The wounded who had kept up with us marvelously were very weak and had lost a lot of blood. I felt that the time for a halt was not far away." The group eventually took refuge in the cellar of an empty house where they were able to rest, dress the wounds of the injured and smoke a cigarette. "I decided," said Newman, "that if we were found I should surrender as the wounded were in a pretty bad way and a single grenade thrown down the stairs would see the lot of us off."

Newman's group was found a few hours later during a house-to-house search. All through that day, the exhausted Commandos were slowly rounded up. Only five managed to avoid capture and make their way back to England with the help of the French Resistance.

The Saint-Nazaire raid did not come cheap. Of the 277 Commandos who took part, 64 were killed and 153 captured. Only four of the 18 motor launches that entered the river that night eventually got home: 105 sailors were killed and 106 taken prisoner. Out of a total of 611 men committed, 403 failed to return from the raid.

Even so, the raid was a brilliant success. At 10:55 a.m. on March 28, after the fighting had long since ceased, the *coup de grâce* was delivered to the *Normandie* dock. The timed fuses in the bow of the *Campbeltown* ignited, touching off a thunderous explosion that killed dozens of German sailors and soldiers poking around on her decks. The blast also blew away much of the dock, putting it out of commission for the remainder of the War. The German battleship *Tirpitz,* denied a proper port, never ventured into the Atlantic.

Five Victoria Crosses were among the many decorations for bravery won at Saint-Nazaire. The Commandos were now so securely established that they would be awarded a role in the forefront of many a battle yet to come. But those who took part at Saint-Nazaire remembered it proudly ever after as "the greatest raid of all."

A FIERY PROVING GROUND

AUDACIOUS ASSAULT ON A NORWEGIAN ISLAND

As Combined Operations planned it, the Commando raid on the German-occupied Norwegian island village of South Vagsoy in December of 1941 was to be an audacious frontal assault on a position bristling with heavy guns. Navy and fighter cover were to keep the Commandos' landing craft from being shot out of the water. Many of the Commandos were to land at rugged spots where the Germans would least expect attack. Indeed, when Admiral Sir John Tovey, Commander in Chief of the Home Fleet, saw that one group was scheduled to anchor its 10-ton craft near the base of a cliff, he warned the Commandos that they might have to swim the last leg of their trip in frigid Norwegian waters. The Commandos later boasted that they had landed without even getting their feet wet.

The smooth landing was only the first of the Commandos' triumphs. In fact, the Vagsoy raid was so carefully planned, so thoroughly rehearsed and so deftly executed that it won praise from its earlier advocates and doubters alike. "Even our old enemies at the War Office applauded," one officer remembered. The London *Times,* ordinarily the most restrained of commentators, trumpeted Vagsoy as "the perfect raid." And Captain Peter Young, who led one of the Commando groups ashore, unashamedly pronounced it "a minor classic of amphibious warfare, which despite the multitudinous accidents inseparable from warfare actually went according to plan." In the space of a seven-hour Arctic winter day, the Commandos achieved every tactical objective: They destroyed the protective gun battery on the nearby islet of Maloy, defeated seasoned German garrisons, demolished all the factories at South Vagsoy and, in the opinion of Captain Young, "made a total mess of everything on the island."

Hoping for as much, and needing a success to bolster public morale in that bleak Christmas season of 1941, the War Office had made room in the troop transports for three photographers—one from Movietone News and two from the Army. The photographers returned with dramatic pictures that documented the historic raid minute by minute.

In the cramped quarters belowdecks on a troop transport bound for Vagsoy, Commandos while away the time by arming grenades with fuses.

Plunging through the smoke screen laid down by RAF bombers to obscure the landing from the Germans, Commandos race up the beach at Vagsoy.

Commandos load explosives into a "beetle," the squat landing craft that tendered them to the beaches of South Vagsoy. Altogether the raiders carried 300 pounds of plastic explosives, 1,100 pounds of guncotton and 1,400 feet of fuse.

Commandos crouch inside a beetle. The ponderous landing craft made only six knots on the still waters of the fjord. "The run in seemed interminable," remembered one tense Commando.

A landing craft approaches South Vagsoy as flames and smoke from the Naval shelling rise from the village. The Commandos achieved complete surprise; one participant reported that the raiders "knocked out a party of four Germans running to their alarm post."

AN EXERCISE IN SPLIT-SECOND TEAMWORK

"Our attack had to be fast and deadly," said Lieut. Colonel John Durnford-Slater, who directed operations on shore. "We had a lot to do and a short time to do it."

The Commandos, the Royal Navy and the Royal Air Force worked with split-second coordination. At the mouth of Vags Fjord, 10 miles from South Vagsoy, sailors lowered five landing craft into the water from the ships that had transported the soldiers across the Norwegian Sea. The Commandos then loaded the landing craft with explosives and headed up the fjord.

As the men approached their destination, RAF bombers blew huge craters in nearby Norwegian airstrips to keep the Luftwaffe grounded, and RAF fighters kept at bay the few German planes that managed to take off. Simultaneously, the Navy ships anchored in the fjord sent shells flying into gun emplacements on the nearby island of Maloy. "The German infantry in Vagsoy jumped into their trenches and wondered when it would be their turn," a Commando said.

Their turn soon came. When the landing craft were within 100 yards of Vagsoy, a Commando in the lead boat sent up 10 red flares to signal for the Navy to stop shelling and for three RAF bombers to provide smoke-screen cover at the landing sites in the village. Despite a freak accident when phosphorus from a smoke bomb burned a group of Commandos, all of the men got safely ashore in minutes.

KNOCKING OUT A FORTIFIED ROCK

Before the Commandos could hope to secure South Vagsoy, they had to capture the islet of Maloy, a 250-square-yard rock less than 200 yards east of the village. The Germans had taken advantage of the islet's strategic location in the middle of Vags Fjord by emplacing four 75mm guns there to cover the only approach. "The idea of steaming straight into the mouths of four guns firing point-blank," said one Commando, "lacked charm."

But just as the plan prescribed, the *Kenya*, the Navy's lead ship, rained 6-inch shells on the rock; within 20 minutes it had silenced the battery. When 105 Commandos went ashore, they found a German officer and 15 soldiers huddling in an underground shelter, ready to surrender.

The remaining 200 Commandos went on to South Vagsoy; the *Kenya* anchored south of the islet and coordinated the actions of the two groups by radio.

From a hilltop above demolished German barracks on Maloy, a British scout looks across the fjord at the action in South Vagsoy. The bombing of the village was so intense that Commandos offshore saw "huts bursting into flame and being hurled into the air."

Radio operators inform the Kenya that Maloy has been taken. Messages to the ship, keeping the commanding officers informed of progress on both islands, averaged one ever 90 seconds at the peak of the operation.

Commandos comb Maloy for Germar survivors. Two Germans were so shell-shockec they had to be half-dragged from a ruin "They looked very miserable," a Commandc said. "I almost felt sorry for them.'

Advancing past two halted comrades, a Commando runs up a snow-covered road toward Vagsoy from the distant point at which his unit had landed.

"STICKY" GOING AGAINST A RESOLUTE FOE

"I don't know what we're getting into, but it looks pretty sticky," a British officer cautioned his men as they entered South Vagsoy. What they were getting into was a bitter contest, for despite the pummeling the village had taken, the Germans had dug in and intended to put up a fight.

In the first rush into the village, only one of the British officers survived unscathed. One captain, looking "wild and dangerous," according to the account of his admiring commanding officer, "waded in, shouting and cheering his men, throwing grenades into each house as he came to it and firing from the hip" until the enemy gunned him down.

The Germans took up defensive positions wherever they could inside the buildings in the village, but when the Commandos stormed their redoubts with grenades, incendiary bombs, gasoline torches and a 3-inch mortar, the Germans had to choose between being taken captive, shot down or burned alive.

As soon as the Commandos had secured the village, their demolition teams turned to the targets they had come to destroy: the fish-oil and canning factories. After charges were set, each team leader blew a whistle, the signal for every man to hit the ground—which within seconds was shuddering from the explosions.

Watchful for hidden Germans, three Commandos steal around the corner of a Vagsoy house

Commandos pull a sled loaded with heavy 3-inch shells and a mortar toward the center of South Vagsoy, where the Germans were headquartered and where the bloodiest fighting occurred.

Photographs taken seconds apart show the destruction of a frame canning factory used by the Germans. A Commando marveled at "the courage of the photographers, who never roamed far from the leading soldiers."

Clutching a white flag of surrender, a German officer leads his men to the beach under close guard by the British. A Commando proudly noted that the raid garnered 98 prisoners, "the first reasonably large collection of German prisoners to be taken to Britain in the War."

MOPPING UP AND GETTING OUT FAST

Their goals accomplished, the Commandos began to withdraw to their ships. They were beset by German planes that broke through the RAF fighter cover, but again teamwork prevailed. "The Naval escort let fly with everything," a captain said, "keeping the planes at a good height."

In addition to their German captives, the Commandos headed home with a cluster of Norwegians who had asked to be evacuated. Aboard ship, the Norwegians and the raiders sang Christmas carols.

The Commandos had discovered a new pride in themselves. "We had an enthusiastic welcome from the Navy, who until then had held the Army in low esteem since they continually had to rescue and evacuate it," a Commando said. "Things were different now."

A British officer inspects a German field gun on Maloy, destroyed by shelling and demolition.

Commandos trundle a wounded comrade up the icy slopes of South Vagsoy to an aid post established near the beach. Sniper fire made this duty perilous, and one Commando reported seeing a medical corpsman "first attending to his wounded, then seizing their rifles to get a few shots at the enemy."

Dragging a bandaged leg, a Commando clutches two medical orderlies for support as he struggles toward a landing craft. Of the British wounded, six died on the return trip and were buried at sea. Miraculously, in all the

Jubilant Commandos and three generations of Vagsoy citizens crowd the railing of their transport for a first glimpse of the English coast. Some civilians left Norway for fear of Nazi reprisals, others to join resistance forces in Britain. A Norwegian-born Commando who fought at South Vagsoy said the raid was "the fulfillment of our dreams."

Commandos ready some of the prisoners taken during the raid for interrogation belowdecks. Many Germans who fought at Vagsoy were not so lucky. A German general who arrived on the island to survey the damage the day after the raid found 150 for whom graves would have to be dug; another 41 were missing in action.

FORGING A KILLER FORCE

At the Basic Training Centre in Achnacarry, Scotland, Commandos-to-be practice close-in combat by slashing at hanging bags filled with rags and wool.

RUGGED QUEST FOR THE GREEN BERET

Lieut. Colonel Charles Vaughan, head of British Commando training, confers with Major William Darby of the U.S. Rangers in July 1942.

The success of the raid on Vagsoy *(pages 42-57)* established beyond doubt the validity of the commando idea. The next step, Prime Minister Winston Churchill told Combined Operations Chief Lord Louis Mountbatten as the year 1942 dawned, was to train enough men in the innovative hit-and-run techniques "to keep the whole of the enemy coastline on the alert, from the North Cape to the Bay of Biscay."

Mountbatten's staff promptly established a Commando Basic Training Centre at Achnacarry Castle, seat of the Scottish Clan of Cameron, rented to the government by Sir Donald Cameron, head of the clan. At Achnacarry, in the Highlands, the murky moors, the sheer cliffs, the deep and icy streams and the broad, rock-rimmed lakes provided terrain as bedeviling as any to be found in enemy territory.

To direct the training, the War Office chose Lieut. Colonel Charles Vaughan, a former drill sergeant in the Coldstream Guards and more recently the deputy commander of No. 4 Commando, the group that had participated in the successful raid on the Lofoten Islands in March 1941. Vaughan had "a rugged determination to exact the last ounce from his trainees," one Commando leader observed. "He knew exactly what he wanted and how to get it."

Vaughan devised a grueling 12-week course that turned out tough, self-reliant graduates who could fire a gun accurately on the run, kill silently with a knife or garrote, climb mountains and cross rivers with a few lengths of rope, or march 15 miles in two hours and 15 minutes. Any whose nerves or muscles failed these tests were sent back to their units. The training was realistic in the extreme; in many exercises live ammunition was used, and some 40 recruits were killed at Achnacarry during the War.

But Allied commanders counted results, not costs, and so did aspiring Commandos. So many volunteers signed up that hundreds had to be turned away. Eventually 25,000 Allied soldiers—French and American as well as British—completed the course. The mark of graduation was a green beret, which came to be much coveted. With it grew a spirit of brotherhood that long outlasted the assault courses.

Two British soldiers in Commando training demonstrate, with painful realism, how an unarmed man could disable an enemy with a knee to the groin.

Commandos flatten a barbed-wire entanglement with their bodies, forming human bridges so the men behind them can cross the obstacle on the run.

CHALLENGE OF SPEED AND STAMINA

The assault course at Achnacarry was a steeplechase of natural and man-made obstacles to be hurdled, climbed or teetered over at top speed by trainees who were burdened with full packs of weapons and field gear. The purpose of this formidable gantlet was to build courage, stamina and agility. Its varied and challenging terrain required a man to churn uphill with legs and lungs pumping, then race headlong toward the next hazard.

Instructors with stop watches shouted constantly for greater speed, which was achieved at the risk of nasty falls. Rock outcroppings spiked the slopes and lurked in the bogs, and the trooper who missed his footing on a peeled-log bridge found a cushion of barbed wire waiting below.

Three candidates test their agility on slender logs that bridge a gully bristling with barbed wire.

Trainees clamber down the roof of a house enveloped in smoke issuing from smudge pots. The exercise was designed to accustom the men to functioning in burning buildings.

A U.S. Ranger leaps from a 20-foot ladder of logs (left) while a British instructor waits to check whether he will emerge from the mire below with his weapon still clean and ready for action. Another jumper (above) moves on, muddied from head to foot.

A French Marine finds natural camouflage among Scottish ferns during an exercise at Achnacarry.

SURVIVAL TRAINING IN THE WILD

Commandos went into battle laden with extra weapons and ammunition, climbing gear and explosives, but without the heavy rations, cooking gear and tents normal to an army on the march.

Because they would operate in enemy territory, at Achnacarry they learned how to live off the land and blend with it—to take shelter under boughs and brush, to scrounge for food and cook it over fires yielding little smoke that would betray their positions. A butcher taught the trainees how to skin and dress game animals, and on rainy field exercises they learned to husband dry kindling in their packs to broil the raw beef and mutton sometimes issued as rations.

One Commando recalled that new men were given an unsavory surprise that they were unlikely to experience in the field. At the end of a lesson in what was called "prehistoric cooking," each was offered a succulent slice from a small animal baked in clay. Only when all had eaten was its provenance revealed: Achnacarry rat.

U.S. Rangers blend into a rocky beach in England while they wait for demolition charges to clear an obstacle during preinvasion maneuvers in 1943.

Two British trainees construct a shelter of saplings and branches as part of an exercise in field survival. Commandos did not carry tents, only rain capes.

With branches loosely arranged to reduce smoke, Commandos build a fire for cooking in the woods.

Commando instructors butcher a doe while students observe the technique. Behind enemy lines Commandos might have to kill game or steal farm animals to survive.

Commando trainees wearing full combat gear demonstrate how to "cat-crawl" across a river over rope cables that have been stretched from shore to shore.

LEARNING THE ROPES, COMMANDO-STYLE

Every Commando trainee carried a four-foot length of rope with a wooden toggle at one end and a fixed loop at the other. He could use it to help a teammate scale a cliff, or to haul equipment across a crevice. By lacing their toggle ropes through three rope cables, trainees could form a precarious bridge. And in a river-crossing exercise gruesomely dubbed the Achnacarry Death Ride, each soldier doubled his toggle rope over a sharply inclined 50-foot cable spanning an icy river and launched himself 40 feet above the water.

Not every Commando used his rope in combat, but the training paid off in other ways. "A man who could climb a cliff," said Lieut. Colonel John Durnford-Slater, the first leader of No. 3 Commando, "got the feeling he could do anything."

A demolition charge explodes in the water beneath two Commando trainees crossing a river on a "toggle bridge" made of three cables looped together with toggle ropes.

U.S. Rangers (left) descend by rope from a guard turret atop Achnacarry Castle as part of the basic Commando course. Below, British Commandos undergoing advanced training use ropes to scale an English cliff similar to those they would find on the coast of France.

Sten guns at the ready, Commandos leap from cover in a mock surprise attack. Shock tactics like this were vital to the success of the lightly armed Commandos.

USING SURPRISE TO KILL IN SILENCE

Operating in small groups without heavy weapons, Commandos relied on speed, surprise and superior skill to overwhelm the enemy. They had to be able to fire from any position and hit their marks with one burst. They learned to kill with a twist of rope or a single knife thrust—or, if necessary, with boots and bare hands. Their operations manual explained: "The Commando seeks to replace firepower with surprise, and to achieve surprise by agility and speed over difficult terrain."

To meet this last prescription, several times a week Commando trainees ran exhausting cross-country "speed marches" of up to 20 miles at a pace of nearly seven miles per hour—better than twice the normal infantry pace of three miles per hour. Without pausing for rest, they completed the march with a mock assault employing all the deadly skills in their repertory.

Commando trainees practice on each other the technique of silencing an enemy sentry with a knee in the back, a hand over the mouth and a knife in the throat.

A French commando yanks a comrade by the hair to expose his neck to a knife thrust in a demonstration of hand-to-hand combat during preinvasion maneuvers in Scotland.

A FINAL TEST AGAINST REAL BULLETS

Only combat itself exceeded the rigors and dangers of Commando training. For their last basic exercise, trainees paddled across a lake and mounted an assault on a beach defended by instructors firing live machine-gun bullets within inches of their bodies. Paddles sometimes splintered in the hail of fire, and hidden explosives sprayed the men with water and mud.

Such exercises did not stop with graduation; to keep fit between assignments, Commandos practiced assaults amid the surf and rocks of the British coast.

The experience paid off in battle. In August 1942, as he ran across the beach at Dieppe through a torrent of German machine-gun fire, a Commando was heard to say to the officer at his side: "This is nearly as bad as Achnacarry."

From a beachhead aerie, a Commando instructor aims a gun at U.S. Rangers approaching in boats.

A barrage of bullets and hand grenades rips the surface of Spean Lake near Achnacarry as Commando trainees in assault boats paddle toward the shore.

Commandos in training slither through bullet-sprayed sand in a pregraduation assault exercise at Achnacarry.

Electrically detonated charges explode in the path of a team of trainees crawling inland toward a barbed-wire obstruction.

A Commando officer brandishes a short sword as he leads his men through surf and smoke during a landing exercise on the shore of Loch Fyne, near the

western coast of Scotland. His troops slog in behind him, carrying ladders that will be used in bridging ditches and scaling cliffs that lie beyond the beach.

2

Private armies with special rules
A mission to kill the Desert Fox
The brigade that did not exist
A raid to win a bet
German Jews form a suicide squad
The turncoat who took the driver's seat
Fiasco at Tobruk
A desert nightmare for the Italians

RAIDERS OF THE SAHARA

On November 12, 1941, the submarine *Torbay* was two days out from Alexandria, Egypt, heading west on a course parallel with the coast of North Africa. In the cramped wardroom, by the yellow glow of the lights, Lieut. Colonel Geoffrey Keyes was writing to the girl he loved back in England. A few weeks earlier he had received the letter that all soldiers away from home dread: The girl was sorry but she had found someone else, one of his best friends actually, and they were going to get married.

For a while, the news had left Keyes numb with shock. But now that he was on his way to a raid, he wanted her to know that he understood; such things happened in wartime, and he hoped she would be happy. "I am writing this now as I am on my way to do more dirty work," Keyes wrote. "It is by no means an easy task, it is my show, my men and my responsibility. The chances of getting away with it are moderately good, but if you get this letter, it means I have made a bit of a bog, and not got back, as I am leaving it with someone. . . ."

Keyes, who was attached to a unit designated the Middle East Commando, was lying about his chances. He had been told the raid meant almost certain death for those taking part. Its mission was as simple as it was dangerous: to kill General Erwin Rommel, commander of the German Afrika Korps, on the night of November 17, 1941.

At 24, Keyes was the youngest lieutenant colonel in the British Army. His Commando unit comprised six officers and 53 men—all that remained of a 2,000-man Commando force that had been sent from England to the Middle East in February 1941. As a fighting group, the Middle East Commando had been the victim of circumstances. By the time the Commandos arrived in Egypt, Rommel had wrested the initiative from the Allies in North Africa. Striking eastward from Tripoli, his Afrika Korps had pushed the British out of coastal Libya, and by mid-April Rommel was threatening to drive deep into Egypt.

The Commandos had attempted a four-pronged amphibious raid on Axis installations on the coast of North Africa but had been thwarted by rough seas. Only one unit of the Commandos got ashore, at Bardia, Libya, and all it managed to do was blow up a small bridge and a few artillery pieces, and set fire to a tire depot. In May, when the Germans invaded the strategic Mediterranean island of Crete,

800 Commandos were sent to cover the withdrawal of endangered British forces there. Although they were ill equipped for the job, the Commandos fought a valiant rear-guard action—at great expense. More than 600 of them were killed, wounded, or left behind on the beaches to face capture by the Germans.

The loss of men on Crete and the lack of assault boats made the prospects for mounting amphibious Commando operations remote. Moreover, the British Army's regular units in the Middle East desperately needed replacements. In July, British General Headquarters in Cairo ordered the Middle East Commando—except for Keyes's small detachment—disbanded and the men reassigned to their former outfits. Churchill, although he saw the logic of the decision, was disgusted. "The Commandos have been frittered away," he noted angrily.

However, the setback to Commando operations was not irreversible. The Commandos, along with their American counterparts, the U.S. Rangers, would make a dramatic reappearance in 1942 in a new role—spearheading the Allied invasion of North Africa.

In the meantime, the ties forged in the Commandos were so strong that many men were reluctant to return to their original units. When a choice was offered, many men elected to remain in a reassignment center in Cairo and look around for duty that offered the chance of action. Such duty was soon available in units that were to make a specialty of desert warfare. These unconventional forces were like little private armies: They made their own rules and eschewed military convention. Their battles had to be fought not just against enemy forces, but against the hostile environment of the desert, where the days were filled with dust and flies and shriveling heat, and the nights were cold enough to chill a man's soul. The raid designed to kill Rommel was typical of the buccaneering approach that characterized their operations.

Keyes, who was leading the raid, was the son of the former Director of Combined Operations, Fleet Admiral Sir Roger Keyes. Young Keyes was an unlikely looking hero. He was tall, with a straggling mustache, jug-handle ears and an owlish expression that belied his fierce military ambition and lionhearted courage. When the idea of raiding Rommel's headquarters and killing the famed Desert Fox was first discussed, many seasoned officers doubted that such an operation was feasible. Lieut. Colonel Robert Laycock, the senior Commando officer in the Middle East, told Keyes privately that he thought the raiders were sure to be killed, but Keyes begged Laycock to keep his opinion to himself lest the operation be canceled. Keyes's enthusiasm, confidence and cool acceptance of the risks ultimately persuaded Laycock and the other senior officers to go ahead with the raid.

Timing would be critical to the success of the operation. Keyes's party was to take Rommel, dead or alive, on November 17, 1941, the night before the already scheduled start of a counteroffensive designed to relieve the besieged British fortress at Tobruk, on the Libyan coast. If the Afrika Korps was suddenly deprived of its leader, the Commandos reasoned, the British Eighth Army's attack would have a much better chance of success.

The night of November 13, 1941, was dark and stormy. Two British submarines, the *Torbay* and the *Talisman,* surfaced off the coast of Libya, miles behind the German lines, and nosed cautiously toward the shore. With Keyes aboard the *Torbay* were the 24 Commandos who would accompany him in the raid on Rommel's headquarters at the village of Beda Littoria, 11 miles inland. They were to disembark first. Aboard the *Talisman* were two more raiding parties with orders to attack Italian camps at Cyrene and Apollonia; also aboard the *Talisman* was Colonel Laycock, who was to set up a rear link on the beach.

Shortly after the submarines surfaced, the Commandos spotted a light flashing from shore. A British intelligence agent there was signaling that the beach was secure. In a strong wind, the men lined up in pairs on the wet and slippery forward casing, holding onto a wire stay that ran from bow to stern along the center of the submarine. The crew passed the rubber dinghies up through the forward hatch, then joined the Commandos on the lurching deck to help unfold the dinghies and inflate them with foot pumps. Inflating the dinghies was no easy job; no man dared let go of the wire stay for fear of slipping into the inky sea.

With the weather steadily worsening, the captain of the *Torbay* partly submerged the submarine with the idea of bringing the dinghies to water level to make their launching easier. It was a good idea that went awry; a wave suddenly swept over the deck, carrying away several dinghies—and Corporal Spike Hughes, who shouted, "I can't swim much!" before he disappeared into the night. Hughes managed to clamber into one bobbing dinghy and grab hold of another, and the current miraculously carried him back to the *Torbay*, where he was warmly congratulated by Keyes for saving two dinghies.

The wind and the waves and the pitching of the submarine were making it increasingly difficult to get the dinghies away. If one man got into a dinghy safely, the next man would tip the flimsy craft and ditch them both into the sea. Two submarine crewmen stayed in the water, retrieving dinghies that had capsized.

Meanwhile, on the *Talisman*, five hours passed as Laycock impatiently waited for the flashlight signal from shore indicating that all the men from the *Torbay* had landed safely. Laycock could not understand the delay. When they had planned the raid they had estimated that an hour would be sufficient for Keyes and his men to reach the shore. Now the submarine would have to put back to sea to recharge its batteries within five hours. Another hour went by and Laycock began to consider postponing his landing until the following night. Finally, at half past midnight, he saw the signal light. Keyes's party had spent six hours launching 13 dinghies from the *Torbay*.

The wind had reached 15 miles per hour by midnight and was now approaching gale force, 32 miles per hour. Moreover, time was running out. With the Commandos on deck clinging to their dinghies, the *Talisman* nosed inshore. Suddenly the vessel touched bottom. As it did so, a wave swept over, washing away 11 men and seven dinghies. The submarine reversed its propellers to clear the bottom while the men in the sea struggled desperately to pull themselves up into the dinghies. The Commandos still on the deck tried again and again to launch their boats; again and again the dinghies overturned. By 4 a.m. withdrawal was the only alternative. The crew of the *Talisman* recovered all of the men and dinghies they could find in the darkness, and the submarine headed back out to sea. Only four dinghies from the *Talisman* reached the beach.

One of those dinghies carried Laycock, who promptly rendezvoused with Keyes and his party. Though the nine Commandos with Laycock were tired and disappointed, he led the whole group on a trek inland to some scrub, where they could shelter and snatch a few hours' sleep. In the morning, Laycock and Keyes decided to abandon the subsidiary targets at Cyrene and Apollonia and concentrate on the primary objective: Rommel. The weather was becoming stormier and there was little hope of getting more men ashore. In any case, there was no time to waste. Rommel had to be eliminated before the British offensive began.

Deep in enemy territory the Commandos could travel only at night. They lay low through the daylight hours. At 8 p.m., in pouring rain, they began the long march inland along rough sheep tracks. Laycock had stayed behind on the beach as originally planned, and Keyes alone led the raid. Just before dawn, the men hid as best they could in the dripping scrub and tried to sleep. This pattern of marching by night and hiding by day prevailed for the next 48 hours.

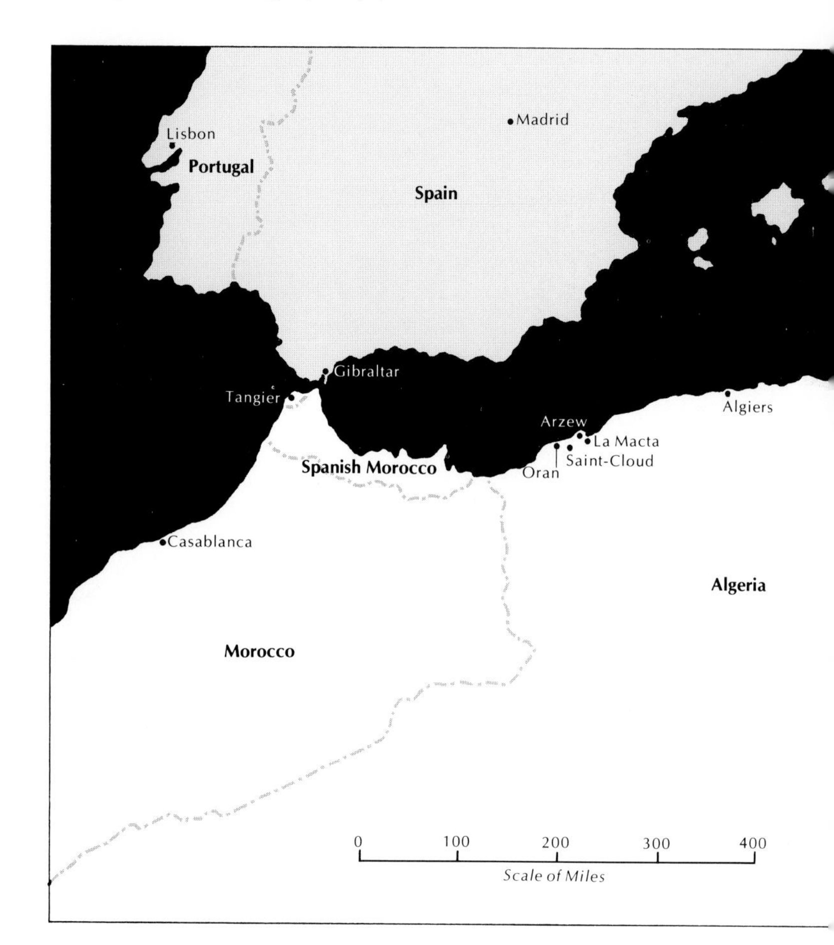

The morning of November 17 found the men resting in a cave about five miles from Beda Littoria, while thunderstorms rolled around the surrounding hills and torrential rain turned the desert into a quagmire.

The weather did not help the flagging spirits of the Commandos. "Every now and then the clouds seemed to open and a deluge of rain fell," recalled Captain Robin Campbell, Keyes's second-in-command. "The country we had to march over turned to mud before our eyes. Little torrents of muddy water sprang up all over the countryside we could see from the mouth of the cave. Also the roof began to drip. Spirits were sinking—I know mine were—at the prospect of a long, cold, wet and muddy march before we even arrived at the starting point of a hazardous operation."

Keyes tried to buck up his men by telling them the weather was just what they needed—the wind and rain would cover their approach on Beda Littoria and the enemy would be taking shelter, so they would be less likely to be spotted. Shortly after 6 p.m. the party had a final meal of bread and marmalade. Then, after blackening their faces for camouflage, the men set out in single file, slithering and squelching in the mud. Soon it was so dark that each of them had to hold on to the bayonet scabbard of the man in front to keep in contact.

About a quarter of a mile from the village, the Commandos stopped by a fork in the track for a cigarette and a final rest. Then Lieutenant Roy Cooke and six men trudged off toward the road to Cyrene to cut Axis military telegraph and telephone wires. Keyes, with the 22 remaining Commandos, continued on into the village. With guns at the ready, Keyes's party crept stealthily into an apparently deserted Arab market about 100 yards from the white stone house

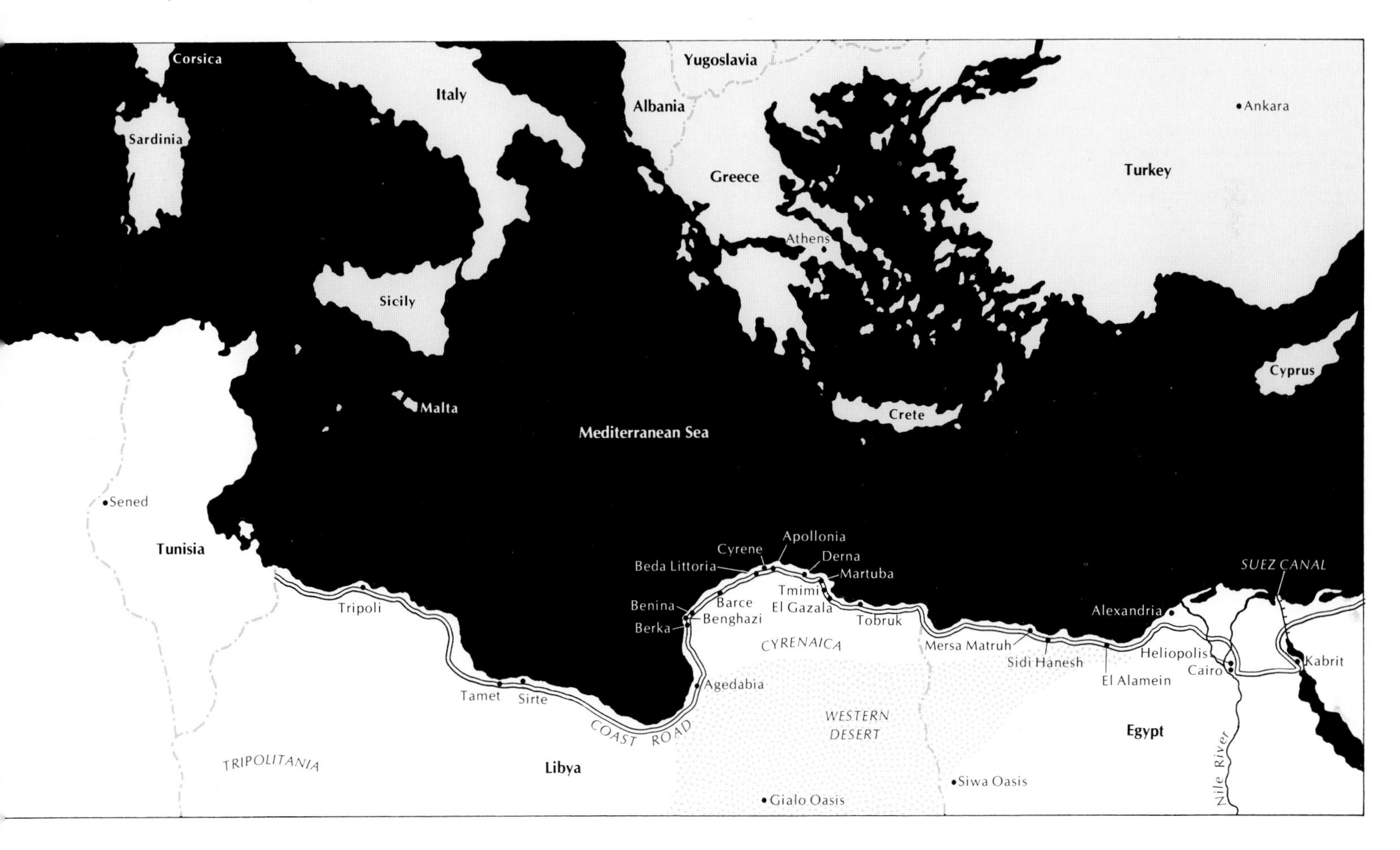

Between 1940 and 1943, Allied special forces operated in inhospitable terrain that stretched more than 1,500 miles from Libya's sand wastelands, where British and New Zealand raiders sabotaged coastal airfields, to Tunisia's rugged mountains and Algeria's bleak beaches, where U.S. Rangers harassed the last Axis strongholds in French North Africa.

that their map identified as Rommel's headquarters. There, in the muddy road, they waited while Keyes and Sergeant Jack Terry went ahead to reconnoiter the house.

The Commandos were tense. One, seeking cover from the rain, tripped over a tin can and disturbed a dog, which began to bark furiously. A door opened suddenly, spilling light into the road, and an Arab officer dressed in the uniform of the Italian Libyan Arab Force demanded to know what was going on. Campbell snapped out a reply in German, stating that his party were Germans on patrol and that the Arab was to go away and keep his dog quiet. Apparently satisfied, the Arab wished them a polite *"Gute Nacht"* and returned to the shelter of his hut.

When Keyes and Terry returned, they reported the way clear. Now the men were given their final orders. Keyes would lead the attack, with Campbell, Terry and three other men. The remaining Commandos were to split up and cover the approaches to the building, lest the assault party be interrupted in its search for Rommel. They had orders to shoot anyone who emerged from the rear of the house.

At about midnight the assault party cut a hole in the wire fence surrounding the house and slipped into the garden among the dark shadows of cypress trees. They could see a single sentry on duty at the entrance to the drive: Keyes raced between the trees and killed him without a sound. Then they all settled down to wait, in the pouring rain, until the one light remaining in a top window went out.

As soon as the building was dark, Keyes led the way around the house to the short flight of stone steps at the front door. The Commandos ran up the steps and hammered on the door while Campbell shouted loudly in German to be let in. The door was opened by a German soldier in a steel helmet and greatcoat. Campbell recorded what happened then: "Geoffrey at once closed with him, covering him with his Colt. The man seized the muzzle of Geoffrey's revolver and tried to wrest it from him. Before I or Terry could get round behind him he retreated, still holding on to Geoffrey, to a position with his back to the wall." As the German started to shout, Campbell shot him with his .38 revolver.

The Commandos ran into the house and found themselves in a wide, dimly lit entrance hall with doors on either side. To the right were stone stairs leading to the upper floors. The Commandos could hear a man in heavy boots clattering down the stairs, and as his feet came into view Sergeant Terry fired a burst from his Tommy gun. The man hastily retreated.

Keyes pointed to a gleam of light shining under a door. He flung the door open to reveal about 10 German soldiers in steel helmets, some sitting around a table, others standing. "I'll throw a grenade in!" Campbell shouted. Keyes slammed the door and held it shut while Campbell pulled the pin from a grenade; then Keyes opened the door again and Campbell rolled the grenade into the center of the room. At the same time, Terry sprayed the room with his Tommy gun. "Well done!" said Keyes. As he spoke, one of the Germans fired and a bullet struck Keyes just above the heart. He fell at the feet of his two comrades.

Campbell jumped forward and shut the door, then he and Terry threw themselves aside as the grenade exploded. Their ears were ringing from the blast as they carried Keyes outside and laid him gently on the grass beside the front door. When Campbell knelt to feel Keyes's heart, it had already stopped beating.

"Are we going to retreat, sir?" a Commando standing sentry duty asked Campbell. "No!" Campbell snapped and went back into the house. A few minutes later, shots rang out behind the building. Sergeant Terry ran around to investigate and found Campbell lying on the ground, badly wounded in the leg: He had been shot by one of the Commando sentries, who had followed the instructions to assume that anyone emerging from the back of the house was an enemy. Campbell handed over command to the 19-year-old sergeant, telling him to place explosive charges inside the house, then withdraw with the rest of the men. Some of them offered to carry Campbell back to the coast, a distance of more than 10 miles, but Campbell knew it was impossible and ordered them to leave him. He was captured by the Germans and imprisoned.

The sad and dispirited little party hurried out of the village in the dark and the rain, leaving bombs exploding behind them. The death of Keyes had affected every man. And where was Rommel, the man they had come so far to kill? No one had seen a hint of his presence at Beda Littoria.

At 5 p.m. on November 18, the exhausted raiders staggered onto the beach where Laycock was anxiously waiting. Sergeant Terry's report could hardly have been worse: Keyes was dead, Rommel was not, and Campbell had been abandoned. The rest of them could do nothing but hide out in caves around the beach and wait for the submarines to pick them up that night. Though the *Torbay* arrived on schedule, the sea was too rough to launch the dinghies. The submarine signaled that it would return the following night.

However, the Commandos had already been spotted by Arab tribesmen eager to earn a little money by passing information to the Italians. At noon, Arab military police wearing red fezzes arrived on the beach and began crawling toward the caves where the Commandos were holed up. Firing broke out. At first Laycock was not unduly worried, but soon a large force of Italians appeared on the skyline, followed by some Germans. By 2 p.m. the Axis troops were within 200 yards of the Commandos. Laycock called his men together and told them to split up into twos and threes, and try to escape into the desert.

Only two men made it. On Christmas Day 1941, Laycock and Sergeant Terry walked into the forward positions of the advancing Eighth Army at Cyrene. They had been scarcely 10 miles from their countrymen all along, but had wandered for 36 days, living for part of that time on berries they picked from the scrub.

Keyes was awarded a posthumous Victoria Cross for his part in the raid. But the bitter irony of the operation was that British intelligence had been wrong. Rommel never used the house at Beda Littoria as his headquarters. On the night of the raid he was not even in the village, but at the front with his forward troops.

Keyes's ill-fated venture occurred at a time when two other eclectic, desert-bred fighting units were beginning to bedevil the Afrika Korps. One of these was the Long Range Desert Group, a band of mobile reconnaissance experts whose skill in negotiating the sand seas excelled that of the nomadic Arabs. The other was a secret unit founded by the foot-loose Middle East Commando to stage hit-and-run raids on German outposts. Initially it was called simply L Detachment, but in time it would gain a respectful reputation from Allies and Axis alike under the name of the Special Air Service.

L Detachment was the brainchild of David Stirling. Stirling, who was six feet six inches tall, had planned to be the first man to climb Mount Everest and was training in the Rocky Mountains when war broke out. Returning home, he enlisted in the Scots Guards, but in 1940, after meeting Robert Laycock in the bar of a London club, he transferred to No. 8 Commando and was sent to the desert.

When the Commando force in the Middle East was disbanded, Stirling and another No. 8 Commando officer, Jock Lewis, got permission to experiment with 50 parachutes that had been unloaded at Alexandria by mistake. The venture was risky; no parachute instructors had yet arrived in the Middle East, and the only plane they could get from the Royal Air Force for practice was an old Valentia, a transport whose tiny belly hatch and large, low-slung tail wheel made for hazardous jumping. These facts did not bother Stirling, although they probably should have. On his first jump his parachute caught on the tail wheel of the aircraft, ripping a large hole in the canopy; he fell too fast and severely injured his back when he hit the ground. In the Scottish Military Hospital at Alexandria, he occupied his time by developing on paper some ideas for a small, highly mobile force able to parachute into the desert behind Axis lines to strike by night at airfields and communications.

In July of 1941, as soon as he was able to get about on crutches, Stirling hitched a lift to General Headquarters in Cairo to present his plans to General Sir Claude Auchinleck, the recently appointed Commander in Chief, Middle East. Unfortunately, Stirling had neither an appointment with the general nor a pass to his headquarters and was refused entrance by the sentries at the gate. He waited until their attention was distracted for a moment, then slipped through as unobtrusively as his height would allow. At the entrance to the building Stirling heard someone shout "Stop that man!" and he ducked into the first office he could find. He was ejected in short order by the infuriated major who was inside.

Back in the corridor, utterly unabashed, Stirling tried his luck at another door and found himself face to face with the Deputy Chief of Staff, Middle East Forces, Lieut. General Neil M. Ritchie. After explaining he had urgent business, Stirling found himself invited—to his surprise—to take a seat. Ritchie listened to the young officer, read the crumpled, pencil-written memorandum he produced from his pocket and finally said: "I think this might be the sort of plan we are looking for."

Three days later Stirling was called to meet with General Auchinleck. At that time, Auchinleck was being pressured by the Prime Minister to mount a major counteroffensive against Rommel. Churchill believed that the German invasion of the Soviet Union the preceding month had stretched the Reich's ability to supply its armies in North Africa. The sooner the British Eighth Army struck, he argued, the better. Auchinleck disagreed. He wanted time to reequip his troops, train reinforcements, repair his armor and stock supply depots. Auchinleck was a thorough, cautious Scot, and not the man to risk entire divisions simply because the Prime Minister was chafing for action. But here was a proposal from a fellow Scotsman. Stirling's plan risked only a handful of men and, with a bit of luck, it might make a considerable contribution to the success of an offensive, when Auchinleck judged the time to be right. He told Stirling to go ahead with his plan.

Stirling was immediately promoted to captain and authorized to recruit six officers and 60 men. His unit would be known as L Detachment of the Special Air Service Brigade, a brigade that did not exist. The code name SAS Brigade had been invented in July 1941 to make the Germans believe that paratroops had arrived in the Middle East in brigade strength. In fact the brigade was nothing more than a figment of the fertile imagination of Dudley Clarke, the staff officer who had suggested the formation of the Commandos a year before.

Stirling had no difficulty finding recruits from among the Commandos in Cairo and Alexandria still awaiting reassignment. L Detachment set up a camp at Kabrit, a village on the edge of the Great Bitter Lake about 60 miles east of Cairo, and began training.

From the start, L Detachment had problems finding a suitable explosive for the projected operations against Axis airfields. They wanted a handy, lightweight bomb, both explosive and incendiary, that would wreck an aircraft through impact, then burn it beyond repair. Experts said those specifications were impossile to meet, but Captain Jock Lewis (the first officer Stirling recruited) refused to believe them. After some weeks of noisy experiments he came up with a mixture of plastic, thermite and oil. The concoction worked beautifully and was known thereafter as a Lewis bomb.

When an RAF officer visiting Kabrit warned Stirling that he was underestimating the difficulty of raiding airfields, Stirling bet £10 that he could get in and out of Heliopolis, the main Cairo airfield, without detection. One morning in October 1941, guards at Heliopolis found holes in the barbed wire surrounding the airfield, and 45 labels stuck on aircraft around the field. On each label was written "L Detachment." Stirling won his £10.

Lieut. Colonel David Stirling, founder of the British Special Air Service for raiding Axis airfields and other installations in the desert, stands by an American-made jeep to talk with Lieutenant Edward McDonald, who led many of the four-man SAS patrols.

Lacking standard training equipment in the desert, Special Air Service recruits practice parachute landings by tumbling off the backs of trucks moving at 30 miles per hour.

After this mock-serious success, Stirling gathered the men of L Detachment and told them they would soon mount a raid to "polish off" Rommel's fighter force. The men greeted the news with enthusiastic cheers. The raid was timed to coincide with Geoffrey Keyes's assassination of Rommel, and for a neophyte outfit the foray was an ambitious one: to raid no fewer than five German airfields in the El Gazala and Tmimi area and destroy the Luftwaffe's new Messerschmitt-109F fighters in the hours before dawn on November 18. The raiders would parachute in, accomplish their objectives, and walk 45 miles to rendezvous with a patrol from the Long Range Desert Group, which would ferry them back to base in trucks.

From the start, almost nothing went right. On November 16, Stirling and 62 of his men sat apprehensively on board five RAF Bombay bombers as they circled above the desert west of Tobruk, bucking and bumping in gale-force winds. The weather, windy at takeoff, had suddenly turned vile, and the aircraft were lost. A violent sandstorm on the ground obliterated all landmarks. More than an hour passed as the Bombays roamed over the desert and the pilots tried to find their bearings. For the men waiting tensely to jump into the night, it seemed an eternity before the green light above the hatch flicked on.

Stirling himself was the first man through the hatch. In the darkness of that stormy night he could see nothing as he plummeted toward the ground. He landed with such force that he was knocked unconscious for a few seconds, and when he recovered he found the wind was so strong it was dragging him by his parachute at a fast clip across the stony desert floor. Stirling disentangled himself from his harness, scrambled to his feet and was almost knocked down by the wind. The air was filled with swirling dust and sand that clogged his mouth and nose. He tried to shout to locate the other men, but the howling of the storm drowned his words. Screwing up his eyes against the stinging sand, he pulled a flashlight from his uniform pocket and began to wave it in all directions. After a minute or so a pinprick of light from another flashlight appeared in the blackness, then another and another.

Stirling spent almost an hour trying to assemble the men who had dropped with him. One man had disappeared; Stirling assumed that he too had been knocked out on landing and dragged away by his parachute. The rest of the party all had cuts and bruises, one had broken an arm, two had sprained ankles and one had sprained a wrist. Worse, they could find only two of their 10 supply parachutes. These yielded half a dozen blankets, 12 water bottles, a day's supply of food and six cans of explosive—but no fuses. The fuses were in one of the missing containers. This was the end of their hopes for "polishing off" Rommel's fighter force. The raid was over before it had begun.

To salvage something from the operation, Stirling decided to make for the Coast Road to reconnoiter the movement of German traffic. He took a sergeant named Tait with him and ordered the rest of the men to head for the spot where they were due to be picked up by the Long Range Desert Group. Stirling reasoned that if they had been dropped in the right place, the rendezvous point would be only about 30 miles away. The two groups wished each other luck and went their separate ways.

With the dawn the sandstorm died away. In the cold gray light of the early morning, Stirling and Tait found themselves surrounded by featureless desert. Stirling had calculated that the sea was 10 miles from where they had landed, yet they had already walked 13 miles and had seen no sign of the distinctive ridged escarpment that bordered the coast. At about 10 a.m. Stirling could just make out, through his binoculars, the silhouette of the escarpment on the distant horizon. The two men took a short rest in a hollow in the sand, slept fitfully, then continued on their way. It was almost 5 p.m. before Stirling and Tait reached the edge of the cliffs. By then the clouds were piling up, thick and black. From the cover of a rock outcrop they watched the traffic moving on the Coast Road below them until the rain started and they could see nothing more.

Wearily, the two men set off again on the long trek to the rendezvous. All through the night it rained, all through the night they walked on. At 7 a.m. the rain stopped and Stirling and Tait lay down on the sodden desert floor and slept for four hours. Then they resumed walking. Shortly before midnight they saw a light low on the horizon. It was the signal lamp with which the Long Range Desert Group marked its camp for the benefit of the men in the desert. Two hours later, Stirling and the sergeant limped in.

The men from another plane had already arrived. They had a similar story to tell. They had been widely scattered during the drop and had lost most of their supplies. Ironically, they had located the fuses, but no explosive. One of the men was missing; another had broken his leg and could not be moved.

The next day, 10 more men arrived with the same sad tale. Stirling waited another 36 hours before giving up hope for the rest of his outfit. Of the 62 men who had set out to destroy Rommel's planes, only 22 were left. For this disastrous loss, L Detachment had achieved precisely nothing.

But the detachment had learned a valuable lesson. The tragedy taught Stirling that parachuting was not the best way to approach a desert objective: The winds were too dangerous, too likely to obscure landmarks and to carry the men to disaster. The solution to Stirling's transport problem was equally obvious: If the Long Range Desert Group could bring L Detachment men back from a raid by truck, surely the LRDG could also carry them *to* a raid. The proposal was received with unqualified enthusiasm by the curious military nomads of the LRDG.

The Long Range Desert Group had been formed in the summer of 1940 by Major Ralph Bagnold, a career Army officer, geographer and desert explorer. Sponsored by the Royal Geographical Society, Bagnold had spent much of the decade between 1925 and 1935 charting the lonely wastes and shifting sands of the Libyan desert while researching a book entitled *The Physics of Blown Sand and Desert Dunes*. During expeditions into the desert in a Model T Ford, he developed an improved sun compass for more accurate navigation, steel channels for freeing the wheels of vehicles stuck in soft sand, and a condenser that radically reduced the amount of water a motor vehicle needed in the desert. Bagnold had also plotted the location of many water holes previously known only to nomadic Arabs.

When the War started, Bagnold suggested to General Sir Archibald Wavell, then Commander in Chief, Middle East, that he could set up a unit capable of living for weeks on end in the desert and able to watch enemy movements from the fastness of the lonely desert wastes. Wavell was enthusiastic, and before long the LRDG was formed.

Bagnold's first recruits were a few British academics and scientists who had accompanied him on his earlier expeditions out of Cairo and Alexandria. By the summer of 1941 the LRDG had established a chain of supply dumps across the desert, extending the potential range of their operations to fantastic distances. They ran reconnaissance and survey patrols with regularity across 1,200 miles of desert from Cairo to Tripoli. Much of the information the Eighth Army received about enemy movements and equipment during this period came via the radio trucks of the LRDG units stationed behind the Axis lines. Its members adopted some of the local garb, wearing Arab headdresses and sandals. The lack of water for shaving forced them to grow beards. The men of the LRDG looked the unlikeliest of soldiers, but their courage was never questioned and their efficiency was beyond doubt.

The desert in which the LRDG operated was about the same size as India, roughly 1,000 miles wide and 1,200 miles long. Much of the terrain was a featureless sand sea widely regarded as impassable, and the only way to cross it was to navigate by compass, sun and stars, as sailors navigate the sea. LRDG drivers learned how to coax trucks up one side of a dune and slide down the other—negotiating dune after dune, hour after hour, mile after mile, frequently stopping to free wheels bogged down to their hubs in soft sand. Living rough, sleeping in the sand beside their trucks, unwashed, unshaven and exposed to climatic extremes, the men of the LRDG considered the desert their personal territory, to be shared only with the Arabs.

The link between L Detachment, soon to be better known as the Special Air Service, or SAS, and the Long Range Desert Group was forged at a dinner attended by officers from both units under the colored lights and palms in the garden of Shepheard's Hotel in Cairo. The union was to be fruitful, for the groups had a healthy respect for each other and the men all shared a love of the desert and a tendency to treat their missions like schoolboy pranks or social outings; they tended to describe their raids as "fun."

Joint SAS-LRDG raids were launched on the 8th of December, 1941, from a base at Gialo Oasis, a scraggy village of mud huts and stunted palms about 600 miles west of Cairo. On the night of December 14, Italian Air Force officers at Tamet airfield near Sirte were in the middle of a noisy party when the door of the mess suddenly burst open and men with blackened faces sprayed the room with Tommy-gun fire, shooting out the lights. A few minutes later, aircraft lined up along the landing strip began to explode as a band of 10 SAS raiders raced away into the night toward their rendezvous with the LRDG, two miles distant. Twenty-four planes were destroyed.

On the following night, five LRDG trucks unobtrusively attached themselves to the end of an Italian convoy moving along the Coast Road. When the convoy halted at Mersa Brega roadhouse, three SAS men raced among the parked transports to plant 30 bombs while their comrades provided covering fire. The trio then ran back to their own vehicles, and as the bombs went off, the five British trucks roared down the road to a point where they could turn off and flee into the safety of the desert.

On the 18th of December, 37 German aircraft at Agedabia airfield were blown up by four SAS men. Seven days later, the SAS returned to Tamet and destroyed another 27 brand-new aircraft that had arrived only the day before.

The sabotage continued. During the next 12 months, the SAS under Stirling would destroy some 250 enemy airplanes and leave a trail of havoc in its wake. No sooner had one raid finished than the next was planned. While the Germans were searching for the SAS in one part of the desert, the raiders would strike in another. Rommel was obliged to withdraw more and more troops from the front line to protect his rear against the ravages of the SAS. German radio began referring to Stirling as the phantom major because he appeared out of the night and disappeared before dawn; only smoking hulks and dead bodies marked his passing.

On occasion, when the pace of the raiding grew excruciating, Stirling would call for a break, and he and his men

A radio operator of the Long Range Desert Group tries to contact his base station. Using a portable antenna affixed to his truck, a skilled operator could extend the range of his radio to as much as 1,000 miles.

would repair to Cairo for rest and relaxation. Stirling's brother, Peter, was a diplomat at the British Embassy and by now was accustomed to having his apartment, on a broad and fashionable avenue opposite the embassy, turned into a temporary headquarters for the SAS.

"In those days when private war could still be waged," said Lieutenant Carol Mather, a young SAS officer, "it was no strange sight to see an SAS expedition parked in the shade of the trees in one of Cairo's quiet residential areas with jeeps bulging with bedding and guns, and drivers lolling against the trees wondering, rather wistfully, whether it was done to brew tea by the side of the pavement."

Peter Stirling's apartment provided an equally incongruous wartime scene. "The flat was crowded out," Mather wrote, describing a typical afternoon he spent there. "David stood at the door having a heated argument with Mo, the Egyptian servant, about an important message he was supposed to have sent to GHQ. On the sofa were sitting some girls and some other officers discussing the racing form at Gezira, whilst across all this we talked about bearings and petrol and ammunition, or sat sprawled on the floor over maps of the desert trying to think above the sound of the gramophone."

The homey comforts of Cairo contrasted strangely with the rigors of the desert. Another SAS officer, Lieutenant Stephen Hastings, described the condition of his comrades a few weeks after an airfield raid. They had driven along the runway in two columns of jeeps armed with Vickers K machine guns, shooting up the aircraft as they went. Then they had raced back into the desert.

In a wadi where low scrub offered some cover from the planes that they knew would soon be on their tails, the SAS troopers took a break. "We looked round at each other," remembered Hastings. "We were indeed a ragged-looking bunch. Faces, hair and beards were covered in a thick, yellow-gray film of dust, eyes were red and strained. Our dirty, open-necked battle dress and loose overcoats hung upon us as upon scarecrows, and they fitted well into the background of the desert. One officer was trying to scrape large, dried and sand-caked bloodstains off his trousers with a stick—the blood of the dead soldier who was lying on his back under a bush with a dirty blanket over the top of his body. Our mouths were dry and ill tasting and there was a burning behind the eyes rather like the symptoms of a hangover. But for the moment we were safe, or at least comparatively so."

At the end of May 1942, Stirling was summoned to Cairo for an interview with the Director of Military Operations. He was informed that a convoy of 17 ships would attempt to reach the beleaguered island of Malta in June. Malta was a critical Allied base in the Mediterranean, and its survival depended on getting supplies through. Stirling was asked to join in a concerted British effort to curtail Axis air attacks on the convoy.

Within 24 hours he produced a plan for simultaneous raids at eight enemy airfields on the night of June 13, using a squadron that the SAS had recently recruited from among Frenchmen who had fled their country after it surrendered to Germany and then formed their own army under Allied command. Most of the proposed raids presented no particular difficulty for the SAS, but three important airfields on Stirling's list were in an area heavily patrolled by crack troops of the Afrika Korps, and Stirling thought the LRDG's chances of getting through the German patrols without detection were remote. When he mentioned the problem at GHQ Cairo he was told of the existence of another group that might be able to help. The group had an utterly meaningless title—Special Interrogation Group—to conceal the desperate nature of its business.

The SIG was virtually a suicide squad. It was composed of a handful of German Jews from Palestine whose job was to infiltrate the German lines dressed as Afrika Korps soldiers. Every man knew that capture meant death. The SIG was the creation of a British officer, Captain Herbert Buck, who had been taken prisoner by the Germans at El Gazala, but later escaped. While he was making his way back to the Eighth Army, Buck acquired an Afrika Korps cap and found to his relief and amazement that he was able to wander freely through the German lines. He spoke German fluently and was readily accepted as just another member of the Afrika Korps. When Buck got back safely to Allied positions, he suggested forming the SIG.

Buck was a perfectionist. Within the SIG only German was spoken, and German military discipline applied. Each man was supplied a false name and cover story, a forged paybook, identification tags and letters from "home." He also carried a photograph of himself with his "girl friend in Berlin"; the girl friend was actually an obliging member of the Army's women's auxiliary who had suitably "Aryan" features, and the Berlin background was added in the darkrooms of Army photographers in Cairo. Captured German weapons and vehicles were discreetly passed to the SIG along with the latest intelligence about the enemy's day-to-day routine. The SIG even took the trouble to learn the slang current with the Afrika Korps.

When Stirling asked Buck if the SIG could transport the French SAS raiding parties to the three airfields in the Derna-Martuba region, Buck immediately offered to lead the expedition himself. On the evening of June 12, a convoy of four vehicles—three German trucks and a British three-ton truck marked as captured by the Afrika Korps—bumped into a German camp on the road to Derna. Several men clambered down from the cabs with their mess tins and casually joined the line at the field kitchen, where lentils and dumplings were being served for the evening meal. These men were members of the SIG. In the backs of their vehicles were the Free French raiders, hiding under tarpaulins and behind packing cases.

The next day, at a camp five miles from Derna, plans for the raids that night were completed. Each of the three raiding parties would consist of five Free French. Only two trucks would be used. One truck would head for Martuba and its sole airfield, the other truck for Derna, where two airfields were to be attacked. Three SIG men would accompany each vehicle. Immediately following the raids, the three raiding parties would return to the camp. From there they would set off together for a rendezvous with the LRDG, 25 miles distant.

Shortly before 9 p.m. on June 13, the two trucks rolled off into the night, with the Frenchmen once more concealed under tarpaulins. Buck, who had reluctantly decided he should remain behind at the camp to coordinate the withdrawal, settled down to await their return.

At about midnight, Lieutenant Augustin Jordan stumbled into the camp alone and gasped out a story that made Buck's blood run cold. The truck heading for Derna had been repeatedly delayed by mechanical troubles. Finally the SIG driver stopped the truck about 200 yards from the airfield and climbed out of it, mumbling something about the engine overheating. From the back of the truck, the 10 Frenchmen suddenly heard the sound of running men. Jordan peeked over the tailgate and saw that the truck was surrounded by German soldiers. One German shouted, "All Frenchmen come out!"

The Frenchmen responded with grenades and bursts of machine-gun fire. In the confusion of the next few seconds, Jordan jumped from the truck and ran for his life. As he did so, the truck, which had been packed with explosives and ammunition, disintegrated in a ball of fire.

Jordan and Buck waited for a week at the LRDG rendezvous in the faint hope that others might return from the raid on Martuba. None did. The men in the second truck had suffered a similar fate: All were killed or captured.

Military intelligence later determined that the SIG driver of Jordan's truck had betrayed the raiders. He was a German prisoner of war who had been recruited by Buck to help the unit perfect its German identity. The driver had been thoroughly screened by British intelligence and passed as trustworthy. But in the end, clearly, his birthright proved too strong. He had manufactured mechanical problems on the way to Derna in order to deliver the raiders into the hands of his countrymen precisely on time.

The other SAS raids that night encountered greater success. At Benina airfield near Benghazi, Stirling and two corporals planted 60 bombs on aircraft, supply dumps and hangars. On their way out, Stirling opened the door of the German guardroom and threw in a grenade, saying: "Here, catch!" As a corporal named Seekings reported, "The Jerry at the desk did in fact catch it, and in a voice of horror cried *'Nein, nein!' 'Ja, ja,'* said Stirling, and closed the door. A moment later there was a big explosion. We then ran like hell as the bombs in the hangars had also started to go off." At one Berka airfield, the SAS found sentries posted beside every aircraft; as the first bomb was being placed, a sentry challenged, shots were exchanged and bullets were soon whining in all directions. The three SAS raiders left the sentries to fight it out among themselves and blew up the gasoline dump instead. Two miles away, at another Berka airfield, the French SAS destroyed 11 bombers and killed many of the guards.

In all, 16 aircraft were blown up that night; so were hundreds of tons of fuel, ammunition and spare parts. These successes, however, were small compensation for the losses among the raiding parties and were little help to the Malta convoy. Axis attacks by air and sea took a devastating toll on the convoy; only two of the ships got through—barely enough to sustain the island in its time of crisis.

More bad news awaited the SAS raiders when they returned to their base at Siwa Oasis: Tobruk had fallen on the 21st of June. Its capture provided the Afrika Korps with an important forward supply base that could enable the German forces to complete their drive on Alexandria and Cairo. Tobruk also was important to General Rommel because with the British gone he would have no resistance in his rear, and because the port facilities there promised to shorten his lines of communication. The British, realizing this, conceived an ambitious plan to render the town worthless to the Germans.

The central figure in the proposed Tobruk raid was one of the most colorful of the many exotic characters who had been drawn, like moths to a flame, to the fighting in the desert. He was John Haselden, an Englishman born in Egypt, where his father owned a prosperous cotton business. Haselden had inherited the family firm and the family's handsome white house on the banks of the Nile at El Minya. In June 1940 he had volunteered for military service with the British, and GHQ Cairo quickly realized his services could be invaluable. Haselden spoke fluent Arabic, and he was known and respected by many of the Bedouin desert tribes. More important, he could easily pass as an Arab.

Disguised as an Arab shepherd, British intelligence agent Lieut. Colonel John Haselden makes rendezvous with a Long Range Desert Group patrol deep in the Sahara. Haselden, who spent weeks in solitude behind enemy lines, used a radio that he carried beneath his sleeping blankets to arrange such meetings.

General Headquarters in Cairo took Haselden on as a British intelligence agent. He preferred to work alone and soon proved himself to be a man without fear. The Long Range Desert Group would take him deep into the sand wastes and leave him at some God-forsaken spot to carry out some mysterious errand. Weeks later the LRDG would return to collect him, and often could hardly recognize the bearded "Arab" who appeared out of the dunes to meet them. In his Arab robes, Haselden wandered freely through towns and villages occupied by the Germans and Italians, and he even infiltrated Axis camps. On one occasion he drove a flock of sheep across a Luftwaffe airfield in order to get a closer look at the aircraft. Because Arab shepherds frequently did the same, the German guards saw nothing amiss in the incident.

After Tobruk fell, Haselden proposed raiding it. He was confident, he told GHQ, that he could get into the town with a small party of men—no more than a dozen—to sabotage the oil storage tanks. His suggestion was greeted with enthusiasm by the military planners in Cairo. Preparations were already well advanced for a battle at El Alamein to drive Rommel's Afrika Korps out of Egypt; the destruction of Tobruk's important supply depots would strike a heavy blow against the Desert Fox.

But what Haselden had conceived as a small-scale raid, depending on surprise for its success, quickly grew in size and scope. By the middle of August Haselden found himself leading an operation that involved most of the special forces in the Middle East as well as amphibious landings and Naval and air support. Instead of exploding a few oil tanks, Haselden was now expected to capture and hold Tobruk for 12 hours while ships and harbor installations were destroyed. Meanwhile, the SAS men would descend on Benghazi harbor and blow up everything they could lay their hands on. The Long Range Desert Group would attack Barce airfield, and the Sudan Defense Force, native Sudanese serving under the British, would strike Gialo Oasis, which had been overrun by the Italians.

The operation was scheduled for the night of September 13, 1942, and given the code name *Agreement*. The name was inappropriate, for there was little agreement about anything. Doubts were raised and widely circulated about both strategy and tactics; many Army officers believed the Tobruk raid was totally impractical. The Royal Navy was worried about losing ships and men in an operation they thought had little chance of success. An LRDG officer who visited GHQ said he was shocked by the "lighthearted" manner in which the problems were tackled with "10 per cent planning, 90 per cent wishful thinking."

Perhaps the biggest worry for the participants in the raid was the lack of security. The raid was openly discussed in the bars and nightclubs of Cairo and Alexandria. Maneuvers for the motor torpedo boats that were to assault Tobruk from the sea were rehearsed in front of the Royal Egyptian Yacht Club at Alexandria; the civilian members did not need much imagination to guess what was in the wind. Axis spies flourished in both Egyptian cities, and it was reasonable to assume that what was common knowledge in Cairo was also known at the headquarters of the Afrika Korps. Yet Operation *Agreement* was not canceled, and during the first few days of September the raiding forces slowly assembled at Kufra Oasis, deep in the desert and some 800 miles from their objectives.

On the evening of the 5th of September, Haselden's raiding party left Kufra for Tobruk. Haselden was to enter the town with a force of 83 men posing as British prisoners of war. Carrying Tommy guns under their coats, they would be transported in three covered trucks with Afrika Korps markings and driven by SIG men in German Army uniforms. Once in the town, Haselden's party would proceed to a small bay not far from the harbor and establish a bridgehead for 400 Royal Marines who were to land at dawn from two destroyers and a force of motor torpedo boats. After destroying the harbor and liberating Allied prisoners of war held in Tobruk, the whole force would escape by sea. That, at least, was the plan.

The first indication of just how bad security had been came from a LRDG patrol that clashed with two Italian vehicles about 20 miles from Tobruk even as Haselden and his men were entering the town. Only one Italian soldier survived the encounter, but he told Captain David Lloyd Owen, the patrol leader, that he was one of many reinforcements recently sent to Tobruk. He also said that the garrison expected trouble and was on the alert. This was, said Lloyd Owen, "disquieting news."

Nevertheless, the three trucks carrying Haselden and his raiders got into Tobruk without trouble. Italian soldiers manning roadblocks waved them through without bothering to check their papers. At 9:30 p.m., precisely on time, Haselden's party reached the bay where it was to establish the beachhead. At the same moment, a wave of RAF Wellingtons droned overhead and began a diversionary raid on the town to occupy the attention of the Germans during the next few vital hours.

While searchlights swiveled across the sky and antiaircraft guns boomed, the raiders moved swiftly into action. One group moved out to capture the coastal guns on the west side of the bay, another tackled the guns on the east side. Their progress was marked by muffled shouts in the night, an occasional scream and brief bursts of Tommy-gun fire. Within a short time the guns overlooking the beach had been captured and the battery's radio station had been knocked out of action. Shortly before midnight, a Very light—a colored flare fired from a special pistol—soared into the sky from the west side, indicating that the raiders were in control. A little more than an hour later a similar signal was fired on the east side. On a high point above the beach, a signal lamp began blinking to guide the fleet of British motor torpedo boats into the bay.

But the 18 MTBs and three Fairmile motor launches out at sea were already in trouble. The column had made landfall, but the sailors could see nothing on shore apart from the searchlights and the burning buildings in the town. The boats nosed about helplessly in the dark searching for the bay while the signaler on shore, unaware that his signal lamp could not be seen, peered anxiously out into the night. At last two MTBs crept into the bay, having stumbled across it almost by accident. None of the other vessels found it.

Meanwhile, farther out to sea, Royal Marines of the 11th Battalion were disembarking from the destroyers *Sikh* and *Zulu* into landing boats that had been hastily constructed for the operation and were proving to be both unwieldy and leaky. By 3:45 a.m. the first wave of boats had all been taken in tow by motorized launches heading for the shore, but a heavy swell was running and the tow ropes began to part. Pitching and yawing, the boats drifted helplessly while the launches maneuvered to pick up the ropes again. When the first boats began to close with the shore, many of them were smashed on the rocks, throwing the heavily laden Marines into the boiling surf. In the end only a handful of men landed safely—to discover they were in the wrong place.

At 5:05 a.m. the searchlights that had been sweeping the sky to pick out the Wellington bombers suddenly turned toward the sea. The *Sikh,* which had moved closer inshore to cover the landing, was spotted within minutes and hit by a shell from a battery a mile west of the landing beach. Her steering mechanism was destroyed. The *Zulu* made valiant attempts to take her in tow, but heavy fire from the same battery forced the *Zulu* to withdraw. The men still holding out around the bay were now engaged in a furious battle with tank-supported German troops that were steadily closing in on their positions. Clearly, nothing could now save the operation, and escape by sea was out of the question; the *Sikh* was burning and slowly sinking, as were a number of the MTBs.

The raiders attempted to fight their way out, even though they must have known it was hopeless. By midmorning, the few of them still alive were pinned in a wadi surrounded by German and Italian troops and tanks. There they made a last

stand, during which the gallant Haselden was killed. Only six men returned from the Tobruk fiasco.

At Benghazi the SAS raid fared little better. The convoy of jeeps was halted by a barrier across the road not far from the town. When an officer in the leading vehicle got out and pulled the barrier aside, he gave a mock Fascist salute and jauntily shouted, "Let battle commence!" To his astonishment, it did. A barrage of machine-gun and mortar fire opened up from German and Italian positions dug in on both sides of the road. The SAS men had run into an ambush. They answered as best they could with their jeep-mounted Vickers K machine guns, but there was no question of trying to continue the raid. The element of surprise had been lost. Stirling ordered a withdrawal. At first light, the fleeing SAS jeeps were pursued across the desert by German and Italian warplanes. By the end of the day the British raiders had lost a quarter of their men and three quarters of their vehicles.

On that disastrous night, only the LRDG's raid on Barce airfield was successful. A small patrol, rather like the one that Haselden had originally planned to take into Tobruk, crossed the sand and swept down on Barce, destroying about 30 enemy aircraft.

The events at Tobruk were soon reduced to insignificance by a resounding British victory elsewhere. At El Alamein on November 3, 1942, a final thrust by the Eighth Army sent the Afrika Korps reeling back from Egypt. Then, the Commandos reappeared to play a brand-new role—as the spearhead of a full-scale invasion force. Operation *Torch,* the amphibious assault of French North Africa, was designed to trap the Afrika Korps and end the Axis domination of the Mediterranean's southern shores. In the vanguard of *Torch,* the Commandos would perform vital jobs—something they did again and again as the Allies staged the great invasions of Sicily, Italy and France. And for Operation *Torch,* the British Commandos would be joined by commandos of another name, the U.S. Rangers.

At 1 a.m. on November 8, Commandos and Rangers served as shock troops for more than 107,000 soldiers in landings along the coast of French North Africa from Algiers to Casablanca. Allied commanders were uncertain about how the French defenders would respond. The British were unpopular in French North Africa because of their attacks on French Navy units, attacks aimed at keeping the ships out of German hands. In the belief that the French were less likely to fire at Americans, British Commandos wore American uniforms. The ploy did not always work. At Algiers, for example, No. 1 Commando split into two groups to capture forts on opposite sides of the bay. On the western side they were received as friends, but on the eastern side they met strong resistance, and fighting there continued for a full day before the French finally laid down their arms.

At Arzew, 30 miles west of Oran, the 1st Rangers under Lieut. Colonel William Darby stormed ashore up a steep and winding cliff path to a fort dominating the approach to the harbor. Scouts cut holes in the wire perimeter and, yelling like dervishes, the Rangers poured through. At 4 a.m. Darby fired a green Very light to indicate to the incoming invaders that the fort was in the Rangers' hands.

The next day, two companies of Rangers were called forward to reinforce the American 16th and 18th Regimental Combat Teams, which were being held up at two points: Saint-Cloud, a fortified village seven miles down the road

The gutted remains of Italian aircraft lie on an airfield near Barce, Libya. On September 13, 1942, units of the Long Range Desert Group destroyed some 30 planes at Barce, stalling the delivery by air of supplies to Rommel.

Miles from their home base, wounded British and New Zealand survivors of the Barce raid rest in a shelter consisting of a tarpaulin stretched over a collection of oil drums.

from Arzew, and La Macta, a village east of Oran where a French battery was threatening the Allied left flank. "Ain't that a stinking shame," one Ranger complained. "We open a port and let those guys come breezing in—now we got to fight their battles for them." The 1st Rangers' C Company pushed the defenders of Saint-Cloud back into the village, while at La Macta, E Company commandeered a squadron of half-track personnel carriers and overran the battery from its flank.

The Rangers may well have thought they deserved a rest on their newly won laurels. Darby disagreed. When the fighting subsided, the training resumed: speed marching, mountaineering, amphibious landings, night fighting. During January 1943, the 1st Rangers slept by day and trained by night. Darby used the time to perfect such tactics as maintaining contact during night maneuvers by means of pin points of light from flashlights with colored signaling filters. Different units were assigned different colors, and a commander could tell at a glance the location of all the units under him.

When it seemed to many of the Rangers that they were destined to spend the rest of the War in training, they were at last given a job to do. On the night of February 11, 1943, the 1st Rangers marched across the boulder-strewn lower slopes of the central Tunisian mountains with orders to destroy an Italian stronghold in the Sened Pass. "We have got to leave our mark on these people," Captain Roy Murray told his men. "They've got to know that they've been worked over by Rangers. Every man is to use his bayonet as much as he can—those are our orders."

The 1st Rangers hid the next day among the rocks in a bowl-shaped valley about six miles from their objective. At dusk they set out again, and soon they could hear the rumble of enemy tanks and trucks rolling along the road through the pass. After all the weeks of training, moving by night was now the Rangers' specialty. At 2 a.m., guided by red and green pinpricks of light, they formed into a skirmish line about half a mile from the Italian positions and advanced slowly and cautiously, without a sound.

They were only 50 yards from the enemy when a machine gun suddenly started firing on the left flank. In the center, the Rangers heard nervous Italian sentries shouting *"Chi va la?"*—"Who goes there?" Then guns along the entire front opened up, their bullets spattering the ground and whining through the air. The Rangers dropped, cradled their rifles in their arms and slithered forward, hugging the

ground as ricocheting bullets showered them with mud and stones. A 47mm cannon joined the barrage put up by the Italian machine guns. The barren slope provided no cover, and here and there a Ranger screamed with pain above the stuttering of the guns.

At last the Rangers crawled under the Italian guns and found a moment's shelter below the line of fire. Someone shouted, "Give 'em hell!" and grenades arced through the air to explode in and around the Italian positions. The Rangers scrambled up the final slope, screaming and shouting. Corporal James Altieri, running forward into the melee, lost his footing and fell into a slit trench occupied by a single Italian soldier. Recovering from his surprise a split second faster than the Italian, Altieri jerked out his commando knife and plunged it into the other man's stomach. The Italian screamed. Altieri rammed in his knife again and again until the man dropped. Then Altieri turned away and vomited.

All along the front demented scenes were played out. "We swarmed over the remaining centers of resistance," said Altieri, "grenading, bayoneting, shooting, screaming, cursing and grunting. The remaining Italians never had a chance. We worked them over furiously, giving no quarter. It was sickening, brutal, inhuman." One by one the machine guns and the cannon were silenced. All that could be heard then were the moans of the dying, the wounded calling for medics and the panting of men fighting for breath after fighting for their lives. More than 100 Italians lay dead around their guns. One Ranger had died and another 18 were wounded.

The attackers destroyed the enemy guns, rounded up their prisoners and prepared to withdraw, carrying the wounded on improvised stretchers slung between rifles. They faced a 20-mile march back to their base. Darby knew they had little time to make their escape; he particularly feared that they might be cut off by German tanks.

The Ranger code regarding wounded was unequivocal: They were to be left behind after a raid if they delayed the withdrawal. But neither Darby nor any of his men had the least intention of sticking to that rule. Through the night the Rangers stumbled and slipped down the rough mountain tracks, their blackened faces streaked with sweat, each man taking a turn at carrying a stretcher or supporting the walking wounded. As the sun came up, Darby was still urging his men on. He was everywhere, up and down the column, taking his turn with the stretchers and encouraging the stragglers: "Keep pushing!" he shouted over and over. "Keep pushing!"

Few of the men later remembered how they had managed to walk the final miles until, at last, they could see the camp shimmering in the heat across the desert. Gaunt, unshaven, filthy, red-eyed and exhausted, the 1st Rangers used their last ounce of strength to get into the camp, then collapsed.

The raid on Sened Pass won for the Rangers a place among the "private armies" of the North African campaign. The Rangers had proved that they possessed the qualities needed to live and fight in that inhospitable theater—not just the courage and determination to defeat the enemy, but the courage and determination to defeat the desert, too.

The war in the desert was by this time virtually over. In April the advance guard of the British Eighth Army, out of Egypt, linked with forward troops of the First Army, out of Tunisia. When that happened, the Afrika Korps was beaten. However, for the private armies that had played such a heroic role in Rommel's defeat—the SAS, the Commandos and the Rangers—there were more battle honors still to win; they would now move on to other theaters.

Men of the U.S. 1st Ranger Battalion guard a captured gun position after a night of fighting at Arzew in the Vichy French colony of Algeria. The Rangers cleared two forts dominating the strategic harbor to spearhead the Allied invasion of French North Africa.

ROVERS IN A SEA OF SAND

Wrapped in kaffiyehs and goggled against sun and sand, men of the Long Range Desert Group huddle in the lee of their truck to wait out a Saharan dust storm.

PATROLLING THE MERCILESS DESERT

The Allied special forces who raided across the Sahara overcame hardships that sometimes made the risks of battle seem almost trivial by comparison. They endured temperatures up to 120° F. in the shade on summer days and below freezing on winter nights. At any hour, howling winds might roil the desert surface into flying torrents of sand capable of stripping their faces of skin and their trucks of paint. Soft, shifting dunes frequently halted the trucks, which then had to be laboriously dug out. Anxiety disturbed the men even when neither the enemy nor the desert did; they never forgot, as one put it, "that we were trespassers and as such were liable to be treated harshly if caught in the act."

That the desert raiders fought as well as they did, smashing Axis airfields and convoys hundreds of miles behind the lines, testifies to a quality beyond toughness: the ability to bend to the desert's demands while bending it to theirs. The special forces learned to operate like bands of motorized Bedouins, as adept at reading the tracks of vehicles as the Arabs were at reading camel tracks. They modified both their trucks and their rations, lightening the former while beefing up the latter until they were eating the best food in the whole desert army—500 more calories per day than the norm. And they looked after their trucks' thirst by setting up secret fuel and supply dumps throughout enemy territory.

The drivers mastered the signs of "good going"—the smooth, hard sand easiest to drive on—and learned to discount mirages and desert darkness, which could trick the unwary into thinking that "every bush was a tank and every dry runnel was a bottomless chasm," as one driver recalled. The navigators charted their courses across immense, featureless seas of sand as mariners once did, using the sun and the stars. The raiders had to map thousands of square miles of desert as they went; the few maps they had were unreliable. "The mountains were all high, as became the dignity of Facist Italy," one intelligence officer wrote of a map captured from the Italians. "Making our way anxiously toward an obviously impassable range of hills, we would find that we had driven over it without feeling the bump."

A desert patrol sets out from a base camp in Egypt in trucks that have been stripped of their doors, roofs and windshields to minimize weight.

Desert raiders load their trucks for a patrol. Each truck was carefully packed to carry up to two tons of supplies—enough rations to last three weeks and enough fuel for a 1,500-mile round trip.

STAYING MOBILE TO STAY ALIVE

Operating in the immense inner desert, where a patrol might be stranded as many as 900 miles from help, the men of the Long Range Desert Group took infinite trouble to keep their trucks in running condition. Repairs in the field sometimes approached the miraculous; when the crankcase of one of the trucks cracked, the men patched it with a hastily improvised mixture of sand and chewing gum.

Patrols carried extra springs and spare tires—about three for each truck—to help them get over jagged rocky stretches that could slow their progress to four miles a day. They decreased the likelihood of getting bogged in the sand by partially deflating the tires, and kept to the upper edges of dunes so they could turn downhill when they hit a soft patch.

Still, "dry quicksand" as fine as flour and the occasional salt marshes that were strewn inexplicably throughout the desert made for long halts on almost every patrol. Troughs had to be dug under stuck wheels so that steel sand channels or mats could be laid down to give the trucks purchase. More than one commander recalled "visions of having to take the trucks to pieces and carry them across" bad soft spots. But unloading—and long, sweaty hours of digging and pushing—usually sufficed to get the trucks moving again.

All hands pitch in to dig out a truck. "At one moment you would be doing a steady 30 miles an hour to the reassuring whine of the tires," wrote one officer, "the next halted dead in five yards with the car up to its axle."

Bundled against the cold, an officer watches as his men prepare to tow a truck out of a marsh. The sturdy tow cables were also used to haul wrecks back to camp rather than abandoning them to the desert and the enemy.

A patrol eases across a rock-studded plain. The raiders traversed a wild mix of terrain, some of it "obviously impassable to motor transport," according to a cocky patrol commander who proved otherwise.

Desert raiders take a noon break to drink a mug of water. Three men have found relief in the only shade for miles around—the shadow of their truck.

WAGING WAR WITH THE ELEMENTS

"The problem," in the words of one desert raider, "is to make yourself so much master over the appalling difficulties of nature—heat, thirst, cold, rain, fatigue—that, overcoming these, you yet have physical energy and mental resilience to deal with the greater object, the winning of the War." That struggle for mastery led the men to fashion uniforms as unusual and varied as the conditions they faced. Coats made of sheepskin offered comfort in the cold winter dawn; the traditional Arab headdresses known as kaffiyehs did double duty, providing warmth against the chill and protection against the blistering desert sun.

But temperature was only one of the raiders' problems. "You don't merely feel hot," one officer wrote of the terrible summer wind called gibleh, "you don't merely feel tired, you feel as if every bit of energy had left you, as if your brain was thrusting its way through the top of your head and you want to lie in a stupor till the accursed sun has gone down." For those times, when the customary ration of six pints of water a day for each man seemed woefully inadequate, the patrols concocted an "anti-gibleh pick-me-up"—equal parts of rum and lime juice.

Bundled-up raiders share a stand-up lunch—"the best that tins could contain," one man remembered.

A soldier pours out a tot of rum—a cherished part of the daily ration that lifted spirits in the heat and gave the illusion of warmth in the winter.

A brush-covered truck blends with the desert scrub that surrounds it. Patrols frequently camouflaged their trucks and left them behind when it was necessary to raid or spy on foot.

Truck crews shroud their vehicles with camouflage nets. When caught with no time to camouflage, the patrols sometimes tried to fool the bombers by putting on what one man called "a spirited show of Fascist friendship"—waving and extending their arms in salute.

FINDING COVER OUT IN THE OPEN

In the open desert, hiding a patrol of 10 trucks—or even one truck—from daylight aerial attack was a life-and-death problem that inspired a brilliant variety of solutions. The Long Range Desert Group used the scant protection of steep dunes, dry wadies and "bushes not big enough to cover a scorpion." They found a measure of concealment in the haze of afternoon heat, and drove pell-mell into dust storms, sandstorms and even the dust clouds of exploded bombs to escape.

The desert raiders abetted nature with camouflage. They draped their trucks with scrub or nets and eventually painted the trucks olive green and rose pink. "The first driver to take over a newly painted truck," wrote one patrol commander, "said he would not dare to be seen in Cairo with such a thing." But colors that might have drawn jeers in the city made the trucks near invisible in the desert, at least when stationary. If a patrol had warning of an approaching plane but no hope of reaching cover, it could sometimes escape detection simply by stopping in its tracks.

Raiders hide out and rest in a dry wadi after a mission. Fast and nimble jeeps were popular with the desert raiders, who used them both for attacking and for scouting ahead of the patrols.

Blessed for once with abundant cover, men of the Long Range Desert Group are able to enjoy a relaxed meal in the shade of palm trees, whose copious branches also hide their supplies.

Screened by a sparse clump of brush, a two-man team behind the lines in North Africa keeps watch on enemy movements. Such duty was both tense and tedious. The raiders stayed out for 24-hour dark-to-dark shifts and hardly dared move lest they be spotted. "You look at your watch at 11," one wrote, "and look again four hours later and it's 11:15."

A WORLD OF HARSH BEAUTY

On a rocky Saharan plateau, New Zealanders of the Long Range Desert Group pause as their navigator sets a course. The painting is by war artist Peter McIntyre.

AN ARTIST'S VIEW OF AN ARDUOUS TREK

Athwart a desert foxhole, Captain Peter McIntyre, the official war artist for the New Zealand Long Range Desert Group, reconstructs a battle scene.

To the average Westerner, the desert is the most forbidding of environments. But to at least one person accustomed to lusher terrain, it also had a terrible and haunting beauty. "By midmorning the heat was coming up in waves," wrote war artist Peter McIntyre of a day in the desert in 1942. "We were in amongst tall, conical hills—black rock at the pointed tops—each a cone so perfect that it seemed man-made, yet there were hundreds of them. As we moved south the cones became larger and closer until we were like ants crawling between pointed buns. Then suddenly there was open desert, flat and smooth to the horizon. The trucks sped over the hard sand with the ease of billiard balls rolling on a table. Not a pebble was visible and in spite of the speed the horizon remained unchanged. We seemed to be gliding into limitless space beyond the edge of the world."

McIntyre accompanied a Long Range Desert Group patrol made up of his fellow New Zealanders, who in three weeks covered some 750 previously uncharted miles from their home base in southeastern Libya to the Nile. Hardly a day of the trek passed without generating some new excitement in the artist, who thrilled to the surprising variety and stark, exotic beauty of the desert landscape. Neither the punishing sun nor the swarms of mosquitoes that plagued the oases could dim his enthusiasm for such startling sights as a petrified forest of hollow black trees set in a field of shifting sand, or for what he called the "mad sandstone world of goblin shapes" that the relentless desert wind had sculpted out of soft stone. As the trek progressed, he discovered that the desert had just as relentlessly eroded his own "sense of normality," until the fantastic had come to seem practically commonplace.

McIntyre drew portraits of some of the patrol's intrepid members and sketched the Egyptian Camel Corps, frontier police who rode out to meet the patrol when it reached the Nile. But his greatest achievement was to capture the unearthly ambiance of the desert itself—where, as he wrote, "colors riot against all sense of reality"—and to record the precarious daily life of the men who had to fight there.

Navigator and commander confer amid a maze of conical sandstone hills. The trucks in the background are spread out as a defense against air attack.

The patrol sets off in the morning aboard its trucks. The mats rolled up on the fenders were reinforced with steel rods and were used as often as once a mile to help the trucks get out of soft sand. The cylinders at the sides caught water from the radiators if they boiled over.

Trooper R. J. Moore of the Long Range Desert Group peers defiantly from under his kaffiyeh. Once, wounded in a battle and separated from his unit, the gritty Moore managed to walk 210 miles toward his home base before he was picked up.

Gunner Edgar Sanders stands confident and relaxed in this sketch by McIntyre, who described him as "one of the toughest men I have ever met." Sanders was awarded the Military Medal for singlehandedly knocking out four Italian armed trucks.

As the navigator sits alone with his maps, the rest of the patrol takes a break near a precariously balanced sandstone formation called Mushroom Rock. The desert wind gouged many such "fantastic monster shapes, towering six and nine meters high," McIntyre wrote.

An escort from the Egyptian Camel Corps accompanies the New Zealanders at the end of their spectacular journey to the Nile. During three years of desert warfare, more than one fourth of the 200 men in the Long Range Desert Group earned medals for conspicuous bravery.

3

A persistent Commando's one-man coup
Invading hostile shores by canoe
"Blondie" Hasler's hazardous inventions
Fighting treacherous waters in the Bay of Biscay
French civilians keep a secret for saboteurs
A long hike home from Bordeaux
The stealthy art of beach reconnaissance
Hard lessons from poorly planned landings
Corsairs at large in the German-held Aegean
The joyous liberation of Simi

THE WATERBORNE IRREGULARS

Second Lieutenant Roger Courtney was an explorer and big-game hunter in Africa before the War. He often hunted in a canoe, and once paddled 3,473 miles down the Nile, from Lake Victoria to Cairo. When he joined the Commandos in July 1940, he asked if he could hunt Germans in a canoe.

Senior officers at Combined Operations Headquarters rejected the suggestion. They considered canoes and comparable small boats more suitable for Boy Scouts than for soldiers. But Courtney, then a recruit at the Combined Training Centre at Achnacarry in Scotland, would not be deterred. He wangled an interview with Vice Admiral Theodore Hallett, the commanding officer of the center, and proposed a plan for using folding canoes—kayak-like craft known as foldboats—in small-scale raids. When Hallett showed no more enthusiasm for the suggestion than his subordinates, Courtney ended the interview with an angry promise to prove that his ideas could work.

Courtney was as good as his word. Four nights later, when Hallett was presiding at a meeting of senior Naval officers in the drawing room of the Argyll Arms Hotel at Inveraray, the door burst open and in walked Courtney, clad only in swimming trunks and carrying a large, dripping bundle. He dropped his bundle on the floor in the center of the room and announced that he had just boarded the *Glengyle* landing ship at her anchorage in the River Clyde and stolen the gun cover from her afterdeck. As proof of his exploit, he had brought the gun cover back with him.

The captain of the *Glengyle,* who was at the meeting, listened with mounting fury as the young officer explained how he had paddled out to the ship in a foldboat, climbed on board unobserved, painted his initials on the door of the captain's cabin, and helped himself to his souvenir.

Under other circumstances, Courtney might have faced a court-martial. Fortunately for him, the officers of Combined Operations, presumably including even the captain whose domain had been invaded, valued flair and initiative in their recruits. The men at the meeting decided that Courtney had proved his point: Foldboats and other small craft propelled by human muscle might have a role in Commando operations. Hallett gave Courtney permission to start training a small team of canoeists. His unit, soon to be known as the Special Boat Section (SBS), pioneered the use of small craft in raiding and reconnaissance work.

Once the SBS began operations, no one offered the opinion that canoes belonged to Boy Scouts. Though the unit never numbered more than 100 men at one time, its members were to play varied and vital roles in theaters as far apart as the Bay of Biscay and the eastern Mediterranean.

Few men fought a lonelier war than those who worked in small boats. They almost always operated at night. They paddled toward strange and hostile shores with the full realization that they would be cut off from any help for hours, perhaps days. Most of the time they worked under the noses of the enemy, and had to rely on stealth and luck for protection. To be cold, wet and dog-tired was normal. Those who made it back to the submarine that had launched them often had to be dragged from their boats in a state of exhaustion. Many were captured because they missed their rendezvous and were exposed by the light of dawn. Others simply disappeared into the night.

The Special Boat Section undertook its first mission in the Mediterranean on the night of June 22, 1941. Lieutenant Tug Wilson and Marine Taffy Hughes pushed their foldboat through the torpedo hatch of a submarine off the west coast of Italy; on the deck of the submarine they opened out the frame, fitted the rubberized canvas skin over it, stowed inside it the gear they would need, then lowered it into the water. They paddled to shore at a point where they knew a railroad ran close to the beach. Wilson and Hughes laid pressure-activated explosive charges on the rails at the entrance to a tunnel and safely returned to their submarine. Before it dived, they had the satisfaction of hearing the sound of an explosion.

By November 1941, Courtney had trained a second SBS unit, known as 101 Troop, to conduct reconnaissance and attack shipping along the coast of France. Their first operation, intended to pave the way for a bigger Commando raid, was not a success. Two-man crews took a pair of foldboats ashore from a motor torpedo boat to reconnoiter a stretch of the Normandy coastline near Houlgate. One craft capsized in heavy surf and both canoeists lost their paddles. They were captured by Germans as they were trying to make their way inland to find a hiding place. The other pair, two privates named Ellis and Lewis, missed their rendezvous with the motor torpedo boat; undaunted, they paddled all the way back across the Channel in the dark and were eventually rescued off the coast of Kent.

Six months later, 101 Troop redeemed its reputation with a daring raid led by its commanding officer, Captain Gerald Montanaro. On the night of April 11, 1942, Montanaro and Sergeant Frederick Preece paddled into Boulogne harbor in a leaking foldboat and attached magnetic mines, or "limpets," to a German tanker. By the time they got back out to sea, their craft was waterlogged and sinking fast; they barely made it to the motor launch that had dropped them earlier. But their risk paid off. Aerial photographs of the harbor taken the next day revealed that only the superstructure of the tanker protruded above the water.

Montanaro's operation paved the way for the most difficult and dangerous 101 Troop raid of the War, and the deepest incursion into Axis territory ever made by small craft. The man behind the raid was Major H. G. Hasler, a 28-year-old regular officer in the Royal Marines, known as Blondie because of his fine, gold mustache. The fact that he was bald added an ironic twist to the nickname.

Hasler was an expert yachtsman who had been recruited early in 1942 to the staff of the Combined Operations Development Centre at Southsea, near Portsmouth. Because of his boating experience, he was assigned to develop a British version of the E-boat, or explosive motorboat, of the sort the Italians had used to raid a British fleet at Crete in March 1941, destroying a cruiser and two tankers.

At that stage of the War, the Italians were far ahead of the Allies in the techniques of attacking ships moored in harbors—and for that matter were experimenting with quite a number of military innovations *(pages 142-151)*. The explosive motorboat—a high-speed launch with a 500-pound explosive charge packed in its bow—was the latest addition to Italy's arsenal of exotic waterborne weapons. The pilot aimed the boat at its target, opened the throttle, then pulled a lever that triggered his ejection over the stern.

As a refinement of the concept, Hasler and his design team began experimenting with an explosive boat that could be dropped by parachute with the helmsman sitting inside. Soon the prototype was ready for a trial. Lieutenant David Cox, the officer who volunteered to sit in the boat when it was released from the bomb rack of a Lancaster, deservedly received the Member of the Order of the British

Empire award for his courage. But his was the only drop ever attempted; swinging through space while strapped inside a boat proved so harrowing for Cox that Hasler abandoned the project.

Hasler's team designed dozens of other devices, including an underwater chariot of sorts—a two-man, torpedo-shaped craft that carried a 500-pound explosive charge. Hasler also tinkered with swim fins and underwater breathing tanks for frogmen, as well as with a terrifying parachute that substituted rotor blades for the usual silk canopy. The spinning blades were supposed to enable the parachutist to steer through the air to a safe landing place. Not surprisingly, only one officer was brave enough to test the parachute, and after trying it out he was so shaken that, Hasler noted dryly, "he had to use both hands to hold a glass."

During these experiments, Hasler became increasingly convinced that only one mode of transport fulfilled most of the requirements for entering an enemy harbor by stealth: the one- or two-man paddle-propelled boat. Hasler had long discussions with Roger Courtney and Gerald Montanaro, who were then honing the techniques of foldboat raiding. Montanaro's team had invented a small magnetic handle, called a holdfast, that would enable Commandos to hold onto the sides of ships while doing their dirty business. To attach limpet mines well below the ship's waterline, Hasler's designers devised a placing rod, a telescoping six-foot steel rod with a U-shaped hook on one end.

Two British Commandos lower a foldboat—a canoe made of rubberized canvas—down the forward hatch of a submarine in 1942. The foldboat had a tendency to leak and even to break apart in heavy seas.

Hasler suggested to Combined Operations Headquarters that he organize a unit to develop tactical use of canoes in combination with explosive motorboats: The canoeists would clear surface obstacles from the path of the motorboats and then pick up the motorboat drivers after they had been ejected. With a great deal of discreet lobbying, he won approval for his proposals. His unit, which was to operate under the puckish name of the Royal Marine Boom Patrol Detachment, was formed on July 6, 1942.

The 34 men who volunteered to join the detachment had little idea of what they were letting themselves in for; they knew only that the work would involve small boats and that it might be hazardous. A month of training winnowed out all but 22 men. These Hasler put through a rigorous course of calisthenics, seamanship, swimming and underwater diving. The men learned how to handle every kind of small boat. They learned techniques of demolition and tricks of stealth and camouflage. They learned to paddle while reclining, to lower their profiles. They were taught to remain motionless when in danger of being spotted, allowing their boats to drift on the wind and tide so that they appeared to be logs. And they learned that knitted sweaters and long woolen underwear soaked in grease gave them some protection from the cold of the water.

Hasler devised exercises during which his men spent four or five days at sea in their canoes without a break. Soon they were as much at home on the water as on land. Hasler shelved the idea of explosive motorboats; the canoes were what now interested him. By early September he deemed his men sufficiently trained to execute a harbor raid.

The Boom Patrol Detachment did not have long to wait, for the British government was growing anxious about Axis shipping, which—despite an Allied blockade of European ports—had substantially increased since Japan entered the War. An intelligence report by the British Ministry of Economic Warfare in July 1942 estimated that during the previous 12 months, 25,000 tons of crude rubber from Asia

The canoeists and raiders of Britain's Special Boat Section operated throughout the Mediterranean Sea and along the coast of France, striking at a coastal railway in Italy, at German ships in Bordeaux harbor and at Axis targets in the Aegean Sea. Other SBS teams surveyed coastlines and beaches, including all the potential invasion sites in Sicily.

bound for Germany and Italy had arrived in the French port of Bordeaux. Shipments to Bordeaux of such vital materials as tin, tungsten and fuel oil were equally alarming.

Bordeaux, therefore, loomed large as a potential target; the question was how to strike it. Both the Royal Navy and the Royal Air Force ruled out the possibility of their making an attack on the harbor. Bordeaux was 62 miles up the heavily guarded Gironde estuary and beyond the reach of deep-draft Navy vessels. The RAF declined to act on the ground that a bombing raid would kill too many French civilians. When the problem of Bordeaux was passed to Combined Operations, planners there decided that an amphibious troop landing was out of the question because it would require at least three infantry divisions, about 50,000 men.

On September 21, Blondie Hasler was asked if his unit could mount a canoeists' raid on Axis merchant ships in Bordeaux harbor. He lost no time in responding; the next day he produced an outline for a plan that he said had "a good chance of success." He proposed that the raiding force paddle up the Gironde in pairs, traveling at night, hiding and sleeping by day. After attaching limpets to enemy ships, they would make their escape overland through occupied France to Spain with the help of the French Resistance. On October 30, Lord Louis Mountbatten signed the order authorizing the operation, code-named *Frankton*.

The canoes that Hasler planned to use had been designed to meet his requirements. Foldboats were ill-suited for the kind of operation he had in mind: They could not be dragged across a beach and could not be lifted when loaded with heavy equipment. Furthermore, foldboats could not be loaded and unloaded through the hatch of a submarine without being dismantled. The craft that Hasler proposed surmounted these problems. Like the foldboats, it consisted of rubberized canvas over a wooden frame. But it was strong enough to carry 150 pounds of equipment, and was considerably more durable. It had a flat wooden bottom and a deck, both made of ⅛-inch-thick plywood; it was fitted with a pair of runners so that on land it could be pulled like a sled, sparing its canvas cover wear and tear. For all its improvements, however, it remained a fragile vessel. It came to be known as a cockle—a term that British seafarers have traditionally given to flimsy craft.

Once *Frankton* had been approved, Hasler had only one major obstacle to overcome. Because the raiders' chances for coming back alive were poor, Mountbatten refused to let Hasler go on the raid; Hasler's services were too valuable to Combined Operations.

But Hasler was determined to go. He stated his case forcefully at a conference at Combined Operations Headquarters attended by Mountbatten himself. After listening to Hasler's arguments, Mountbatten polled the other officers present. All but one of them said that Hasler should stay behind. Mountbatten thought for a moment, considered Hasler's crestfallen expression and—being a man who

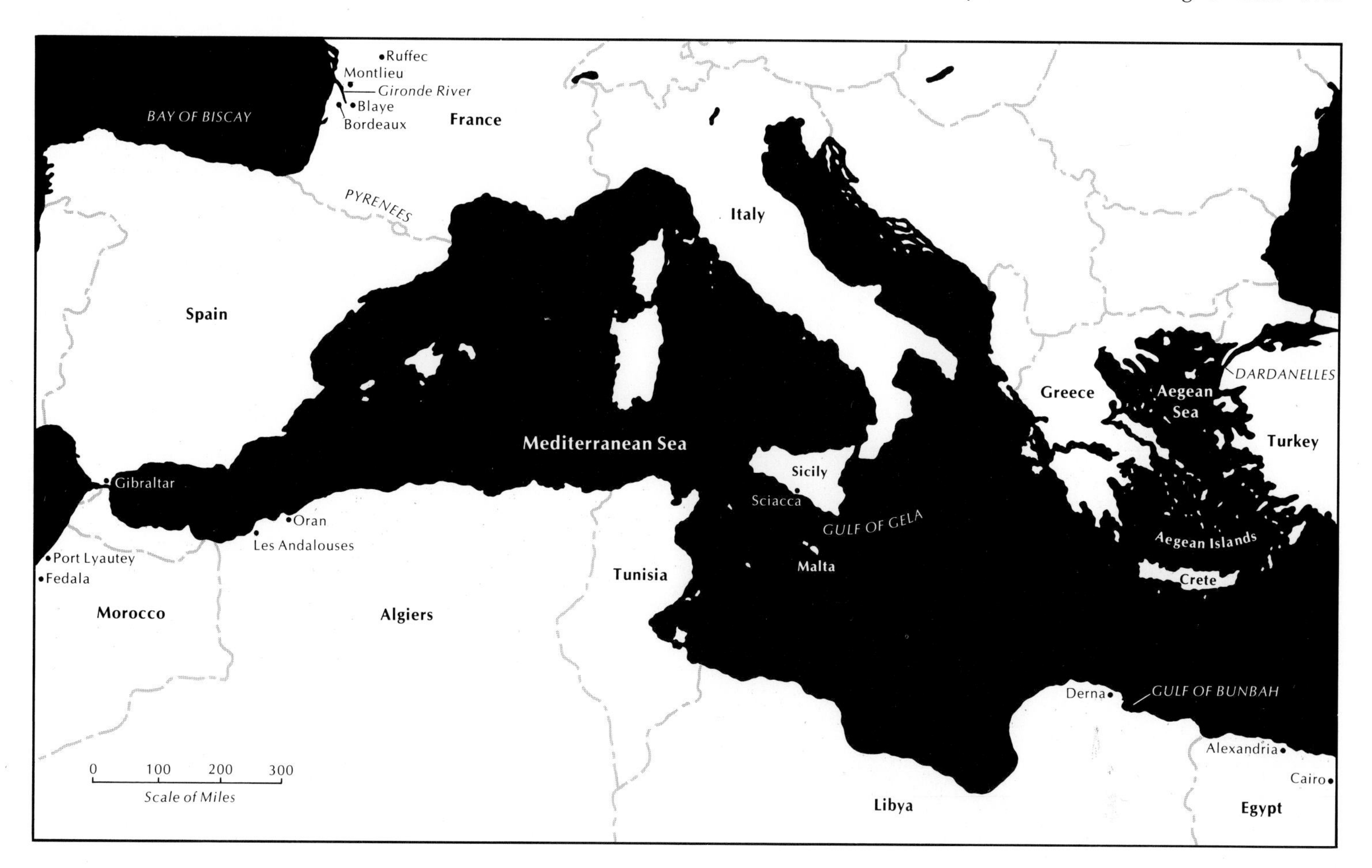

loved adventure himself—smiled. "Much against my better judgment," he said, "I'm going to let you go."

Early in November, No. 1 Section of the Royal Marine Boom Patrol Detachment moved to Holy Loch on the western coast of Scotland to practice launching their cockles from the deck of a submarine and to train further in the handling of limpet mines. Apart from Hasler, none of the men knew what was afoot; they were told only that they would no longer be allowed to go ashore from the submarine depot ship on which they lived. Clearly, however, something important was in the offing. A senior Naval officer came on board to give the men a pep talk, at the end of which he solemnly saluted them. "We really started to worry then," said Marine Corporal William Sparks. "If the Navy are saluting the Marines, it must be something big."

On the morning of November 30, six cockles were lowered carefully through the torpedo hatch of the submarine *Tuna* and stowed below in the torpedo racks. Hasler and 11 Marines of No. 1 Section embarked immediately. Talking among themselves, the Marines decided that their most probable target was the German battleship *Tirpitz,* which was then skulking in a Norwegian fjord.

As soon as the *Tuna* sailed, Hasler set up a blackboard in the forward torpedo space and called his men together. "I am sorry to disappoint you," he told them, "but we are not going to Norway. We are going to France." He went on to explain the purpose of the mission, not neglecting to point out that the expedition had the personal support of the Prime Minister. On the blackboard, he showed the men how they would make the approach up the Gironde and attack the ships in Bordeaux harbor. Then Hasler informed the men that it would be too dangerous for the submarine to wait to collect them after the raid. The news that they must all make their escapes overland across France was greeted with stunned silence.

"We were a bit shaken that they would do that to us," reported Sparks. "My first thought was that we would be dead lucky if we got away with it. But after the briefing, Blondie tried to teach us a bit of French with a phrase sheet, and everyone laughed. We soon got used to the idea."

After dark on December 6, 1942, the *Tuna* surfaced in the Bay of Biscay, four miles off the French coast. The night was cold and clear; the sea was calm, with a slow swell running. The crewmen opened the torpedo hatch and manhandled the cockles up onto the submarine's deck. One craft snagged on a corner of the hatch clamp and ripped open from end to end. Hasler examined the damage and told the crew, Marines William Ellery and Eric Fisher, that they would not be able to go. Fisher broke down in tears.

For launching the cockles, Hasler had designed an ingenious sling crane that was now attached to the submarine's gun. The Commandos took their seats and the crewmen hoisted each cockle, swung it out over the sea and lowered it by means of the gun's elevating gear. Hasler and his partner, Sparks, were first in the water. Moments later, all five cockles were safely launched and in formation. After whispered farewells to the crew of the *Tuna,* the Commandos paddled away into the night.

At about midnight the canoeists heard a roar that resembled the sound of a waterfall. The sound grew louder and louder as they approached the mouth of the Gironde. Hasler knew its cause—a tide race, a stretch of steep, breaking waves created by conflicting currents. He also knew that none of his men had ever negotiated such a hazard. Signaling the cockles to close together, he told the Commandos that they had nothing to worry about; all they had to do was carry out normal rough-weather drill and they would be all right.

Hasler and Sparks were first to go through. As they surged into the foaming breakers, they had to fight with their paddles to keep the bow of their bucking craft head on into the race. When they burst into the calmer water on the other side, Hasler and Sparks turned to wait for their companions. The second cockle came through safely, and was shortly followed by the third and fourth. But there was no sign of the fifth craft. The men shouted above the roaring of the waves, but received no answer. Hasler and Sparks fought their way back through the race to search for the missing

Stroking in unison, two canoeists whisk along in a cockle, hardier than its predecessor, the foldboat. The paddles' two blades were feathered, or turned at right angles to each other, so that while one blade was pulled through the water, the other knifed the air—reducing both wind resistance and the canoeists' silhouette.

cockle. They found nothing. Sergeant Samuel Wallace and Marine Robert Ewart had disappeared somewhere in that fierce and tumbling water.

Now they were eight.

The Commandos continued on their way, heading toward the shadowy outline of a lighthouse on the Pointe de Grave, a promontory at the mouth of the river. They had paddled for only a few minutes when they heard the dreadful rushing noise again, this time louder and apparently closer. The second tidal race was even faster and rougher than the first. Three cockles got through, but the fourth capsized. The cockle came swirling out of the race upside down, with Corporal G. J. Sheard and Marine David Moffat clinging grimly to the hull. There was no possibility of bailing the boat out. Hasler ordered it scuttled, and told Sheard to hang onto his cockle and Moffat to hold onto another.

As the little flotilla moved on, the drag of the two men holding onto the cockles reduced their speed to about one knot. Hasler now faced a grim decision: He had to choose between the mission and the men in the water. It was about 3 a.m. and the Commandos were in an area where both riverbanks were heavily guarded. If they tried to tow the men ashore, the cockles would almost certainly be spotted. Even if they reached the banks safely, the team would never be able to find a place to hide before dawn. Time was short. The tide would soon turn against them. Hasler knew what he had to do: Abandon the men. With a heavy heart he told them so, and bade them try to swim to shore.

"It was so terribly cold I didn't see how they could possibly do it," said Sparks. "We all shook hands with them and said we'd see them back in Portsmouth. It was a terrible moment. I was crying my eyes out—I think we all were. But they were wonderful lads. When Blondie told them we would have to leave them, they said 'Yes sir, that's all right sir.' After we had said good-by, they let go of our canoes and we carried on, leaving them behind."

Now they were six.

Heading into the river with the precious night hours quickly waning, the three crews paddled on until they could see, looming out of the darkness, three German patrol boats moored on one side of the river. On the other side was a jetty where a sentry was on duty. The cockles were going to have to try to slip unobserved between the jetty and the patrol boats, which would certainly have sentries on board.

Hasler and Sparks went first, leaning forward to lower their silhouettes. As they were going through, a patrol boat started to signal to the jetty. Both men were certain they had been detected. They tensed, expecting bullets to start flying around them at any moment. But nothing happened, and they slipped quietly out of sight of the Germans to wait for the other two cockles. Only one arrived. Inexplicably, the third cockle, with Lieutenant John Mackinnon and Marine James Conway aboard, did not come through, although no shots were heard.

Now they were four.

Exhausted and sick at heart, the men continued on their way, conscious that the sky was lightening in the east. Shortly before dawn they found what they thought was an island in the middle of the river, and dragged their cockles ashore. They hung camouflage nets over the boats and threw themselves onto the ground. Hasler said he would take the first watch.

Half an hour later, he heard voices and wakened the sleeping men. The Commandos were not on an island but a promontory where, they later discovered, the wives of the local fishermen met the fishing fleet every morning with baskets of food. A sudden lull in the chatter indicated to all

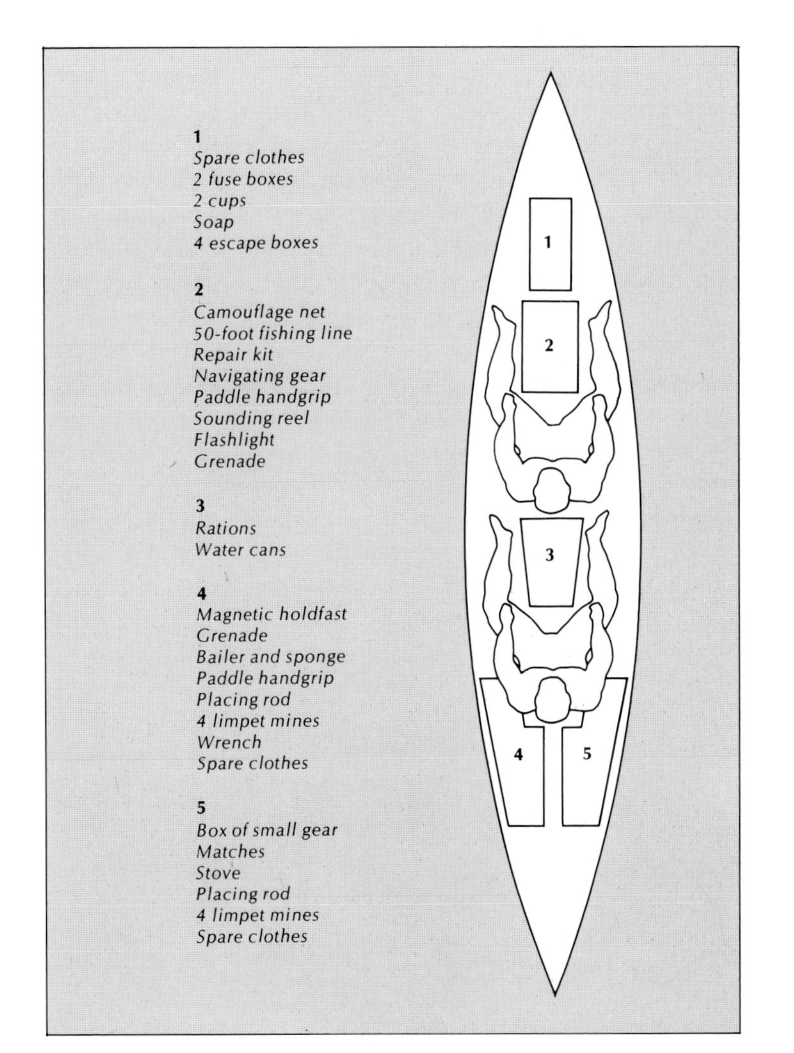

This contemporary sketch of a fully loaded cockle details the equipment—and the method of stowing it—used during the raid against German ships in Bordeaux harbor in late 1942. The canoeists practiced reaching blindly under the cockpit covers and opening the sewed-up bags until they knew by touch how to find everything from grenades to sea-water soap. Each canoeist supplemented the boat's cache with a Colt .45, a commando knife and a bird-whistle signal.

four men hiding under the camouflage nets that their presence had been noticed.

Hasler, the only French speaker among the crew, decided to tell the truth and hope that the women would not betray them. The women listened gravely and departed without making any promises. But as the day wore on it became clear they had kept the secret; the four Commandos were not disturbed. However, at dusk they thought they saw a line of German troops approaching. "We lay there with our silenced Sten guns and grenades, ready to give them a fight," related Sparks. "But as it got darker they didn't seem to come any nearer and then we realized that what we thought were Germans was nothing more than a line of invasion stakes," he said, referring to the poles that the Germans had planted along the shore to stop landing craft.

After dark, the Commandos waited for low tide before moving and then had to drag their heavily laden cockles across a wide expanse of glutinous mud. Once the boats were safely launched, Hasler set a quick pace; the other three men were grateful for the exertion, because the night was even colder than the one before. After covering about 25 miles in six hours, the Commandos found a perfect hiding place for the coming day—a dry ditch bordered by hedges between two open fields.

While they were brewing tea in the early morning, a dog appeared and barked furiously at their camouflage netting. His owner, a French farmer, soon arrived to investigate the commotion, and once again Hasler explained who they were. This time they had no worries. The Frenchman was delighted to discover that they were British Commandos and immediately invited them to his house for a drink. When Hasler explained that such conviviality would not be convenient, the farmer seemed disappointed.

That night the four Commandos found the river buzzing with activity. They lost some time dodging patrol boats, and dawn caught them still on the move. In a hurry to find cover, they nosed into a little island—this time a real one—in the middle of the river. Hasler got out first, as usual, to make sure there was no one about. He came running back seconds later and whispered: "Quick! Push off!" They had landed a few yards from a German antiaircraft post.

The sun was already up by this time, so they could not safely paddle far. Instead they moved the cockles into a field of high marsh grass, hoping the reeds would be tall enough to hide their craft. Positioned under the noses of the Germans, they found that time passed slowly. "We lay there all day," Sparks recalled, "not daring to move or speak. We could hear the Germans talking and laughing and two of them walked quite close to us. To make things worse, a herd of cows came into the field and formed a big circle round us and stood there for the rest of the day just looking at us."

At dusk the two cockles moved on, reaching the outskirts of Bordeaux before dawn on December 10. The four men paddled their craft into tall reeds and spent that day and most of the next resting there. Toward evening on the 11th, they began fusing the mines. The Commandos planned to drift into the docks on the last of the flood tide, plant their limpets during high water and then escape with the ebb.

Corporal Albert Laver and Marine William Mills were to take their cockle a mile or two upriver to search for suitable targets at docks on the east bank. If they found no targets there, they were to return and sink two ships moored at a jetty opposite the reeds where the four men were hiding. Hasler and Sparks would go into the main docks on the west bank, three miles upriver.

The four men blackened their faces with grease paint and donned mottled-green camouflage hoods. At about 9 p.m. they shook hands, wished one another luck, edged the cockles out of the reeds and went their separate ways.

Hasler and Sparks needed a little more than an hour to reach the main docks. As they rounded a bend in the river they saw, for the first time, the ships they had come so far to sink. There were seven of them moored in the harbor. Unlike the blacked-out docks in England, these were brightly lighted. Across the water the Commandos could hear the creaking and rattling of cranes that were busy unloading several of the vessels.

Despite the dock lights, Hasler decided that he and Sparks had a good chance of not being seen so long as they stayed in the deep shadows close to the hulls of the ships. Silently, the two men crossed the river and slid along the file of vessels to a big cargo liner that Hasler had selected as the first target. Sparks leaned out with his magnetic holdfast and clamped it to the bow, and Hasler fixed the first limpet mine on the hook of the placing rod. He gently lowered the mine into the water and gripped the rod tightly with both hands; then he felt the mine's magnet draw it toward the side of the ship. Both men held their breath; if the mine was not controlled, it would make a terrible clang when it attached itself to the ship's hull. Mercifully, the mine settled in place with only a soft click. The men edged along the waterline, fixed another mine amidships and then a third at the stern. Then they moved to the next ship.

They had mined the bow of the second vessel and were about to plant another limpet amidships when a sentry on the deck above directed a flashlight onto them. Both men ducked their heads against the decking of the cockle and froze. They could only hope their camouflage would save them. Sparks was still clinging to the ship with the holdfast. Gently he slipped the holdfast loose and let the tide take the cockle alongside the ship. The sentry followed the cockle; his boots clumped on the iron deck and his flashlight still played on them. Both canoeists felt their backs had been stripped naked as they waited for the inevitable shots.

But luck was with them. Under the flare of the bow, they passed out of sight of the watchman on deck, and Sparks clamped on the holdfast to keep them still. Again they waited. They could hear the sentry shuffling his feet above them; the beam of his flashlight still swept the water. But eventually the light went out. "Thank God for the camouflage," Sparks wrote later. "He must have decided, in the end, that we were just a lump of wood. While we were waiting under the bow, we slapped on another mine."

The ebb tide was now flowing, and time was running out. Two ships lay side by side and Hasler decided to mine them both at the same time by slipping in between their rusty iron hulls. The Commandos had just fixed the second limpet when the towering iron walls began to close in, squeezing the frail cockle in a viselike grip. For a moment it seemed that nothing could save the men from being crushed; they saw the deck of the cockle warp and heard the boat's framework creak in protest. Instinctively, both men reached out to push the huge ships apart, although they knew that was impossible. Then, at the whim of the tide, the pressure began to ease and the Commandos were able to edge out of the trap. As they went, they planted their last two limpets.

"That was our job done," Sparks recalled. "We paddled out to the middle of the harbor as quickly as we could. Then Blondie turned round, shook hands and said, 'Bloody good show.' I was over the moon that we had pulled it off. I felt like going ashore and having a drink to celebrate."

Celebration was somewhat premature, for the pair still had to escape. Paddling swiftly back downriver on the ebb tide, they reached the clump of reeds where they had spent the previous day. Soon they heard a splashing behind them. It was the other cockle. Hasler laughed out loud when Laver and Mills appeared out of the night.

Laver and Mills were also in good spirits. They had found no targets in the eastern docks, they said, but they had plastered the two ships at the jetty opposite the reeds. One had five limpet mines stuck to it, the other three.

Now it was crucial for the Commandos to put distance between themselves and Bordeaux before the mines began to explode. After a minute or two of whispered conversation they set off together, driving the cockles downriver as fast as they could. At 6 a.m. the tide began to turn against them, and Hasler judged it time to split up and continue overland. The men were some 20 miles from Bordeaux, near the little town of Blaye. The four men solemnly shook hands again and wished one another luck. Then the crews made their separate ways to shore.

The two crews never met again. The only survivors of the Bordeaux raid were Hasler and Sparks. After several days of stumbling across country, relying on French peasants for civilian clothes, food and shelter, they eventually made contact with a Resistance escape organization at the town of Ruffec, 90 miles northeast of Bordeaux. From there they were smuggled across the Pyrenees into Spain, where they parted. Each made his way alone to England.

Not until after the War was the fate of the other eight men pieced together. Wallace and Ewart, who had seemed to be lost at the first tidal race, actually got past that obstacle and continued upriver some distance, but then they were swept into surf near Pointe de Grave; their cockle capsized and they swam ashore where, in a state of collapse, they were captured. The body of Moffat, one of the two men Hasler had abandoned in the river, washed ashore on December 17. His companion, Sheard, disappeared without a trace.

Mackinnon and Conway, who became separated from their companions while slipping by the German patrol boats, carried on by themselves for three days. On the night of December 10, their cockle struck a submerged obstacle and was wrecked. Both men got ashore, cadged civilian clothes, and made their way across country to the southwest, hoping to reach Spain and relative safety. At the village of La Réole, however, they were betrayed to the Germans and arrested.

Laver and Mills, neither of whom could speak a word of French, were unable to find civilian clothes. They managed to cover about 20 miles, but were finally picked up, still in uniform, on December 12 in a suburb of Montlieu. It was Mills's 21st birthday.

In October 1942, the German High Command had issued a directive that all Commandos, whether in uniform or not, whether armed or not, were to be "slaughtered to the last man." As a result, the six captured canoeists were shot.

But the raiders had left their mark in Bordeaux harbor. When their limpet mines exploded at dawn on December 11, 1942, two ships were sunk, and three others heavily damaged. Hundreds of tons of cargo that had been meant for use by the Axis was sunk or destroyed in the blasts. Hearing of the losses, Hitler was furious and demanded an explanation. The High Command was slow to give him one. They thought at first that the British had devised a way to float mines into Bordeaux on the tide. Not until they found an unexploded limpet mine on one of the ships, and two of the abandoned cockles, did they know the answer.

While Hasler was perfecting the techniques of raiding by canoe, an innovative Royal Navy lieutenant commander named Nigel Willmott was embarked on another novel amphibian enterprise, one that would eventually save the lives of thousands of Allied soldiers. Willmott's specialty was beach reconnaissance. His expertise, which was self-taught, grew out of a frustrating mission he had attempted in the Mediterranean theater in 1941.

In January of that year, Willmott was appointed navigating officer for a proposed British invasion of Axis-occupied Rhodes, the largest of the Dodecanese, an island group situated in the Aegean off the coast of Turkey. The Luftwaffe was devastating Allied shipping in the eastern Mediterranean from air bases on Rhodes—a menace that the British

SERGEANT SAMUEL WALLACE

MARINE ROBERT EWART

LIEUTENANT J. W. MACKINNON

MARINE JAMES CONWAY

MARINE W. H. MILLS

CORPORAL A. F. LAVER

MAJOR H. G. HASLER

CORPORAL WILLIAM SPARKS

urgently wanted to neutralize. Willmott was given the job of determining where on its coastline landings could be made.

Charts of the coast of Rhodes were sketchy and unreliable. A study of the island through the periscope of a minelaying submarine failed to supply the information that Willmott needed. Would the landing craft be able to get to the shore, or would they be halted by false beaches and submerged sand bars, beyond which lay water deep enough to drown men and tanks? Was the beach firm enough to support trucks and tanks, or would they bog down and become easy targets for the defenders? Was there an exit from the beach, or would the invaders be trapped in a cul-de-sac and unable to move inland? As Willmott saw it, the only way to answer the questions was to go ashore and look for himself.

When Willmott first sought permission to explore landing sites, he was turned down flat. He was told that if he were captured by the Germans, British intentions would be revealed. Willmott replied that without an inshore reconnaissance, any landing attempt could become a massacre.

Willmott's argument prevailed in the end. Twenty-four hours after his proposal was rejected, his superiors reversed themselves and asked him how soon he could proceed. Willmott made his plans. His original intention was to paddle ashore from a submarine in a rubber dinghy, but he later changed his mind, deciding that a foldboat would be more maneuverable and capable of carrying much more equipment. He had just one problem: He knew nothing about foldboats. To learn more, Willmott sought out an expert—Roger Courtney, who had first persuaded Combined Operations of the value of the craft.

By then Courtney was in the Middle East, in a tented camp at Kabrit, Egypt, where he was training Special Boat Section recruits on the nearby Great Bitter Lake. When Willmott arrived at Kabrit, Courtney agreed to help—on one condition. "I go with the boat," he said matter-of-factly.

He and Willmott made an unlikely pair. Courtney was a big, happy-go-lucky character with a fund of stories about hunting lions from canoes and a capacity for drinking any other man under the table. Willmott was thin and rawboned, a strict disciplinarian and a physical-fitness buff.

Courtney taught Willmott the essential skills of the canoeist, and together they developed a team approach to reconnaissance. Because landing a canoe would invite detection, they decided that one man should remain offshore in the canoe while the other swam in to survey the beach.

They discovered that swimming ashore without being seen was difficult enough. For practice, one stood watch on the beach while the other swam in, and if the lookout spotted the swimmer, he threw a stone at him; the stone showed the swimmer that he had failed and must try his approach again. With further practice the two men found that the soft hiss of even a small wave breaking on the shore would cover the crunch of footsteps on gravel, and they timed their movements to coincide with the breaking waves.

After two weeks of improvised but intensive training, the pair embarked on the submarine *Triumph* for Rhodes. On the night of March 21 the submarine surfaced four miles off the coast of the island. Willmott and Courtney eased into their foldboat and, with a whispered farewell, pushed off and paddled quickly into the darkness.

The first landing site they wanted to survey was a small bay southeast of Marizza, where there was a German airfield. About 100 yards from the shore, Willmott shipped his paddle and prepared to go overboard. He lifted his legs out of the cockpit, twisted sideways and rolled over so that he was lying across the boat on his stomach. Then he slipped into the water, gasping involuntarily at its coldness. The plan was that he would spend three hours ashore.

Using a breast stroke, Willmott swam cautiously toward the beach, occasionally probing with his feet for underwater obstacles. When he touched bottom, he worked his way along the shoreline to find out whether its gradient was shallow enough to land tanks. Then, using the waves to cover any sound he might make, he crawled slowly onto the beach. Seeing two German sentries standing directly ahead of him on a road overlooking the bay, he froze, knowing that in the darkness he would look more like a rock than like a man if he lay still.

Eventually the sentries moved on, and Willmott was able to continue his survey. He noted the gun positions and sentry posts around the bay, then moved back into the water to walk and swim the approach lanes that landing craft would take. About 15 yards from the beach he found a shoal that would certainly have blocked an amphibious assault. Any vehicles attempting to drive off the shoal would have foun-

Of the eight British canoeists who took part in the daring raid on Bordeaux harbor in October 1942, only the pair at lower right, Major H. G. Hasler and Corporal William Sparks, survived. By train, cart and foot they traveled some 500 miles to Barcelona in neutral Spain, trading their compasses to the Resistance for guide service and sometimes eating snow to satisfy their thirst. In Barcelona they separated. The British Consul gave Hasler a plane ticket to London and provided Sparks with papers that enabled him to go by train to British-held Gibraltar.

dered in five feet of water. He measured the shoal's length and width, taking notes with a grease pencil on a piece of slate strapped to a waterproof bag at his waist. Before leaving the beach, he grabbed a handful of the coarse beach gravel and stuffed it under his sweater. Later analysis of the gravel would determine whether the beach could support the weight of trucks and tanks.

By then Willmott was chilled to the bone, and his teeth were chattering violently. The swim out to meet Courtney was agony; he was exhausted and ached in every joint. Two hundred yards off the beach, he held up his hooded flashlight and began shining it out to sea in a wide arc. He signaled for five minutes, but saw no sign of Courtney. For the first time, Willmott wondered if he would make it.

By the time Courtney finally arrived, Willmott barely had enough strength left to drag himself into the foldboat. Courtney gave him a swig from a whisky flask and then a Thermos full of hot coffee spiked with brandy. Willmott revived sufficiently to help paddle farther out to sea for the rendezvous with the submarine. A swirling and impenetrable mist caused them considerable anxiety, but the night was clear by the time they were scheduled to signal, with an infrared light, to the *Triumph*. They were picked up within minutes.

The pair surveyed other beaches on Rhodes during the next two nights, Willmott going ashore again on the second night and Courtney on the third. Then they packed up and returned to Cairo, where Willmott set about preparing detailed intelligence reports. He had barely finished when the Admiralty announced that the invasion of Rhodes had been canceled. The Navy needed all of its landing craft for the impending evacuation of the British from Greece. Courtney returned to the SBS with a Military Cross for his trouble. Willmott was awarded the Distinguished Service Order.

The findings convinced Willmott that the Navy needed a unit trained to specialize in the techniques of beach reconnaissance. No one concurred, however, and his proposal was pigeonholed and more or less forgotten. The Navy did not consider such investigations essential to the success of amphibious operations. If reconnaissance was needed at all, the Navy could call in the obliging SBS, though its men were not specifically trained to survey beaches.

On one occasion, however, the SBS proved invaluable. In May 1942, Captain Kenneth Allott and Lieutenant Duncan Ritchie of the SBS were dropped in a foldboat in the Gulf of Bunbah, on the North African coast near the Libyan port of Derna, to determine whether the beach was suitable for tank landing craft. The British plan called for driving a tank wedge into Axis forces behind their lines at the gulf; at the same time, elements of the Eighth Army would advance in a frontal attack from positions west of Tobruk. The success of the entire assault would depend on getting the tanks ashore.

Allott and Ritchie landed safely just before dawn and dragged their foldboat into a patch of scrub, where they would wait out the daylight hours. At noon, to their dismay, truckloads of off-duty Italian soldiers began arriving at the beach. The Italians were plainly planning to spend the afternoon there. The Commandos stared miserably at the track their craft had left in the sand; it stretched directly from the water's edge to the bush where they were hiding. Soon about 200 troops were on the beach, and some of them cavorted around the bushes that hid the Commandos. The Italians were apparently too intent on enjoying themselves to notice the track, and Allott and Ritchie were not detected.

After dark the two Commandos pushed off again in their foldboat and quickly discovered a shelf of rock running across the gulf about 150 yards from the shore. The formation would have made it impossible for landing craft to get close enough to shore to unload tanks. On the basis of the Commandos' report, the proposed landing in the Gulf of Bunbah was canceled.

Allott and Ritchie's findings should have provided a salutary lesson about the treacherous nature of the Mediterranean coast of Africa—and the need for beach reconnaissance anywhere. But the lesson was one that Allied military planners at times chose to ignore. When, for instance, the Allies mounted Operation *Torch* in North Africa, the neglect of beach reconnaissance almost caused a debacle.

For a time it seemed as though this particular Commando art would be given its rightful due in preparations for the invasion. As *Torch* was being planned in the spring of 1942, Lord Louis Mountbatten remembered that there was a Royal Navy officer experienced in locating suitable sites for amphibious landings: Nigel Willmott. In May, he was posted to the staff of Combined Operations, which was helping to map out the North Africa invasion. At a high-level meeting presided over by Mountbatten, Willmott explained his theories, emphasizing the danger of making a major landing on unfamiliar shores. He told the planners about faulty charts, underwater obstacles, sand bars, beaches where anything on wheels would bog down, beaches without exits. And he told them how he and Courtney had explored Rhodes.

What he had to say was politely noted. But more than three frustrating months passed before Willmott was given permission to start recruiting and training beach reconnaissance teams to do the advance studies for the North Africa invasion. Then, despite a "top priority" classification, he encountered endless bureaucratic stumbling blocks to obtaining the equipment he needed.

In September, Willmott and seven other canoeists flew to Gibraltar. There, they boarded submarines that would take them to the North African coast so that they could make surveys. But by the time they arrived in North Africa, the Admiralty had issued instructions prohibiting any preliminary landings on any of the *Torch* beaches for fear of compromising security. Reconnaissance of the landing sites would be made from submarines only.

Willmott and his men spent nearly two weeks examining the planned landing areas through periscopes. They averted a potential disaster by discovering that one beach earmarked for a landing by a motorized division was completely enclosed by tall cliffs. Even so, their survey was inadequate. Willmott feared there was much they did not know.

His fears were amply justified. When Operation *Torch* got under way at dawn on the morning of November 8, 1942, scenes of considerable chaos were played out. At Port Lyautey, on the Atlantic coast of Morocco, only tracked vehicles could negotiate the soft sand, and the beaches soon were choked with mired trucks and jeeps. At Fedala, a little to the south, the surf was so high that 18 out of 25 landing craft were lost, and many heavily burdened soldiers were swept off their feet by the undertow and drowned.

At Les Andalouses, west of Oran, landing craft ran afoul of a submerged sand bar about six yards offshore. As they hit the hidden bar, dozens of landing craft were damaged, and many broached to and spilled their loads. Vehicles that tried to drive off the sand bar foundered in the deeper water separating it from the beach. Near Algiers, a key beach thought by the planners to be 2,000 yards long turned out to be usable over only 200 yards. A monumental jam of men and machines resulted from the miscalculation.

Though Operation *Torch* eventually succeeded, the mishaps on the beaches placed the assault in dire jeopardy at the outset. *Torch* hammered home a great lesson about beach reconnaissance, the very lesson that Willmott had been preaching for more than a year.

The next time Willmott appeared at Combined Operations Headquarters, he found a much more receptive audience. On December 12, 1942, Mountbatten authorized a letter to the Secretary of the Admiralty urging the creation of a new unit specifically trained and equipped to undertake beach reconnaissance. The letter was well received; a few days later, the unit was officially constituted. It was called Combined Operations Pilotage Parties—COPP for short. Willmott was given command of the new unit.

The aim of COPP was to train 50 reconnaissance teams made up of volunteers from both the Commandos and the Royal Navy. Willmott set up his headquarters at a yacht club on Hayling Island, a remote spot near Chichester on England's south coast. There he instituted a spartan training regimen, which began with a swim in the nude every morning, regardless of the temperature. The swim was followed by calisthenics and hours of canoeing. In the evenings the men practiced night landings, and on Sundays the unit marched double time two miles to church and back.

Gradually the COPP unit acquired equipment: seaworthy boats, waterproof night compasses and flashlights, rubber suits and a vital little gadget for measuring beach gradients underwater. The device consisted of two reels of fishing line marked with lead pellets at specific intervals. The swimmer attached the end of one line to a stake driven into the beach at the water's edge, then slowly swam out, unreeling the line. Whenever a pellet passed through his hand, he took a sounding with the other line and noted both the distance from the shore and the depth. From the resulting figures, the swimmer could later diagram the sea bottom to determine whether it was too steep for a landing.

In February 1943, four COPP teams under the command of Lieut. Commander Norman Teacher were sent to the Naval base at Malta for their first job: preparing the way for the Allied invasion of Sicily. They were to swim ashore from foldboats to survey possible landing sites along four different sections of the coast. The teams were dispatched over Willmott's protests: He feared that his men had not trained long enough to be able to endure the rigors of their mission.

The four submarines assigned to the mission left Malta with the canoeists on the evening of February 27. What happened next justified Willmott's fears and underscored the extreme hazards of beach reconnaissance.

Teacher and his team were to explore a 15-mile segment of the southwest shore between the coastal town of Sciacca and the Belice River. At about midnight, he and his paddler, Lieutenant Noel Cooper of the Royal Navy Volunteer Reserve, jumped into their foldboat and headed away from the submarine *Unbending*. The sea was rough and a strong wind whipped spray from the crests of the waves. About 200 yards from the beach, Teacher pulled on his rubberized canvas suit and prepared to swim ashore. As he slipped overboard, his eyes rolled from the shock of the icy water; he murmured a hoarse farewell to Cooper and struck out for the beach. He was never seen again.

Other COPPs from the *Unbending* took over on following nights, and for a while they had better luck. Under the noses of Axis sentries, the swimmers accurately measured beach gradients and gathered other information. But on March 4, their fifth and last night, Cooper went ashore again, this time with Captain George Burbridge, a volunteer from the Canadian Army. They never returned.

Elsewhere along the coast, similar disasters occurred. None of the four COPPs aboard the submarine *Unrivalled* returned from surveys of the southern tip of Sicily; two men were lost and two captured.

On the north coast, Lieutenant Neville McHarg and a companion, paddling toward shore from the *Safari*, ran into sardine nets and were searching for a gap when RAF bombers began a raid on the nearby harbor of Castellammare. Flares turned night into day and forced the canoeists to abort the mission. The next night they were turned back by the weather. On the third night Army Captain Theodore Parsons reached the shore, but as he was wriggling up the beach he heard a challenge and found himself looking down the barrel of a rifle. His paddler, a seaman named Irvine, came ashore to look for him and was also captured.

On the south coast, the crew of the *United*, lingering off the Gulf of Gela, thought that all four of their COPPs had been lost on the night of February 26. In fact, two had been captured. The other two, Naval Lieutenants Robert Smith and David Brand, overstayed their time while surveying a sand bar and were beset by a violent storm when they tried to return to the *United*. While struggling to stay afloat in increasingly wild seas, Brand broke his paddle.

Dawn came, and still the storm gave no sign of stopping. On the crests of the waves the two canoeists had a grandstand view of the coast of Sicily; in the troughs they could see nothing but walls of gray water. Every few minutes they had to bail out with tin cups. By 8 a.m. they had given up hope of finding the submarine and decided to try to paddle back to Malta, a distance of 80 miles.

Taking a bearing from the misty silhouette of the Sicilian volcano Mount Etna, Smith and Brand set out with only the faintest hope of success. The rain and the seas were so heavy that one man had to bail while the other paddled. All that day they fought the storm and their own fatigue as the little foldboat rose and fell, shuddering up one side of a wave and corkscrewing madly down the other. Shortly after dusk, the sea tore a hole in the boat's stern canopy, and for a time both canoeists had to give over to bailing.

The storm finally died around midnight. By then Brand was in poor shape; an old wound in his hip had reopened and was excruciatingly painful. The most he could do was bail feebly. But with the dawn, a smudge appeared on the horizon directly in front of them. It was Malta. Smith kept paddling, and early in the afternoon they were picked up by a passing British motor torpedo boat.

Back at Hayling Island, Willmott was deeply distressed by the losses at Sicily. When he was urged to produce more COPP teams for the inshore reconnnaissance of the island,

he held out until he was reasonably satisfied that his men were ready. His stubbornness paid off. In better weather and with new, stronger boats built specially for the job, the four men of COPP 5 and COPP 6 successfully explored all of the proposed landing sites in Sicily with the loss of only one canoeist. On the night of the invasion, July 10, 1943, the COPPs went out again in their canoes to act as markers for the incoming assault craft. Seven divisions went ashore with little difficulty, and took just 38 days to seize the island. The handful of brave men who had spent so many nights exploring the beaches—some at the cost of their lives—played no small part in the triumph of that landing.

Jobs for canoeists were meanwhile proliferating. A few days before the invasion of Sicily, 23 members of the SBS landed secretly on the south coast of German-occupied Crete from a Royal Navy motor launch. Their orders were to attack three airfields on Crete and to destroy as many aircraft as they could find, reducing the Luftwaffe's capacity to strike the invasion force at Sicily, some 480 miles to the west.

The raiders climbed up into the mountains and made contact with Major Paddy Leigh Fermor, a British liaison officer who had been left behind in Crete to organize local guerrilla bands after the Allies evacuated the island in 1941. The next day, they split up into three groups and, following Fermor's directions, set out across the mountains for their separate objectives.

In command of one group was a young Dane, a former merchant seaman by the name of Anders Lassen, who was soon to become a legendary figure. Though he had only recently joined the SBS, Lassen had already won a Military Cross for a Commando raid in West Africa. During SBS operations in the eastern Mediterranean he would kill or capture more Germans than any other single man.

On Crete, when Lassen's group reconnoitered Kastelli Pediada airfield, south of the port of Heraklion, local villagers warned the men that an attack was impossible because of the number of guards posted around every plane, day and night. Lassen was not in the least perturbed. He decided that he and another soldier, a corporal named Jones, would stage a diversion on the west side of the airfield while his two remaining men attacked the Stukas and Ju-88s parked on the east side.

Lassen's diversion grew to the proportions of a pitched battle. At 11:30 p.m. on July 4, he and Jones cut a hole in the airfield's perimeter wire and crept toward some hangars, near which they could see a group of Italian soldiers sitting around a bonfire. When a sentry challenged them, Lassen pointed to the fire to distract his attention, then shot him twice at close range.

Chaos ensued. Bullets whined in every direction, Very signal lights soared into the sky and Italian and German guards blazed away at flitting shadows. Lassen and Jones slipped away from the action to what Lassen later described as a "quiet area," where they started another fight. Exactly as Lassen had planned, trucks roared across from the east side with reinforcements, leaving the two SBS men on that side free to tiptoe among the aircraft and plant their bombs.

Lassen and Jones became separated during the fighting but—despite being hotly pursued by German search parties—both escaped, as did their companions. When time fuses triggered their bombs, six German aircraft were destroyed and three others put out of commission.

The four men made their way together back to the camp in the mountains. A week later they reached a rendezvous point on the coast, where the motor launch picked them up and they rejoined the two other patrols. The others had not been as successful; the airfields they had been sent to attack were deserted.

After the Crete raid, the SBS temporarily abandoned canoes in favor of a fleet of caïques—two-masted, 30-to-50-ton Mediterranean fishing craft—for operations in the Aegean Sea. A major shift in the tide of the War prompted their incursion into the Aegean. Early in September 1943, Italy capitulated to the Allies, withdrawing its troops from many of the Aegean islands. The islands were strategic prizes. Whoever held them could control the flow of shipping from the east and west Mediterranean through the Dardanelles and northward into the Black Sea. Shortly after Italy's surrender, the Italian commandant on Rhodes surrendered his forces to the Germans. Alarmed at this turn of events, the Allies moved swiftly to secure the remaining islands of the Dodecanese group. The SBS, then commanded by Lieut. Colonel the Earl George Jellicoe and based in Palestine, was ordered into the Aegean in their caïques.

In September, Special Boat Section detachments landed

In this sketch, a COPP swimmer determines the contour of a beach with two fishing lines—one attached to the shore by a foot-long brass peg, the other dropped to the bottom. The distance from shore was measured by pellets affixed to the line at intervals of one fathom, or six feet; the weighted bottom line told the water's depth in one-foot intervals.

on Cos, Samos, Leros and Simi, but the Germans quickly responded with overwhelming force to drive out the intruders. By November, all the Aegean islands, from the Sporades group in the north to the Dodecanese in the south, were in German hands.

The SBS struck back hard, with an ambitious goal in mind: to pin down and demoralize the three German divisions in the Aegean, 28,000 men or more. To improve the odds, the SBS sought and received help from the Royal Navy and Royal Air Force, enlisted the aid of local Greeks, and at times engaged a special unit of freedom fighters—the Greek Sacred Squadron, named for an ancient Greek force that fought the Spartans in 379 B.C. With such resources, the men of the SBS began to attack German shipping and island garrisons, varying the timing and location of their strikes to keep their foe off balance. By the summer of 1944 they had raided every German-occupied island in the Aegean, hitting some islands two or three times.

The SBS headquarters ship was an old wooden caïque, the *Tewfik,* anchored off the Turkish coast in a blue-water cove. It presented a picture of almost idyllic tranquillity; the sunlight sparkled on the sea, the air was heavy with the scent of wild geraniums and of the olive, lemon and fig trees that covered the nearby hills. The picture was completed by the tanned young men who could often be seen lounging in wicker chairs on the *Tewfik's* deck, playing cards and drinking champagne they had "liberated" from some luckless German ship that had crossed their path.

This mobile base in the territorial waters of neutral Turkey was a brazen violation of international law. But the Turkish government turned a blind eye to the *Tewfik's* presence and to the constant activity of armed caïques in other remote coves on the Turkish coast. The Turks' lack of interference was an important contribution to the Allied war effort, for it put every island in the Aegean within easy striking distance.

At the end of January 1944, the Special Boat Section kicked off a flurry of raiding with a mission led by the indefatigable Anders Lassen, who by then had added two bars to his Military Cross. He and four other Commandos ambushed a German patrol boat as it entered the harbor on the island of Calchi, capturing vessel and crew. Thereafter, one raid followed another in quick succession. Five German

caïques were blown up at Stampalia; at Simi, grenades were thrown through the windows of a German billet; at Archi, two German caïques were blown up and a third was captured and taken back to the SBS base with a cargo of champagne, beer and wine. At Nisiros, when German troops arrived at an orphanage with orders to remove the children to Rhodes, SBS men—forewarned by the Greeks—stepped out of the shadows, killing two Germans and capturing 10 others. At Piscopi, a similar trap was laid. There, the German commandant was offered a fat pig by the islanders, and the SBS was waiting for him when he went to pick it up; he resisted capture and was killed.

On a single night in April 1944, SBS raiders wiped out all of the German garrisons on the outlying islands of the Cyclades group north of Crete. The fighting was savage. At Santorini, Lassen and an SBS sergeant stormed a German billet on the first floor of the Bank of Athens building. The sergeant kicked the door open, Lassen threw in two grenades, the sergeant sprayed the room with a Sten gun and Lassen used his pistol to deal with any German showing signs of life. The toll of the Cyclades operation was particularly one-sided: 41 Germans were killed, 27 wounded and 19 captured. Of the 39 SBS men who took part, only two were killed and three wounded. Anders Lassen survived; his career was to end later during a fire fight in Italy, for which he was posthumously awarded the Victoria Cross.

In the early summer of 1944, men of the SBS and the Greek Sacred Squadron made preparations for the most ambitious raid yet: a full-scale assault on the island of Simi, a steppingstone to nearby Rhodes. The plan for the operation hung on the elimination of a formidable German threat—two destroyers based at the island of Leros.

Colonel Jellicoe remembered the success of the Royal Marine Boom Patrol Detachment's cockle raid on Bordeaux harbor, and he asked if the detachment could send a few men to the Aegean to deal with the destroyers.

The response was quick. On a night in June 1944, three canoes penetrated Portolago harbor at Leros and headed toward the anchored ships. Two of the crews attached limpets to the destroyers and several escort craft without incident, then made their way back to a waiting motor torpedo boat.

The third crew had a harrowing experience. As Marine Corporal Edward Williams Horner and his crewman approached their first target, a sentry on board one of the destroyers spotted and challenged them. According to their drill, the men froze, but the tide carried them closer to the ship. The sentry challenged again, and when he slammed home the bolt on his weapon, Horner figured that the situation was hopeless. "All right," he yelled. "We surrender."

The Marines paddled to the side of the ship to find the gangway and give themselves up. But no gangway was in view. This fact, coupled with the confusion they could hear on board the ship, prompted second thoughts about surrendering. They kept paddling, hid momentarily under the flared bow of the ship, and then headed for shore. Not a shot was fired. The men reached the shadows of the cliffs that ringed the harbor. While a German gunboat charged about in search of the tiny craft, Horner and his partner edged along the shore to the harbor entrance and paddled furiously to the British motor torpedo boat. The next morning, a series of explosions erupted in Portolago. The last two German destroyers in the Aegean had been wiped out.

The assault on Simi could now proceed. On the night of July 13, ten motor launches and two caïques, carrying 81 men of the SBS and 132 members of the Sacred Squadron, left a cove on the Turkish shore and headed for their target. They landed unobserved at three separate beaches and by dawn had settled themselves on a promontory overlooking the main German strongholds. At first light, the raiders swooped down on the German positions; five hours later, the entire island was in their hands. The people of Simi greeted the victory with wild rejoicing. They roasted an ox in celebration and delivered many speeches from the steps of the town hall. Meanwhile, the Commandos destroyed fuel and ammunition dumps, gun emplacements and 19 German caïques anchored in the harbor. At midnight they departed, taking 151 prisoners with them.

The Simi raid signaled a change of scene for the Special Boat Section. The Greek commandos, who had been performing with increasing skill under SBS tutelage, were judged ready to fight the Germans on their own. The bulk of the SBS moved north to the mainland for operations in Greece and Yugoslavia. Though their buccaneering days in the Aegean were over, the men of the SBS would continue to harass the Germans—with a dash and energy that belied their small numbers—until peace came to the Balkans.

Raiders of the Special Boat Section unload supplies from a camouflaged Greek caïque on a German-occupied island 70 miles north of Crete. The British Commandos and Greek freedom fighters who roamed the Aegean Sea often distributed to the local islanders the food and fuel they captured from German ships and supply depots.

4

A school for sabotage
Violating a military taboo
A scheme to capture Gibraltar
German commandos in Soviet uniforms
A mission to keep the Danube open
The savage soldiers called Nightingales
A baron and his "wild bunch" play havoc behind the lines
A Russian withdrawal spurred by trickery
The demise of a proud command

MASTERS OF DECEPTION

In the autumn of 1939, a special training camp was built in the dense pine forests on the shores of the Quenzsee, a lake near Brandenburg, Germany. Heavily guarded from the outside world, the camp was a school for sabotage, silent killing and other nefarious arts. On graduation, men joined a unique unit called the Brandenburgers. They were Germany's commandos.

Brandenburgers, like all special forces, were trained to wage warfare behind enemy lines, to strike swiftly where least expected and then to disappear quickly. Their task demanded the same qualities of outstanding courage and initiative expected of British Commandos and U.S. Rangers.

But the Brandenburgers were remarkable in one regard. Unlike the Allied commando groups, who relied mainly on surprise and force of arms, the Germans used deception as their chief weapon. They often carried out their missions in disguise, wearing civilian clothes or the uniforms of the enemy. They spoke the language of the enemy, carried his identity documents, mimicked his habits, and when he least expected it, struck him from behind, causing havoc and generating confusion. Brandenburgers mingled with enemy soldiers, countermanded enemy orders and redirected convoys, cut enemy communications, gathered firsthand intelligence and seized strategic installations during undercover operations that sometimes lasted for weeks.

The tactic of deception was both an asset and a liability for the Brandenburgers. It enabled them to worm their way into the very heart of the enemy's camp in order to undertake and complete audacious missions. But posing as the enemy in his own territory violated military taboos, both official and unofficial. According to international laws governing warfare, such deception was punishable by execution—as the Brandenburgers well knew. Nor could the Brandenburgers count on approval in the Reich: Many members of the Wehrmacht's regular officer corps regarded their methods of waging war as ungentlemanly and underhanded. The effectiveness of the German commando group, however, was rarely in doubt.

The elite unit was the creation of Captain Theodor von Hippel, an officer attached to the Abwehr, or German military intelligence. Before the War, Hippel had been a colonial officer in German East Africa. However, unlike many of the men who had served the Empire abroad, he was far from being a traditionalist, and after he became an Abwehr officer in 1939, he began toying with ideas for irregular action behind enemy lines.

A special force of Abwehr agents had already been formed specifically for the invasion of Poland. Though the agents were called *Kampf-Truppen,* or combat troops, they were saboteurs rather than soldiers and operated largely on their own, without firm ties to the Wehrmacht. Their successes helped to crystallize Hippel's theories. A few days before the German Army crossed into Poland on September 1, 1939, several hundred *K-Truppen* dressed as coal miners and workers slipped over the border. Their orders were to seize certain strategic industrial installations in the region of Upper Silesia and to prevent them from being destroyed by the Poles when Germany attacked. The agents were equipped only with small arms and hand grenades, but they needed nothing more; though some of their groups were attacked by Polish troops, the agents managed to hold out until the arrival of the advance guard of the regular German columns and to save a number of factories important for the Reich's war production.

Meanwhile, other *K-Truppen* detachments, who were also operating in civilian clothes but wearing red kerchiefs to identify them to the Wehrmacht, were assigned to safeguard bridges and roads. Still others captured the huge electricity station at Chorzow, threw the switches and blacked out eastern Upper Silesia, thus deactivating electric detonators that the Poles had placed on demolition charges at key industrial sites.

In the mountains near the Polish-Czechoslovakian border, a separate detachment of some 360 men occupied Jablunkov Pass, a principal avenue for the German invaders. The detachment held out for four days against attacks by Polish frontier troops and managed to remove all of the dynamite charges previously set in a crucial railway tunnel.

Hippel was impressed by the accomplishments of the *K-Truppen,* who were disbanded following the conquest of Poland. At a meeting in Dresden attended by Abwehr chief Admiral Wilhelm Canaris, Hippel proposed the formation of another special combat unit, with *K-Truppen* as the nucleus, to carry out clandestine missions under Wehrmacht command in the coming campaigns in Western Europe.

At first Admiral Canaris was cool to the idea. He had little taste for the kind of planning and organizing that would be involved in the creation of an entirely new outfit. But Hippel was undeterred and sought support from other Abwehr officers. His persistence paid off when a former superior officer, Helmuth Groscurth, who had influential connections in the Army General Staff, endorsed his proposal. No record remains of how Canaris reacted, but at the beginning of October, Hippel was authorized by the General Staff to assemble a "company of saboteurs" from ethnic German Abwehr agents. The unit was given the cover name 800th Special Duties Construction Company, but soon it came to be known as the Brandenburg Company.

Though the earliest volunteers for Brandenburg duties came from *K-Truppen,* Hippel also recruited extensively among expatriates who had recently returned home to Germany and from *Volksdeutschen,* German nationals living in the countries bordering the Reich—Lithuania, Latvia, Estonia, Poland, Hungary and Yugoslavia. Intimate familiarity with foreign customs was essential: For German commandos to be accepted in the ranks of enemy armies—a role Hippel intended for them from the start—they would have to be able to talk, drink, drill, swear and even spit without any hint of their alien status.

During the spring of 1940, Hitler was brewing numerous schemes for conquest, and the Brandenburgers figured in most of them. Among the targets of the Reich were Scandinavia and the Low Countries. The Brandenburgers served in the vanguard of the troops invading these areas. On the night of April 8, detachments of Brandenburgers dressed in Danish Army uniforms crossed into Denmark to seize principal road and railway bridges in preparation for the German invasion the next morning. The commandos took every one of their objectives.

On May 10, Germany attacked Belgium and the Netherlands. A few hours before the onslaught, Dutch police could be seen escorting a group of prisoners across the bridge over the Maas River at the town of Gennep near the German border. The "police" were Dutch Nazis, and the "prisoners" were Brandenburgers, who had machine pistols under their overcoats and grenades in their pockets. With the advantage of surprise, the commandos overpowered the sentries and held the bridge long enough to secure a gateway into the Netherlands for the troops of the 265th Infantry, who were soon moving across.

Another Abwehr unit, the 100th Special Duty Battalion, undertook similar surprise attacks on the Maas River bridges at Maastricht in the Netherlands. These assaults all failed, making the success of the Brandenburgers at Gennep even more vital for the German advance; General Walther von Reichenau, commanding the Sixth Army, was able to divert to the open bridge at Gennep a number of units that were stuck at Maastricht.

During the invasion of Belgium, a detachment of more than 100 Brandenburgers dressed in civilian clothes infiltrated the ragged columns of refugees fleeing from the Germans. Pushing baby carriages that had weapons concealed under the mattresses, the German commandos maneuvered through the crowds to secure their objectives—the main bridges over the Meuse and Dender Rivers and the Scheldt River tunnel near Antwerp. Another detachment, dressed in berets and overcoats, commandeered a bus and raced toward Nieuport to prevent an incident like one that had occurred in World War I. When the Germans invaded Belgium in that war, the defenders at Nieuport opened the floodgates on the Yser River, inundating the low-lying regions and frustrating the German advance. This time the Brandenburgers won out; despite fire from a British detachment across the river, the Germans captured the floodgates before the Belgians could open them.

Canaris, who had previously exhibited little interest in the Brandenburgers, now realized that they had become something of a jewel in his crown. The fact that at first he had not wanted the unit formed was forgotten, and he proudly accepted the plaudits that were being heaped on "his" commandos. On May 14, 1940, the Führer himself sent congratulations, and the next day, Canaris received orders to expand the battalion into a regiment, to be known as the *Lehrregiment Brandenburg*.

A worthy challenge for the enlarged force was in the works. After the surrender of France in June, the Brandenburgers were ordered to train for Operation *Sea Lion*—the

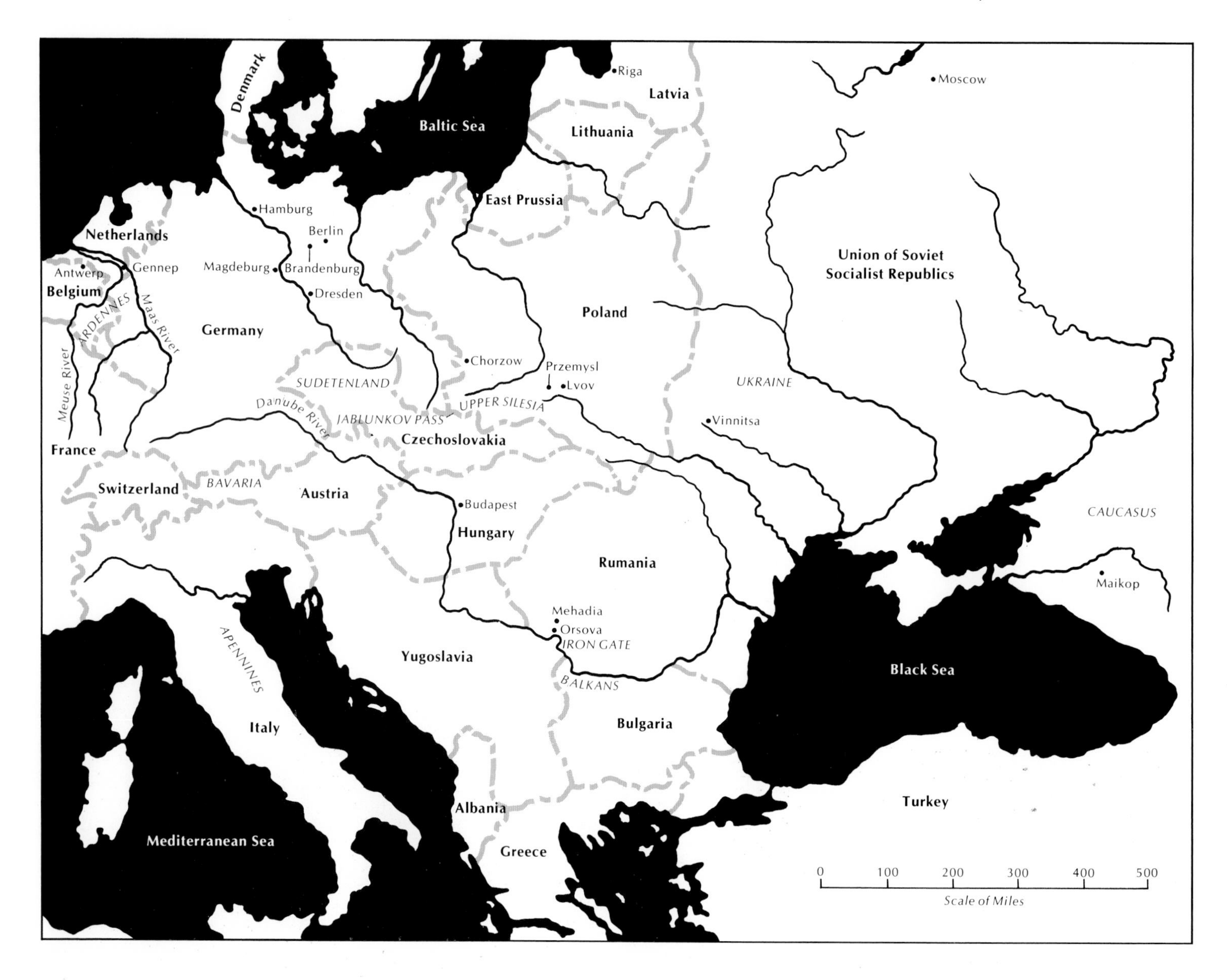

invasion of England. One company dressed in British Army uniforms was to parachute into Dover to secure the harbor and seize the coastal batteries on the cliffs. A half-company, wearing *Ueberwurf-Uniformen* (cloaks that would cover their Wehrmacht uniforms), was to land with the first assault wave west of Hastings, race along the southern coast road on motorcycles and attack the coastal batteries at Beachy Head from the rear. And one company was to land at another point on the south coast of England to storm Allied strong points there.

However, the launching of Operation *Sea Lion* hinged on the Germans' winning air superiority over the English Channel. When the Luftwaffe failed in its attempts to subdue the Royal Air Force during the summer and autumn of 1940, Hitler gradually lost enthusiasm for the invasion and set his sights elsewhere.

One of his schemes was to seal off the Mediterranean Sea by capturing the Rock of Gibraltar, the 2¼-square-mile Iberian headland where the British maintained a garrison. Unknown to the Führer, Canaris had been secretly considering a similar plan.

In July 1940, Canaris summoned Captain Hans-Jochen Rudloff to the Abwehr headquarters in Berlin. Rudloff was the commander of No. 3 Brandenburg Company, which had been singled out for particular praise after the operations in the Netherlands and Belgium; his men had won a total of 92 Iron Crosses. When the commandos were expanded into a regiment, No. 3 Company became the 3rd Brandenburg Battalion.

Rudloff's interview with the Abwehr chief was memorable. He listened with growing astonishment as Canaris outlined a wildly ambitious plan for the 3rd Battalion to enter neutral Spain from southern France, cross the country secretly in covered trucks and take the British garrison at Gibraltar by surprise. Rudloff thought the proposal "fanciful in the extreme," but kept his opinion to himself and dutifully flew to southern Spain for a feasibility study. It did not take long to confirm Rudloff's gravest misgivings. Spain teemed with British agents. Smuggling an entire battalion from the Pyrenees to Gibraltar would, he thought, be impossible.

Rudloff returned home with a negative report, and Canaris reluctantly shelved the idea until he discovered that the Führer was thinking along similar lines. Then, with the approval of the German High Command, Canaris helped draw up plans for Operation *Felix*—a full-scale assault on Gibraltar in cooperation with the Spanish government. Brandenburgers disguised as Spanish Foreign Legionnaires were to blow up the heavy steel fence between Gibraltar and Spain, and sabotage Gibraltar's airfield, oil depots, power station and water distillation plant. One hundred and fifty commandos stood by for the raid. They waited in readiness for more than a month, only to have the operation finally and irrevocably canceled: After concluding that Spain's military forces were in no shape for a prolonged fight, Spanish dictator Generalissimo Francisco Franco refused to join the War.

The cancellations of *Sea Lion* and *Felix* were frustrating to Canaris and his officers. But they took advantage of the lull in operations by mounting a recruiting campaign and expanding the training program at Quenzsee.

Located only 40 miles or so from Berlin, the Quenzsee camp was isolated on one side by the lake and screened on the other by tall pines. People living thereabouts became accustomed to gunfire and explosions emanating from deep within the forest.

Early in the War, the Brandenburgers and other German special forces raided deeply into nations targeted for attack, paving the way for the invasions of Poland, Denmark and the Low Countries. Later they struck eastward into the Soviet Union as far as the oil fields of Maikop in the steppes of southern Russia and northward to Riga in Latvia.

After crossing the Maas River by rubber dinghy at Maastricht in the Netherlands in 1940, Brandenburgers scramble up the fallen span of a bridge that had been demolished only a few hours earlier by Dutch guards.

The recruits were taught many of the same tactics the British Commandos learned at Achnacarry in Scotland—surprise, stealth and speed—but the Brandenburgers' training program stressed the techniques of deception. Students learned not only how to use false papers with confidence, but how to forge their own. The subtleties of wearing disguises were instilled by having the men turn out for inspection in foreign uniforms perfect in every detail, down to their underwear and the contents of their pockets. For gathering the materials for such masquerades, the men were left to their own devices.

"If a man had a photograph of his sweetheart in his wallet and there was an incriminating landmark in the background, he would be in trouble," Helmuth Schwinker, a Brandenburger from the Sudetenland, recalled. "But it was that kind of attention to detail that saved lives time and time again when we were on operations.

"The course had a very leveling effect on everyone. Independence and intelligence counted more than rank. It was typical of the place that the officers and soldiers shook hands rather than saluted each other. Unlike the rest of the Army, who were told to 'leave the thinking to the horses because their heads are bigger,' we were encouraged to think for ourselves, and to develop intuition and resourcefulness.

"In the evenings, the canteen at Quenzsee was amazing. Recruits came from all over the place, so there would be dozens of different languages being spoken by men of very different backgrounds exchanging ideas and opinions. We tended to be very idealistic about our involvement in the unit. It was certainly nothing like being in an ordinary German regiment."

Exercises at Quenzsee were designed to test ingenuity as much as military skill. One group of recruits was ordered to get the fingerprints of the Brandenburg police chief—without his knowledge. Their first attempt was to arrange an interview during which a young officer tried repeatedly to press a silver cigarette case into the hand of the police chief; the interview ended with the officer being turned over to the Gestapo as a suspicious character. After the officer had been bailed out by the training-camp commandant, his group succeeded in a second attempt by mounting a 24-hour watch on the police chief and eventually taking the prints from his car.

The exercises grew progressively more difficult. On one occasion, students were told at noon that they had five hours in which to capture 10 uniformed and armed soldiers

of the Wehrmacht and deliver them to the Quenzsee camp. The students' leader rushed into Brandenburg and wheedled Gestapo military-police badges and patches from a local supplier with a cock-and-bull story about needing the insignia for the camp's annual dramatic production. The students ripped the insignia from their own uniforms and sewed on those of the feared Gestapo. They then commandeered a truck and tore out of the camp to the nearest highway. As precious minutes ticked away, the students waved down another truck, which was carrying a guard company from Magdeburg to Berlin, and announced that they had orders to divert both truck and men to Brandenburg. Their imperious demeanor brooked no protest, and they arrived on the deadline with their captives.

These unconventional antics, and in fact the entire thrust of the training program at Quenzsee, were not calculated to appeal to military traditionalists. The Brandenburgers' emphasis on individualism and independence was an anathema to regular Army officers, who demanded rigid discipline and blind obedience from their own troops. But as long as the Brandenburgers followed one triumph with another—and in the early years of the War, they did—they had little reason to care about enemies in the regular military. Their feats made them impervious to criticism. Later, as the commandos' fortunes declined along with those of the Wehrmacht, the situation would be different.

During the winter and spring of 1941, the Brandenburgers added to their list of accomplishments with commando operations in the Balkans. Disguised as civilian workmen, a number of Brandenburgers slipped into Rumania, Hungary, Bulgaria and Yugoslavia. Their orders were to protect Axis war matériel against possible sabotage inspired by Allied agents. The Brandenburgers got jobs as watchmen in oil fields, and worked as guards on freight trains traveling in Hungary and on oil tankers plying the Danube River.

The Danube, which winds through the Balkans, was crucial to Axis designs for that region. Hitler intended to launch an invasion of Greece and Yugoslavia on April 6, 1941. If the Yugoslavs took the natural defensive precaution of closing the Danube to shipping, the invading forces would lose a supply artery vital to sustaining their thrust into the Balkans. To keep the river open, Brandenburgers were stationed, ostensibly as employees of the Danube Shipping Company, in the Hungarian and Rumanian ports along the Yugoslavian border.

In occupied France, German special forces ride assault craft toward shore in rehearsal for the anticipated 1940 invasion of England.

Hans-Jochen Rudloff inspects the elite 3rd Brandenburg Battalion. "It became like a special club," one Brandenburger said. "We were superbly fit, and ready for anything."

The biggest detachment—some 54 men of the regiment's 2nd Battalion—was sent to Orsova, Rumania, where the Danube flows through the Iron Gate, a narrow gorge between sheer rock walls nearly 2,500 feet high. There the river could be most easily blocked. The Brandenburgers, posing as sailors, stevedores and office workers, were charged with making sure it did not happen.

In March 1941, the detachment at Orsova noted that many small freighters were congregating on the Yugoslavian side of the river suspiciously close to the Iron Gate. Sergeant Hans-Jurgen Frey was working as a deck hand on a small coal barge based at Orsova. "We thought the freighters would probably be used to block the river in one of two ways," he explained. "Either they would be loaded with cement and scuttled in midchannel, or they would be packed with explosives and blown up close to the riverbank at a point where the rock face would tumble into the water."

Early in April, the Brandenburgers played out a tactical ruse intended to get the Yugoslavs to relax security around the freighters: They abruptly left Orsova, making certain that their departure was observed by Yugoslav agents in the town. At Mehadia, some 20 miles north of the river, the detachment linked up with the remaining men of the 2nd Battalion, who had been flown in to a makeshift airstrip the day before. On the evening of April 5, the day before the scheduled invasion, the battalion drove in convoy back to the banks of the Danube, to a lonely wooded area on the cliffs a few miles downstream from Orsova.

The commandos, now wearing gray German Army uniforms, roped their way down the steep cliffs under the cover of darkness. "It was raining heavily and as black as it could be," recalled Frey. "As we edged down the slippery rock face, it seemed at times we would never get to the bottom."

At the edge of the river, they uncovered small boats that they had earlier arranged to have hidden among the rocks and scrub. The commandos settled down to wait. Shortly before 3 o'clock in the morning, they began paddling silently upstream. Reaching the dock area, the Brandenburgers stormed ashore before the Yugoslav guards realized what was happening. "Everyone knew exactly what he had to do," reported Frey. "We swept through the docks and then separated into small groups to board the blockade ships. I was lucky; my group had to take the first freighter in the line, and we were on board before a shot had been fired. Once we got control of the ship, we lifted the hatches to see what she was loaded with. It was cement."

On the Rumanian side, a German Army assault force was waiting. In less than 30 minutes' time, the raiders signaled the success of their landing, and the German troops across the river began to launch their boats. Elsewhere along the invasion front, in both Yugoslavia and Greece, Brandenburg detachments were taking over power stations, bridges and railway crossings. Brandenburgers with special knowledge of the target countries acted as guides for the first waves of the German invasion smashing across the frontiers.

The Balkans were now secured, and in June 1941 the *Lehrregiment Brandenburg* was committed to the Führer's most ambitious operation: *Barbarossa,* the invasion of the Soviet Union. For this military venture, Hitler had assembled three Army groups—designated Army Group North, Army Group Center and Army Group South—that comprised more than 2,400 tanks, some 2,000 aircraft and about three million troops. Units of Brandenburgers were assigned the task of dashing across the border into Russia and capturing such critical targets as bridges and railway tunnels in advance of the Army Groups.

On the evening of June 21, while Canaris dined at Horcher's, the most fashionable restaurant in Berlin, the first Brandenburg detachments were moving into action for the invasion, set to begin at 3:15 a.m. the next day. Lightly armed and equipped, dressed mostly in Soviet uniforms, the commandos approached their objectives on foot and by boat, glider, parachute and truck. The German advance into Russia was to mark the zenith of the *Lehrregiment Brandenburg,* for the impetus of the invasion was maintained in large part by a series of commando operations, each more daring than the one before.

For sheer nerve, few of the missions could compare with the first action of three companies of Ukrainian volunteers attached to the regiment's 1st Battalion. The companies bore the unlikely name of Nightingale Group, an allusion to their talented choir. In the early morning hours of June 22, just before the invasion began, the Nightingales crossed into Soviet Ukraine with orders to occupy the town of Przemysl and to establish a bridgehead on the San River. Both actions were aimed at keeping the road eastward open for the main assault forces. The commandos wore Wehrmacht uniforms to capitalize on local sympathies, which leaned more toward the Germans than the Soviets.

On the way to their objectives, the Ukrainian commandos literally ran into a Soviet patrol. So surprised were both parties that neither fired. The lieutenant leading the raiders was the first to collect his wits. He loudly demanded to see the Soviet commanding officer. The Russian captain in charge responded with a hesitant suggestion that the intruders should surrender. Nonsense, said the German lieutenant, and he proceeded to explain that his men were actually on a secret Soviet mission; they were dressed in German Army uniforms because they had been on a long-range patrol. So deep was the penetration, he continued, that his men only carried German papers!

Incredibly, the Russian accepted the story, and the two groups cheerfully joined forces and marched toward Przemysl, which was heavily fortified by Soviet troops and weapons. The captain obligingly gave the Brandenburgers safe conduct into the town. Then, before any further questions could be asked, air-raid sirens began to wail and everyone scattered for cover.

Brandenburgers in Yugoslavia wear Serbian dress, their "Abwehr civvies"—or civilian clothes for undercover work. "We learned how to operate in disguise and ensure the disguise was perfect," one recalled.

Immediately following the air raid, the Red Army began to withdraw. The Brandenburgers stayed out of the way until the majority of the Russian troops had gone—whereupon they gleefully emerged from their hiding places in fighting spirit, mopped up the Soviet rear guard and secured the nearby San River bridge. Within hours, lead elements of German Army Group South were rolling across the span and heading east.

As the Red Army was driven back all along the front, the Brandenburgers employed a tactic that became one of their hallmarks—using captured Soviet trucks to tag onto the end of retreating Soviet columns. In the northern sector of the front, a detachment of Brandenburgers disguised as wounded Russians linked up with the Red Army rear guard during the German advance into Latvia. As the last Soviet vehicles rolled across the bridge over the Dvina River, the "wounded" commandos threw off their bandages, killed the Russian engineers preparing to blow up the bridge, and held it until the leading German troops arrived. The commandos' coup enabled German Army Group North to maintain its thrust toward Riga, the major Baltic port in Latvia, with no loss of momentum.

Elsewhere in the U.S.S.R., long-range Brandenburg patrols penetrated hundreds of miles behind the Soviet lines on reconnaissance, intelligence and sabotage operations. To collect current information on movements by enemy troops, these patrols sought contact with Red Army units rather than avoiding it.

The Brandenburgers' disguises, necessarily, were as foolproof as ingenuity could make them. Their Red Army uniforms were authentic down to the last button; their fake letters from Russian wives and sweethearts were even addressed to the correct field postal numbers. Language, however, posed a dangerous problem for some Brandenburg units that moved among Soviet soldiers. Commandos who were unable to speak Russian fluently enough to pass muster often tried to protect themselves by posing as wounded; they would swathe themselves in bandages and either fake unconsciousness or groan loudly to avoid being questioned by the genuine Russians.

Other commandos pretended to be members of Soviet ethnic groups that did not speak Russian—a ruse that sometimes got them into uncomfortable predicaments. A Brandenburg detachment ran into trouble that way at a Soviet checkpoint in the Caucasus. The commandos were traveling in a Red Army truck and posing as exhausted stragglers from the front. They were ordered down from their vehicle so that it could be searched. While they were lounging at the side of the road, a suspicious commissar, or political officer, walked across to question the men. As it happened, he chose to address a young noncom from Hamburg who was unable to speak a word of Russian.

The Brandenburg commander quickly stepped in. "You won't get much change out of that fellow," he said. "He's an Armenian." The commissar, unfortunately for the Brandenburgers, was a real Armenian, and in his native tongue he began to gabble at the young German. Getting no response, the commissar drew his pistol. The German commander was a shade faster. He leveled his own gun at the same instant and killed the commissar, simultaneously signaling general action. The commandos had practiced many times what to do in such a situation; now, firing furiously to cover one another, they clambered back onto their already rolling truck and raced away before the Russians at the checkpoint dared to lift their heads.

Sometimes patriotism proved as much of a problem as language for the Brandenburgers. On the 29th of June, 1941, the Nightingale Group was camped on the outskirts of Lvov, with orders to stay in reserve until the 1st Mountain Division of the German Army launched a full-scale attack on the town the following day. However, the Nightingale soldiers were in a state of agitation. Information filtering out of Lvov indicated that the Soviets there were committing frightful atrocities against the pro-German Ukrainian population and that mass executions were being carried out in the NKVD, or secret police, prison. The news was more than the fiercely patriotic Ukrainians of the Nightingale Group could stand.

Lieutenant Albrecht Herzner, commander of the Nightingales, feared that his troops might bolt unless he allowed them to act quickly, and so he sought authority to raid the town in advance of the main attack. To his great relief, he was given permission to unleash the Ukrainians. Within 20 minutes, the Nightingale Group was ready. They carried a motley assortment of weapons; some even held knives in their teeth.

At about 11 p.m., the Ukrainians roared through forward German positions in trucks of the 1st Brandenburg Battalion and headed toward Lvov. When they reached the first line of Soviet defenses, there was no stopping them. They rushed headlong toward the Russians with bloodcurdling yells, oblivious to the defensive fire. Sheer fury carried them forward through one position after another.

The commandos' primary aim was to rescue their countrymen from the NKVD prison. They were too late. When they smashed down the prison doors, an appalling sight greeted them. Hundreds of prisoners lay dead in the inner courtyard; they had been ruthlessly machine-gunned. That scene spurred the Nightingale Group to savagery. For the rest of the night they combed the streets of Lvov, killing every Soviet soldier they could find. Wehrmacht units followed their bloody path, quietly and efficiently occupying the vantage points.

On the morning of June 30, the Nightingale Group took over the radio station in Lvov and broadcast a proclamation announcing the formation of a free and independent West Ukrainian state and citing the atrocities committed by the Russians as grounds for breaking away from the Soviet Union. The gesture was brave, but futile; the Reich had no intention of allowing "free and independent" states to exist within its captured territories. But the Nightingales were not aware of this.

Buoyed by patriotism, the group went on to distinguish itself again during the advance of the Wehrmacht through the Ukraine. At Vinnitsa, where the Red Army was firmly ensconced in the cover of a huge forest, a group of Nightingales disguised as Russian partisans was assigned to pinpoint the Soviet headquarters.

Stealing quietly between the trees, the Nightingales made contact with a band of genuine partisans and were promptly invited to join them for a meal. The Nightingales were ready with a cover story: They had been overwhelmed by the German advance, had slipped through the lines and were seeking to join the Red Army. The real partisans eagerly offered to help by conducting them to Soviet headquarters. There, the commandos were questioned suspiciously for several hours, but their cover story was finally accepted. That night, using a miniature transmitter developed in Berlin for just such an occasion, one of the Ukrainians radioed their position to the Brandenburg battalion that was waiting at the edge of the forest. The commandos struck the next day, captured the headquarters, and held it until regular German troops arrived.

The Vinnitsa operation was the Nightingales' last major mission. Their action in declaring a "free West Ukrainian state" proved extremely unpopular in Berlin, and the newly formed German Ministry for Eastern Territories stepped in to assume authority in the West Ukraine. Disillusioned, the Nightingales lost heart for the battle, and at the end of 1941 the group was declared "unreliable" and disbanded.

The overall success of the Brandenburgers on the Eastern Front gave Hitler considerable satisfaction. But he was not pleased by events elsewhere. In particular, the Führer began expressing increased irritation at the frequency of raids made by Allied special forces along the coast of France. At times he would spend the better part of an hour with his military chiefs of staff, discussing ways of preventing the commando strikes.

Hitler was particularly disturbed that German intelligence was giving no warning of the incursions of the Allied raiders. In fact, all the Abwehr agents in England had been captured by British intelligence and executed or turned into double agents; as a result, they were sending home no useful information on Commandos or grand strategy or anything else. Hitler complained bitterly that this was a pitiful performance, considering that Germany was separated from England by a "ditch" only 23 miles wide. Much of what he knew, he said, he had to "gather from the newspapers."

Canaris, as the man in charge of spy operations, took the brunt of Hitler's ire. The Führer's disenchantment marked the beginning of a rift that would widen as the War progressed. And as the fortunes of Canaris declined, so would those of his Brandenburgers.

On the Eastern Front, Hitler faced disappointment on a grand scale. Wehrmacht operations against the Red Army in late 1941 proceeded dismally. An attempt to capture Moscow failed, and the German Army was obliged to endure an agonizing winter without adequate protection from subzero temperatures. Hitler had perversely insisted that winter uniforms would not be necessary because the Russians would be defeated before the summer was out. Lacking warm clothing, thousands of men who had escaped Russian fire froze to death in the cold.

Desperate to regain momentum, Hitler informed his generals in April of 1942 that a new offensive would commence in the Caucasus, in the southwest of the U.S.S.R., to deprive the Soviet Union of its vital oil fields. The *Lehrregiment Brandenburg* was ordered to join forces with Army Group South. In June, Brandenburg units donned their now-familiar Red Army uniforms to precede the German advance on the Don River. The commandos' assignments, as before, were to keep the roads open and to prevent the destruction of strategic installations.

During July, a curious little private army operating as a Brandenburg unit went into action for the first time. It was commanded by Baron Adrian von Fölkersam, the grandson of a Russian admiral. Fölkersam could speak fluent Russian (as well as French and English), had studied economics at universities in Berlin and Vienna, and at the age of 27 was widely regarded as the most audacious officer in the *Lehrregiment Brandenburg*.

Early in 1942, Fölkersam had recruited and trained a special task force of 62 Russian-speaking Balts and Sudeten Germans. He called them "the wild bunch" and planned to take them farther behind Russian lines than any other Brandenburg unit had ever gone. In July, the men were given

Members of the Nightingale Group, three companies of Ukrainians attached to the Brandenburgers, march to the city of Lvov, where the anti-Soviet populace welcomed them as liberators. The Nightingale's German commander noted that, when the group withdrew after less than a month and a regular German occupation force asserted control, "Ukrainians were shattered that their fight for freedom seemed to be over."

their first job: They were to make their way into the Caucasus and prevent the oil fields at Maikop from being destroyed before the German troops arrived.

Dressed in NKVD uniforms, members of the unit slipped through the Soviet lines under cover of darkness and headed for Maikop in captured Red Army transports. On the afternoon of their first day in enemy territory, Fölkersam and his men came across a huge encampment of Red Army deserters. Fölkersam stopped to talk to them and soon discovered that they were planning to defect to the German side.

To the amazement of his comrades, Fölkersam launched into a stirring speech exhorting the Soviets to continue the struggle for the glory of Mother Russia and Stalin. His impressive performance prompted a considerable number of the deserters to reassert their allegiance to the Soviet Union. They eagerly agreed to follow Fölkersam. He was delighted. He had realized at once that the Soviet troops would provide his group with a perfect excuse for moving about at will. What could be less suspicious than a unit of NKVD men in charge of a large number of Soviet soldiers in the heart of Russian territory?

On the morning of August 2, the Brandenburgers and their band of followers mingled with a retreating Russian convoy on the road to Maikop. At a bridge over the railway line on the outskirts of the town, they encountered a detail of genuine NKVD men who were directing troops and traffic. Fölkersam, who was dressed in the uniform of an NKVD major, made one of his typically brazen overtures. He stopped his truck and approached a harassed NKVD officer trying to sort out the confusion.

"So you finally bothered to show up," said the Russian. "Well, I don't need you now. Clear the road." The German officer had no way of knowing what the Russian might be alluding to, but he saw no need to ask questions. Happy to oblige, Fölkersam climbed back on board his truck and continued into Maikop.

In the town, the Brandenburgers stopped outside the building being used as NKVD headquarters, and Fölkersam went inside to "report." He presented himself to a Russian general as "Major Truchin from Stalingrad" and explained that he had brought in a large contingent of Red Army soldiers whom he had persuaded not to desert. The general, in fact, had already received word of the coup; he complimented Fölkersam on his timely action and promised to ensure that his superiors in Moscow were informed. In the meantime, Fölkersam and his men were offered billets in private homes; no further questions were asked.

That evening Fölkersam and his "adjutant," a young German officer named Franz Koudele, were invited to have drinks with the general. Between vodkas, Fölkersam asked if he might inspect the town's defenses the following morning, and the general amiably offered to show him around Maikop personally.

Next day the Brandenburger was given a conducted tour and was highly disturbed by what he saw. The Russians had heavy artillery and a great deal of armor protecting the point at which Fölkersam was sure that the Germans would mount their main assault on the town. When the general asked for his opinion, Fölkersam tried tactfully to make a case for spreading the defenses in the event that the attack came on a broader front. The general readily agreed to disperse his artillery.

For the next five days, the Brandenburgers in their NKVD disguises roamed freely, familiarizing themselves with the defenses of the town and the nearby oil fields. By August 8, the German Army was reported to be only 12 miles from Maikop. That night Fölkersam could hear the distant rumble of the panzers' guns and every window in the town was rattled by the responding booms of Russian artillery.

Fölkersam called his men together in the house where he was billeted and gave them last-minute instructions. In small teams, they were to generate maximum confusion among the Soviet defenders and prevent them from destroying the oil-field installations. After the briefing, the Brandenburgers separated to carry out their various tasks.

The streets of the town were choked with a rabble of refugees, partisans, troop reinforcements and military trucks. Fölkersam and his team headed first for the NKVD headquarters in search of the general who had been so friendly to Fölkersam. They found that the general and his staff had already left, and in the sudden absence of authority, looters were already at work.

Their next stop was on the northern outskirts of the town, where a Red Army communications center was set up in an isolated house. The center controlled the terminals of the

Shadowed by an aide, SS Major Otto Skorzeny (left) and his chief of staff, Captain Adrian von Fölkersam (right), cross a square in Budapest, where their battalion, modeled on the British Commandos, abducted the Hungarian regent to Germany in 1944 to be a "guest of the Leader."

Army's network of field telephones, which linked the front-line positions with the sector headquarters. However, the center was indifferently guarded, and Fölkersam was quick to exploit this shortcoming.

On his orders the Brandenburgers, hugging the deep shadows close to the walls, quietly surrounded the house. Then, at a signal from him, they hurled a shower of grenades through every window. From within the building came a series of explosions; clouds of black smoke began pouring from the roof. In moments the house looked as if it had sustained a direct hit from an artillery shell, Fölkersam observed with satisfaction.

The counterfeit NKVD men raced away before they could be unmasked as saboteurs, and headed for the front line. Fölkersam was now relying not only on the authority of his spurious NKVD rank but also on the fact that he had often been seen during the previous days in the company of the Russian general. He was gambling that he would be able to issue orders without being questioned.

At the first defensive position they reached, Fölkersam affected surprise to find it still manned. "Why are you still firing?" he demanded of the Soviet officer in command. "Did you not know there has been a general withdrawal to the rear of Maikop? You had better get moving, but make sure that not a single piece of equipment falls into enemy hands. Get going." The trick worked; the soldiers hastily began gathering their belongings.

Fölkersam tried the same trick farther along the line, but this time encountered a stubborn and suspicious Soviet officer who insisted on confirming the withdrawal order before agreeing to move. Fölkersam, knowing that the communications center had been destroyed, urged the officer to telephone his commander. Sure enough, the officer discovered that the line was dead, and he was compelled to take Fölkersam's word.

By that time the Brandenburgers were manipulating another vital communications post. Koudele had been given the job of seizing the local telegraph office, with orders to occupy it by force if persuasion failed. In fact, the Red Army major in charge of the office was in no mood to argue with the NKVD. When Koudele marched in and told him the town was being abandoned, the director tried to reach the Army communications center, received no reply and assumed it had already been vacated. He and his staff hurriedly joined the refugees streaming out of town, leaving the Brandenburgers in command of a telegraph system that reached most of the northern Caucasus.

As messages flooded in from all quarters, many from dif-

ferent military units, Koudele and his men passed out the same response: "I can no longer connect you. The city is being evacuated."

Communications were in a state of utter chaos, and all semblance of order broke down among the Russian ranks. Troops that were pulling back from the front under Fölkersam's instructions encountered reinforcements moving up. Officers shouted conflicting orders at each other and their men. No one knew what was happening, but the temptation to withdraw was strong: Certainly no one wanted to be left at the front alone to face the German onslaught.

At the oil fields, Russian engineers were standing by to blow up wells, pumps and storage tanks. Brandenburgers in NKVD trucks raced around the installations issuing orders to delay the demolition. By quoting the general as their authority, they succeeded in preventing much destruction, even though the noise of the battle made it obvious that the Germans were getting perilously close.

Only in the suburb of Maksde did the Brandenburgers' tactics backfire. The engineer in charge at the Maksde oil field, unable to raise headquarters on his field telephone, signaled the telegraph office at Maikop and was told by the Brandenburgers in charge that the town was being abandoned. He waited no longer and ordered his men to start blowing up the field. The blasts signaled other engineers nearby to do the same, and most of the oil fields around Maksde were destroyed.

But the loss detracted little from the commandos' accomplishment. On the morning of August 9, 1942, advance German troops reached the fringes of Maikop and were amazed to encounter little resistance. By midday the town was in German hands at a cost of few casualties, thanks largely to the extraordinary night's work done by Fölkersam and his men.

By autumn of 1942, however, the German thrust into the Caucasus had stalled. The advance to the oil fields was enfeebled by Hitler's decision to give top priority in men and matériel to support the sieges of Stalingrad and Leningrad. Faced with inadequate supplies of men, armor, artillery, fuel and ammunition, the German offensive in the south ground to a halt. When the effort by the Germans to capture Leningrad and Stalingrad failed, the Wehrmacht armies on the Eastern Front were forced to go on the defensive.

Once the Wehrmacht's advance in Russia stalled, the demand for undercover operations by specially trained commandos in Red Army uniforms ceased. The glory days of the Brandenburgers came to an end. There were some contingency plans that might have kept the outfit occupied: The general directives for the *Lehrregiment Brandenburg* had foreseen a role for commando units during withdrawals as well as attacks. In the event of a withdrawal, the Brandenburgers would stay put, allow themselves to be overtaken by the enemy and then hamper his advance from the rear. But they were never given the opportunity to put these contingency plans into practice.

In October of 1942, the Wehrmacht High Command ordered that the *Lehrregiment Brandenburg* be enlarged to division size and sent to the Eastern Front, where troops were desperately needed. During the crucial defensive battles of that winter, Brandenburgers were increasingly called upon to serve as infantrymen in the front lines, and many were wounded or killed. Although the Brandenburgers had been highly trained for complex, dangerous and daring commando operations, the special skills of these men were wasted in front-line action.

At one time Canaris had reserved the right to decide how to assign the Brandenburg division, but now he was powerless to prevent its gradual dissolution. The questionable per-

American military police guard two captured Germans who had operated behind Allied lines in American uniform during the Battle of the Bulge. The German saboteurs spread so much confusion that, according to Lieut. General Omar N. Bradley, "half a million GIs were playing cat-and-mouse with each other every time they met."

formance of the Abwehr as an intelligence-gathering agency had eroded the Admiral's credibility. The all-powerful members of Hitler's inner circle were growing contemptuous of Canaris, and the Führer himself spoke of the Abwehr chief with sarcasm. Canaris secretly returned the contempt; though he was an ardent German patriot, he had come to the conviction that the Nazis were bringing his country to ruin, and he despised them for it. Indeed, he had made the Abwehr a haven for anti-Nazis, many of whom were conspiring against Hitler.

As Canaris fell from grace, his opponents in the Nazi hierarchy chipped away at his domain. Heinrich Himmler, head of the Schutzstaffel, or SS—the Nazi security police—had always been jealous of Canaris' "private army." Now that the Abwehr chief was out of favor, Himmler poached on his territory. Early in 1943, Himmler formed a separate commando force that was to eclipse the Brandenburgers for the rest of the War.

The new unit was commanded by Otto Skorzeny of the SS. His command rapidly expanded from a company to a battalion and drew many of its recruits from among the disaffected ranks of the *Lehrregiment Brandenburg*. Adrian von Fölkersam was among the first to apply for a transfer to the new unit. "He told me that there was great dissatisfaction in the ranks of the Brandenburgers," Skorzeny recalled. "The division was no longer employed on special service, but used as a stopgap at various points along the front—a role which any other division could have played equally well."

While the Brandenburgers were buried—many of them literally—on the Eastern Front, the reputation of Skorzeny's special force grew apace. In September 1943 the force astonished the world by rescuing Italian dictator Benito Mussolini from a ski lodge in the Apennines, where anti-Fascists were holding him in an attempt to break Hitler's grip on Italy. In July 1944, Skorzeny's men helped maintain order in Berlin after an assassination attempt on Hitler's life. In October, they infiltrated the citadel of Budapest, kidnapped Admiral Nicholas von Horthy, Hungary's regent, and imprisoned him in Bavaria to ensure the installation of a pro-German government in Hungary. And in December, during the Battle of the Bulge, the massive German counterattack against the Allies in Belgium, Skorzeny and his men undertook the sort of operation that the Brandenburgers had pioneered. Dressed in U.S. Army uniforms, English-speaking commandos under Skorzeny infiltrated the Allied lines and caused considerable havoc during the German counteroffensive in the Ardennes.

For nearly a full year the Brandenburg division had been sinking into ignominy. In the early months of 1944, several top officers of the Abwehr, including Canaris, were being investigated by the Gestapo on suspicion of conspiracy. The Brandenburg division, by association, was regarded with a baleful eye. Manfred Roeder, a lawyer and one of the investigators, contemptuously referred to the division as a collection of drones. When Canaris got word of the insult, he was incensed. He insisted that the division's commander, Major General Alexander von Pfuhlstein, take some kind of action against Roeder.

Pfuhlstein at first refused, but when Canaris accused him of lacking the "necessary personal courage," Pfuhlstein and his aide-de-camp barged into Roeder's office at Lvov on January 18, 1944. "I am the commander of the Brandenburg division," Pfuhlstein shouted. "You have gravely insulted my men. I am here in their name. This is my answer!"

With that, the general slapped Roeder across the face with his right hand and stalked out of the room. No duel ensued. Pfuhlstein was sentenced to seven days' confinement to quarters as a result of the incident. In February, Canaris was dismissed as head of the Abwehr and placed under house arrest. He was later tried and executed for plotting against Hitler's regime.

Pfuhlstein's slap was the last blow to be struck in defense of the Brandenburgers. In the autumn of 1944, the outfit was dismantled and re-formed as a panzer grenadier division, its earlier skills and achievements virtually forgotten.

ITALY'S INNOVATIVE ARSENAL

Carrying their rifles lodged in holsters that are affixed to their ankles, Italian special forces line up to board a plane for a practice parachute jump in 1942.

NOVEL IDEAS FOR THE DUCE'S "BOLD ONES"

The Italians proudly called their version of commandos *arditi*—the bold ones—and since the 1930s they had pioneered an arsenal of special equipment on which the *arditi* and other special forces could draw. Dictator Benito Mussolini was so pleased with the results that he frequently showed off this equipment to visiting German generals.

Like the Allies, the Italians had a submachine gun. The Italian weapon, manufactured by the venerable Beretta foundry, was known as a MAB (for Moschetto Automatico Beretta—Beretta automatic rifle). It differed from the Tommy gun and the Sten gun in having two trigger settings—one for automatic firing and one for single shots. The Germans—who were accomplished arms makers themselves—liked the MAB so much that they outfitted some of their troops with it.

The Italians gave particular attention to innovative naval and air operations. They developed two-man torpedoes that Italian frogmen used to wreak havoc on Alexandria harbor in 1941. And they found a practical, if odd-looking, way for paratroopers to tote their rifles. The muzzle fitted into a pocket at the paratrooper's ankle; the rifle butt was secured at the trooper's thigh and attached to a 15-foot cord that was coiled under the paratrooper's arm. After a man jumped and his chute opened, he would slip the rifle from its holster, uncoil the cord and let the rifle dangle below him as he descended. When he hit the ground it was still tethered to him, so he could quickly retrieve it.

At least one Italian innovation won the admiration of some Allied officers, who encountered it when fighting in the desert. It was an assault vehicle called a *camionetta* that had four-wheel drive, six forward and four reverse gears, and a two-position steering wheel that could be remounted in the rear to drive stern-first if a narrow track or an obstacle made turning around difficult.

Double fuel tanks and space for 20 cans made it possible to carry 800 liters of fuel, and to drive 1,000 miles. The *camionetta* could churn with equal ease through the sands of the desert and the snows of the Russian steppes *(page 150)*.

Italian dictator Benito Mussolini leads German officers in an inspection of a paratrooper's equipment at the paratroop training center in Tarquinia.

An airman tests an experimental parachute above the plowed fields of central Italy. The chute's tulip shape increased the rate of descent; when the parachutist came within a few seconds of landing, he could slow his fall by pulling a control rope that converted the canopy to a conventional umbrella-like configuration.

"A PINCH OF ARTISTRY" IN THE AIR

With his parachute attached to his lower back, a trooper plunges earthward in a spread-eagle position that the Italians called the "angel leap." Said one paratrooper proudly: "The British, like the Germans, jumped like automatons. The Italians invested even this unnatural act with inspiration and imagination—and a pinch of artistry."

A parachutist wears a windbreaker smock and the harness for his parachute. Leather pads, gauntlets and a sausage-like helmet visor protected the parachutist's knees, knuckles and nose against the impact of the angel leap, which often caused him to land on all fours.

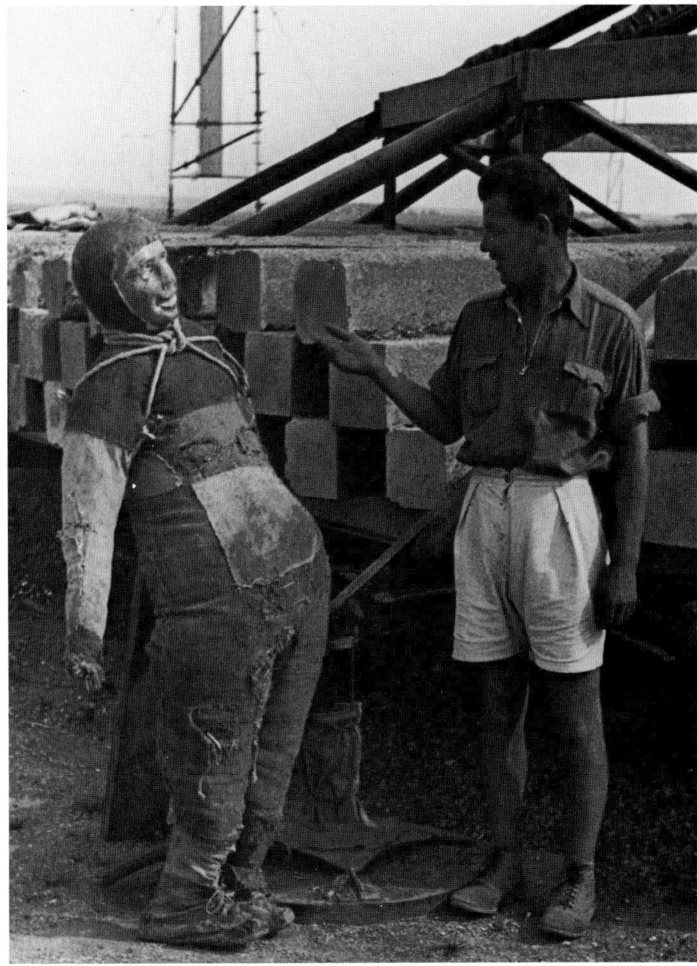

A technician addresses a smiling cloth dummy that Italian parachute troops dubbed "Sigismondo." The stuffed dummy was used instead of a man in the early tests of new parachutes.

Equipped with canvas packs to carry automatic rifles and 40-round magazines on their backs, Italian paratroopers practice firing during a beach landing exercise.

SHIELDS AND CHUTES FOR RAIDS BY SEA

Wearing tight-fitting paratroopers' helmets and vests equipped fore and aft with ammunition pouches, Italian Naval commandos stand ready for review. Once the ammunition pouches on his chest were emptied, the trooper turned his vest around.

In an amphibious exercise, Italian special forces crouch behind body shields braced on the gunwales of their assault boat (above). At right, carrying their shields, which were grooved to hold rifles, the men charge inland.

Learning to parachute into the sea, the trainee at left makes a leap from a tower into a water tank. Below, an advanced chutist drops toward the water near a rescue boat.

Three frogmen in flippers and wet suits crawl ashore with a floating equipment pack as two comrades swim toward the beach with a second pack to join them.

A COMBAT TRUCK FOR ALL SEASONS

Bundled against the cold, Italian special forces in Russia (above) crowd aboard the versatile assault vehicle known as a camionetta. At right, two camionette carry a patrol across the North African desert. The outsized tires provided better traction and clearance and an easier ride; the racks on the sides carried spare fuel, and the perforated iron plates above the rear wheels could be detached to provide traction in snow or sand.

5

Noisy decoys to mislead the Germans on D-Day
Survival training at an English manor
High-risk night drops into France
Withdrawing from a blazing Breton forest
An ambush saves an ancient viaduct
Riding into battle in "mechanized mess tins"
Major Farran's cross-country run
Drilling the maquis in the guerrilla arts
Supply line in the sky
Exuberant welcomes that triggered reprisals
German gunners caught looking the wrong way

PHANTOMS IN ARMS

At 11 minutes past midnight on June 6, 1944, Lieutenant Noel Poole, a former bank clerk from Somerset, England, jumped through the hatch of a Stirling bomber circling over the Cherbourg peninsula. He misjudged the jump, smashed against the plane's tail assembly and floated half-conscious down through the drifting clouds, landing with a thump in a meadow near the village of Isigny. He was the first Allied officer to reach France on D-Day.

Poole was a commando of the 1st Special Air Service. Only minutes after he jumped, scores of other commandos tumbled into the night sky and floated silently toward the dark fields of Normandy. Still others were parachuting into the Côtes-du-Nord and Morbihan areas of Brittany.

They came equipped for various tasks. Within minutes of landing, Poole and his comrades were firing off flares and playing highly amplified recordings of gunfire and men's voices to simulate the sounds of an airborne invasion, hoping to draw the attention of the jittery Germans away from the real invasion on the Normandy beaches. Commandos in the Côtes-du-Nord and the Morbihan were stealing quietly to rendezvous with French Resistance forces, who would join them in a campaign to sever all communications between Brittany and the rest of German-occupied France.

These men were only the first of hundreds of Allied commandos to land in occupied France. They were followed, in the gray dawn of D-Day, by the British Army's 1st and 4th Commando Brigades, both of which stormed ashore in the vanguard of the invasion. The mission of the 1st Brigade was to seize two bridges at Benouville and Ranville so that when the main Allied assault forces arrived, the Germans would have neither an exit for escape nor an entry for reinforcements. The mission of the 4th Brigade was to seize a radar station at Douvres, thus denying the Germans a vital source of intelligence.

Between the men who landed at midnight and those who landed at dawn there were some notable differences. The first contingent were special forces trained to operate in small squads and wage guerrilla war behind enemy lines in coordination with the Resistance and the Allied high command. The second were battle-tested assault troops operating at brigade strength to spearhead the Allied offensive. The mission of the guerrilla fighters would essentially be completed in three months; the mission of the assault troops would continue until the last shot had been fired in Europe.

The Allied high command highly valued both kinds of commando operations and credited both with hastening the collapse of the German armies and saving the lives of tens of thousands of men.

The commandos recruited for guerrilla action were an oddly mixed bunch. Some were special forces under the aegis of the U.S. Office of Strategic Services and the British Special Operations Executive—two nonmilitary government bureaus that disseminated agents throughout German-occupied Europe to aid the resistance movement. Others were veterans of the Special Air Service, a British Army unit that was air-dropped behind enemy lines to sabotage communications and supplies. And their numbers also included hastily trained Frenchmen chafing to liberate their country.

Operating sometimes in uniform and sometimes in civilian clothes, this motley collection of fighting men ranged for weeks through territory supposedly held by the forces of the Third Reich, spreading confusion and destruction wherever they went. They called in airdrops of men, supplies and food, they trained and armed the Resistance, and they disrupted enemy movements by road and rail. Their presence alone boosted the morale of the French people and enmeshed the Germans in a web of uncertainty and fear. Their combat effectiveness was attested by increasingly shrill directives from the German High Command exhorting its harried troops to eradicate "terrorism."

The formation and training of these various units went hand in hand with the detailed planning for D-Day during the early months of 1944. At first the planners thought it better to use all commando forces independently and not to employ underground forces at all. Reports from France indicated that the Resistance was deeply divided between the Gaullists—followers of General Charles de Gaulle, self-appointed leader of the Free French Forces, who was fighting in exile to free his countrymen from German rule—and the French Communists, who looked to the Soviet Union for inspiration and leadership. The rank and file seemed as likely to fight among themselves as against the Germans. Could a movement so divided be trusted and effectively controlled? Prime Minister Churchill, among others, had grave doubts, but he also strongly believed that the French must be given a part in their own liberation.

Churchill's decision to include them had far-reaching consequences, for it meant that commando forces would now play an unaccustomed role. Although they would continue to attack the enemy in independent hit-and-run operations, they would also have the responsibility of training and advising the French Resistance forces popularly known as maquis. (The literal translation of *maquis* is "brush," and the term was applied to Resistance fighters because they used forest and brushland as cover.)

Among the most important of the forces assigned to work with the maquis were the so-called Jedburgh teams, who took their name from the town in Scotland where they trained for their special missions. Each team comprised an English or American officer, a radio operator, and a second officer from the country in which the team would be functioning. A Jed, as a member of the team was known for short, was supposed to be not only a military leader but also a counselor, doctor, woodsman and gunsmith, and an expert in the handling of explosives. Except in emergencies, Jeds were to wear the uniform of their country of origin, both to augment their authority and to give the maquis a sense of being in touch with regular Allied military forces.

Jedburgh recruits came from all quarters in response to an appeal for volunteers for hazardous duty. Nearly 100 French-speaking OSS officers stepped forward, among them 24-year-old Major William Colby—a future director of the U.S. Central Intelligence Agency. They were joined by British officers and noncoms from many different regiments, as well as the cream of the Free French Forces and a number of Belgians, Norwegians and Dutchmen.

By January of 1944, three hundred Jeds had been assembled for specialized training at Milton Hall, an Elizabethan manor and park near Peterborough in northeast England. At Jedburgh they had undergone the traditional Commando training: how to slosh through bogs and ford rivers, make forced marches lugging heavy packs, find their way at night by nothing but the stars, move and kill silently, fight unarmed and master the art of living off the land. Now some refinements were added. When they left Milton Hall, the men were proficient in Morse code. They could operate and assemble scores of small arms and field weapons of British, American, German, French and Italian manufacture. They were able to parachute into unfamiliar terrain in pitch-blackness, and they knew how to derail a train or blow up a bridge with the smallest possible charge. Graduates of the program, recalled William Colby, were honed "to the sharpest edge humanly possible."

Just as important as the Jeds and equally well trained were the Special Air Service Brigade units. The success of the SAS in North Africa, the Aegean and Italy, where they throttled Axis movements and choked off Axis supplies by blowing up airfields and sinking tons of shipping, had been so impressive that the Allied high command deployed 2,500 SAS men in Normandy.

SAS men were the most mobile of all the commando groups. They used the cavalry-raid techniques they had perfected in the desert to disrupt transport and communications far behind the enemy lines. More exposed than the other groups, they also suffered heavier casualties: Roughly half of the men serving in the SAS were killed or wounded.

Of the other agencies that prepared uniformed units to parachute into France, Britain's Special Operations Executive recruited and trained groups of soldiers in exile—Belgians, French, Poles and others who had escaped when their countries were occupied by the Germans. The groups were known as Inter-Allied Missions, each consisting of from two to 25 men led by experienced SOE officers, and were among the first units to be dropped into France. They arrived as early as January 1944 and established crucial contacts with maquis leaders in the Rhone Valley.

There were also so-called Operations Groups that the American OSS had formed to "train, supply and lead guerrilla forces in enemy territory." The OSS units learned their trade on the wooded grounds of plush Congressional Country Club outside Washington, D.C. In the spring of 1944, four of these groups, each with a complement of 34 men, were ordered to England to prepare for missions in occupied France. All were capable of either scouting functions or hit-and-run raids, and all were under the command of Lieut. Colonel Serge Obolensky, a Russian prince who had once served in the Saint Petersburg Imperial Guards and who had emigrated to the United States after the Revolution. He had become a darling of New York society, and in London he spent most of the evenings before his departure for France at dinner parties and dances.

Obolensky was not the only one who celebrated. There was, William Colby recalled, an almost festive air among the hand-picked men waiting to parachute into France. In part this was a defense mechanism: "None of us dwelt on

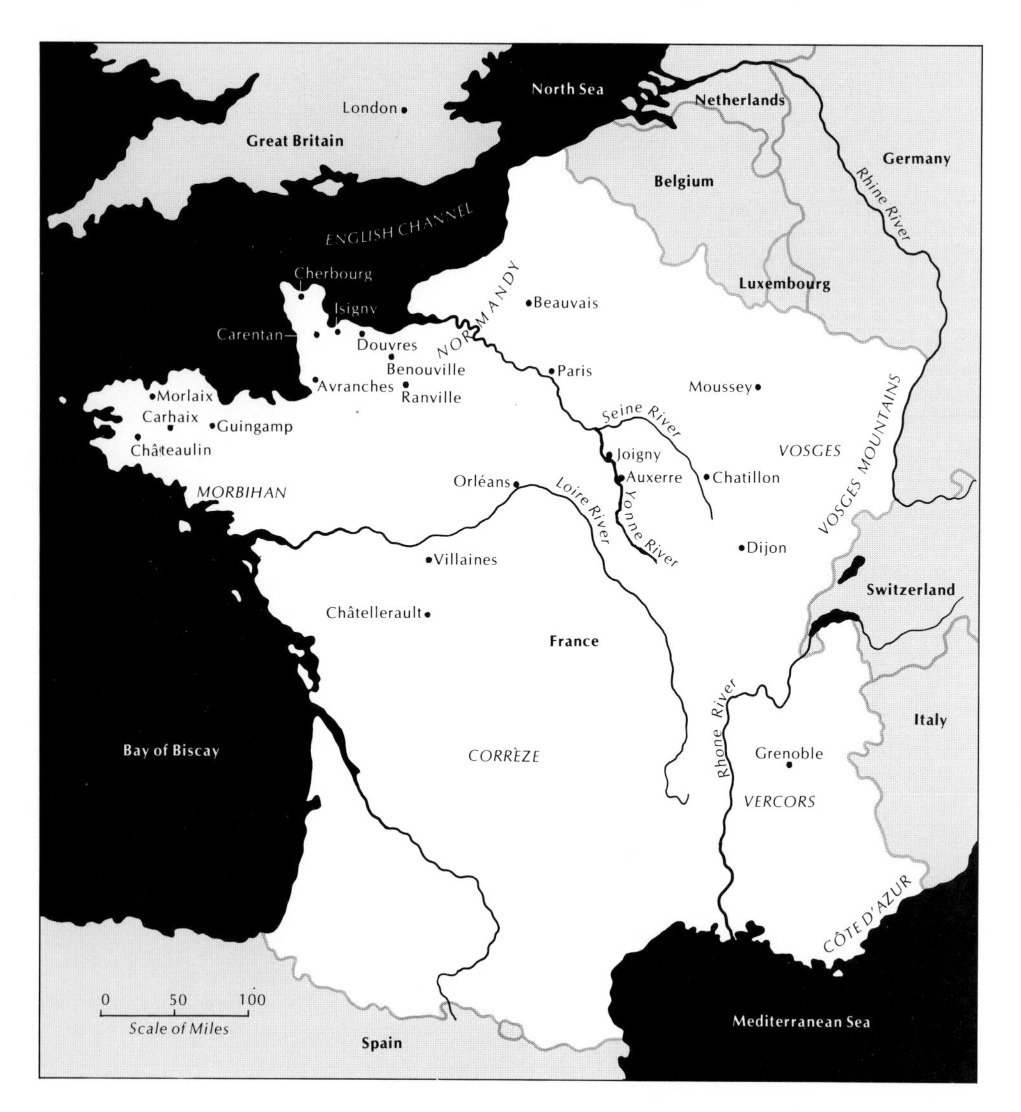

Commandos played a vital role between June and September of 1944 in the liberation of France. They spearheaded the Normandy invasion, staged diversionary attacks in the Cherbourg peninsula and led the maquis in raids near Guingamp and Morlaix, behind the lines of the retreating Germans.

On D-Day, commandos cling to the slippery decks of small assault craft ferrying them across the English Channel in the vanguard of the Allied invasion forces.

the dangers of what we were preparing to do," he said. But the attitude also reflected confidence in their training and in their ability to cope with the unexpected. For most of the special forces, under whatever command, this flexibility would spell the difference between success and failure—indeed, between destruction and survival.

Most members of the teams did not know until just before they took off when or where they would be dropped. Day after day, recalled SAS Captain Derrick Harrison, they would go to the airfield and try to glean what information they could from parachute instructors, pilots and airport personnel. "Are we flying tonight, Frank?" "What's the weather going to be, Leo?"

The official word of a mission came first to the team captain, who was given large-scale maps of the drop area. If it was to be a blind drop, with no one on the ground to receive the parachutists and guide them to a forest hideout, the team captain studied the maps for indications of cover in which to establish a base. When he thought he had found what he needed, reconnaissance planes flew over the area and returned with aerial photographs, which the team captain examined with a stereoscope.

An experienced special-service officer like Derrick Harrison could get to know a terrain in remarkable detail simply by poring over photographs. Preparing for his own drop into a forested section of central France near Auxerre, some 300 miles behind German lines, Harrison spotted a likely base area and began puzzling out from the photographs how to get there. "A rough bearing of 200 degrees from our rendezvous should bring us to a large rectangular clearing in the wood. Given a clear night, we could do that stage of the trek by the stars. Four miles on was a valley that would cut across our route at right angles. The woods ended halfway down the slope. The only cover was afforded by a strip of hedge that ran down into a sprawling village. What to do? Run the gantlet down the moonlit slope, or follow the hedgerow and risk blundering into the village? I decided to wait until we faced the situation on the ground."

Commandos parachuting into France frequently landed outside the drop zone—and had to blunder around in strange terrain at night, always in danger of running into German patrols. One trooper who was dropped off target near Rambouillet had hardly touched ground when he heard a man coming toward him in the dark, speaking German. He shot the man, fled into the night, and was lucky to eventually make contact with Resistance forces.

On the first of several drops he made into Europe, Major Colby had the equally unnerving experience of looking down through the night for the secluded pasture where he was supposed to drop and finding to his horror that he was descending instead on a city rooftop. His pilot, it turned out, had mistaken a burning train for a line of signal fires. Colby managed to swing his legs up, clear the roof and its chimney

pots, and land with a crash in a backyard. He was followed a moment later by the other two members of his Jedburgh team. Fortunately, the citizens who flung open their shutters to investigate were sympathetic; they warned the Jedburghs that a German garrison stood just a few hundred yards up the street. The three stole out of town by back alleys and made their way across wooded farmlands to a rendezvous with members of a maquis network in the Yonne region.

Men who descended close to the front lines often had worse luck than Colby and his companions. The early-morning D-Day drops were particularly hazardous. One SAS team of four enlisted men and two officers dropped just south of Carentan on the Cherbourg peninsula 40 minutes after midnight on June 6. They landed some two kilometers off target, and the officers and most of the equipment got lost. The team's mission was to deceive the Germans into thinking that a full-scale airborne landing had taken place; the four enlisted men did the best they could by igniting 20 small bombs they still had with them and firing their carbines in the air. Then they fled north. Eventually they found their two wandering officers, but all six were captured in a fire fight with a German patrol.

Farther south, in Brittany, SAS Corporal Émile Bouétard, a 28-year-old Breton sailor who had escaped from occupied France, was involved in another bad drop; he ran into a German patrol and was shot dead, the first Frenchman to be killed in the battle to liberate his homeland.

For all that, most of the 150 SAS men who parachuted into Brittany in the first minutes of D-Day landed safely and soon began operations against the Germans. Allied commanders put a high priority on operations in the Breton peninsula, for eight German divisions were stationed there, presenting a considerable threat to the success of the Normandy landings. It was the job of the SAS and the Breton maquis to seal off the peninsula and delay the movement of reinforcements to the beachhead by blowing up railway lines, ambushing convoys and cutting communications.

In charge of the Brittany operations was Commandant Pierre Bourgoin, the one-armed leader of the 4th SAS. Under him were six Jedburgh teams, and 18 SAS demolition teams that specialized in railway sabotage. Bourgoin's orders were to establish bases where he could assemble the maquis and launch harassing raids against the Germans. Then, when Lieut. General George S. Patton's Third Army was ready to break out of the beachhead and wheel into Brittany, Bourgoin was to unleash the maquis in a general uprising against the Germans. His signal to spring into action would be a nonsense phrase radioed from London: *LE CHAPEAU DE NAPOLÉON EST-IL TOUJOURS À PERROS-GUIREC?* (IS NAPOLEON'S HAT STILL AT PERROS-GUIREC?)

Soon after they landed in the early hours of D-Day, Bourgoin and his lieutenants made contact with local maquis leaders. Several thousand unkempt volunteers had already gathered in the Duault forest, near the old walled city of Guingamp, where German troops were quartered. There the SAS set up a redoubt code-named Samwest. Farther south, in the Morbihan, SAS troopers found the maquis sheltering in huts at a woodland farm near the village of Saint-Marcel. This became the nucleus of a second SAS redoubt, code-named Dingson.

The SAS men quickly learned that working with the maquis would not be the kind of strictly disciplined operation they were accustomed to. Word that the SAS had arrived soon spread the length of Brittany, and within hours hundreds of men and boys were milling about the Samwest and Dingson camps, creating a carnival aura that shocked and worried the SAS officers. Captain Jules Leblond arrived at Samwest to find "a continual procession of visitors—well-wishers and sightseers—around the base," and almost no attempt at security. At Dingson, Bourgoin likened the atmosphere to that of a village fair; lights were everywhere, people were shouting and laughing, and local peasant women paraded in national costumes donned for the occasion.

The Germans easily infiltrated both bases, and at Samwest a woman and man suspected of being enemy agents were "shot and daggered respectively," according to the official SAS report. But the German command was at first too busy redeploying troops after the Normandy landings to worry about moving against a ragtag guerrilla force. Then on June 11, two German officers stopped at a farm on the outskirts of the Duault forest to ask directions to Carhaix. They were met with a burst of machine-gun fire from maquis in the farmhouse. The Germans tossed a grenade and fled, one of them badly wounded.

The next morning, German troops burned down the farm,

which had supplied the Samwest base its water. Though he had not yet received London's message to start full-scale operations, Captain Leblond decided to send 30 SAS troopers to rescue the farm workers from execution for harboring the maquis. "I thought it would have a disastrous effect on morale if we let a farm be burned within a kilometer of the base without raising a hand," he later reported to London.

It was a debatable decision. The SAS troopers swooped down on the farm and in a brief but bloody fire fight killed 10 German soldiers while losing two men of their own. The raid saved the farm workers but so alarmed the Germans that they brought in 13 truckloads of infantry to mount an attack on the Samwest base. In the face of this heavy force, Leblond ordered the maquis to disperse in the forest. Before they left they destroyed their precious supply depot of arms and ammunition, which had been painstakingly built up from airdrops.

Captain Leblond and a small body of men made for the Dingson base, marching at night and hiding by day. They arrived to find the camp extraordinarily well organized and growing fast. New recruits had walked great distances to get there, recalled Lieutenant Nicholas Marienne, hobbling in with "feet swollen and bleeding through their worn shoes. But they don't care; all they want is arms."

All told, Dingson covered 1,200 acres, on which 3,500 men were gathered. The camp boasted a field kitchen, a vehicle workshop, a shoe-repair shop and a hospital, as well as a tailor and a dentist. Inevitably, the traffic into Dingson was noticed by the Germans; they offered a reward for the capture of Commandant Bourgoin and set about arresting all the one-armed men they could find—including an infuriated 75-year-old pensioner. (They never caught Bourgoin.)

At first light on the morning of June 18, Dingson sentries heard a rattle of rifle and machine-gun fire to the west of the camp. A German patrol had run into a maquis outpost. Two hours later, on the other side of the camp, Germans in brigade strength tried to storm a château held by an SAS detachment but were beaten back by machine-gun fire. By 9 a.m. a German brigade was moving up the main road to Dingson, and armored cars were advancing from nearby villages. Bourgoin radioed for air support. Through the long, hot day the camp fought off constant German infantry attacks. But the maquis had to abandon one position after another as the Germans sprayed the forest with tracer bullets, setting fire to the trees. At 4 p.m., 40 American P-47 Thunderbolts streaked overhead and plastered the German positions with gunfire and bombs.

The attack lifted maquis morale but failed to halt the Germans. Bourgoin ordered his forces to scatter as soon as night fell. In the dark, they filtered out between the burning trees by twos and threes. Their losses were moderate—about 200 maquis and 50 SAS troopers—but again they had lost tons of supplies, enough to equip 5,000 men.

In the aftermath of the capture of Samwest and Dingson, London sent a team of agents to find out what had gone wrong. Their conclusion was that the maquis and special forces should above all avoid massing in numbers, which made them easy prey to the superior German firepower. Yet there was evidence that the commando presence was already making itself felt. In addition to tying up German forces that were badly needed elsewhere, guerrilla activity in conjunction with bombing had slowed German troop movements to a crawl.

In one classic case, guerrillas under Jedburgh leadership

In liberated Paris, Commandant Pierre Bourgoin marches down the Champs Élysées on Armistice Day, 1944, at the head of the Special Air Service unit that helped him to organize the French Resistance in Brittany.

so harassed the 2nd SS Panzer Division that its arrival at the Normandy front was delayed by two weeks. A crucial attack occurred in the Corrèze, in south central France, where a Jed team blew a small bridge on the main road, then opened fire on the halted panzer column. The ambush cost 20 French lives, but it delayed the Germans for six hours.

The destruction of the two Breton redoubts by no means incapacitated the commandos there. Having dispersed to isolated farms and forests, they began guerrilla warfare in earnest. Small bands roamed the Breton peninsula, striking according to the maquis dictum of *surprise, mitraillage, évanouissement*—surprise, machine-gunning, disappearance. Testimony to their effectiveness can be found in the July intelligence reports of the German Army Group West. One report noted that "experienced leaders" were being parachuted into France by the Allies in increasing numbers and that their presence was already apparent in the "better planning" of operations and in the "disciplined performance" of the men carrying them out.

By the end of July, some 400 commandos were operating under Bourgoin's direction, along with about 8,000 armed maquis and untold thousands who were only partially armed. On July 31, advance elements of Patton's Third Army broke through at Avranches. With American tanks rolling virtually unopposed into Brittany, the commandos were ordered to keep open the two main highways running along the peninsula and to prevent retreating German sappers from blowing the bridges. On August 2, some 100 French commandos from the 3rd SAS were dropped near Morlaix to seize the great stone viaduct spanning the gorge at the town's edge. They attacked immediately and after a brief fire fight took the viaduct.

At dawn the next morning about 1,000 men from the German 2nd Parachute Division moved toward Morlaix with orders to recapture and destroy the viaduct, blocking the American advance on Brest. Shortly before 10 a.m., as the column was leaving the little town of Châteaulin, it ran into an ambush organized by Jed officer Bernard Knox.

Knox had 2,000 maquis hidden in the bushes on both sides of the road. Before dawn he and his men had scattered hundreds of "tire busters"—mines disguised as cow dung—across the road. Knox held his men in check as the Germans came trudging up the road behind their slow-moving trucks and guns. When the lead vehicle struck the first mine and burst into flames, the maquis attacked with bazookas, light machine guns and grenades. Within minutes, 30 Germans lay dead and 20 had been wounded. Those who fled into the fields were pursued by maquis killing squads, on forays they referred to as "Boche hunts." The shattered German column was forced to abandon its mis-

sion, and the viaduct remained in the hands of the SAS and the maquis. American armor rolled on to Brest.

By mid-August the battle was moving beyond Brittany, and the four German divisions remaining there were either surrounded or too badly battered to be effective. The commandos and the maquis not only had kept the roads open and the bridges intact but had mopped up pockets of German resistance that might have diverted large segments of Patton's army. Brigadier Roderick McLeod, commander of the SAS Brigade, noted that his men had suffered 40 per cent casualties but considered themselves, with some justification, Brittany's liberators. General Eisenhower went out of his way to acknowledge the "great assistance" given by the guerrilla forces. He ordered that the maquis be allowed to mark their vehicles with the Allied white star.

Patton by now was moving eastward so rapidly that his right flank was wide open. Commandos were assigned to protect that flank by setting up posts along it, blowing the Loire bridges and harassing the Germans in wide-ranging attacks.

The commandos involved in these missions relied heavily on the armored jeep, which gave them an elusive mobility that frustrated the Germans. Although one tankman referred to the jeeps as "mechanized mess tins," they were formidable vehicles when fully equipped for battle. They had twin Vickers K machine guns fore and aft, and a single Vickers mounted beside the driver so that he could fire one-handed as he drove. A Bren gun was carried loose in the back, and grenades were stowed all over the vehicle. Four men rode in the jeep, and each carried his own carbine, together with a haversack full of survival supplies and ammunition in case he had to flee the vehicle on foot. With auxiliary gas tanks, the jeeps had a range of 900 miles.

The jeep commandos were constantly amazed at how freely they could operate behind German lines. Often they were under greater threat from trigger-happy maquis—who regarded all transport as German—than from the Germans. To protect against maquis attack, the commandos took to flying silk Union Jacks and sounding a "dot dash dot" on the horn—the Morse code *R,* for Resistance—when approaching a sharp curve in the road or an area that offered easy cover for ambush. If they found a German convoy approaching, standard procedure was to make a 90-degree turn and tear away across country at breakneck speed.

The SAS men found that in areas where the roads were thick with enemy convoys, the best protection often was to act like Germans—a ruse employed successfully by Major Ian Fenwick, a well-known *Punch* magazine cartoonist who commanded an SAS group of about 60 men operating in the gap between the Seine and the Loire, some 50 miles south of Paris. If the Germans were driving at night with their lights ablaze, Fenwick and his men turned on their lights as well; if the Germans masked their lights, so did the SAS. For several weeks they rampaged around the country, shooting up trucks and trains with amazing impunity.

In one scrape after another, the men of the SAS seemed to survive on sheer luck. Captain Jock Riding and some companions were bowling along a road one night in their jeep when they ran almost head on into a column of German tank transporters. Riding turned out his lights; then, spotting a narrow track leading through the fields to the right, he wrenched the wheel. But he turned too quickly and overturned the jeep. Riding and his men struggled desperately in the dark to right the jeep as first one and then another of 80 German trucks slowly rumbled past. To their astonished relief, not a single truck stopped.

A favorite tactic of the jeep units was to attach themselves unobtrusively to the rear of a German column. At a signal, they would race the length of the column, firing on everything in sight. An equally popular technique was to ambush the last vehicle in a convoy, make their escape, and race along secondary roads to catch the convoy and again pick off its last vehicle.

Some Allied officers derided the jeep commandos as mere cowboys who were engaged more in games than in warfare. But the terror they spread behind the German lines was real and the perils of their tactics all too evident. Of the

Teams of Jedburghs—trained for the special mission of harassing German panzer divisions driving north to defend Normandy—receive a bold daylight drop of supplies near Corrèze, France, in July 1944.

Escorted by commandos, a French farmer and his horse cart trundle air-dropped supplies to cover. Most airdrops were made at night, with no more than the moon and a few signal flares to guide the pilots.

80 or so jeeps landed successfully in France by parachute or glider during the early weeks of the invasion, more than a third were destroyed. The Germans learned to insert in their columns trucks with sides that dropped to reveal 20mm cannon, which could knock out a jeep with one burst. Major Fenwick, while riding in a jeep, was hit in the head and killed instantly by a cannon shell. Of the four men with him, two were shot, one was captured and only one escaped.

As commando strikes mounted, the Germans reacted with increasing savagery. A commando officer who was wounded and taken prisoner was later clubbed to death with rifle butts by the Germans as a lesson to villagers.

Yet the commandos continued to take outlandish risks. SAS troop commander Derrick Harrison, operating in the valley of the Yonne, launched an attack on more than 200 SS troops with just four men and two jeeps. They were on their way to a maquis workshop to get a gun mounting rewelded when they heard the crackle of machine-gun fire coming from the village of Les Ormes. An elderly French woman, tears streaking her face, was pedaling a bicycle toward them. She told Harrison that between 200 and 300 German soldiers were setting fire to the village and executing hostages. The SAS troopers decided on a lightning raid, relying on speed, surprise and firepower.

"Union Jacks fluttering in the wind," recalled Harrison, "we tore down the road, round the bend and into the village. I took in the scene in an instant. The church in the middle of the square . . . a large truck . . . two German staff cars . . . the crowd of SS men in front of the church."

The commandos raked the square with machine-gun fire, setting the vehicles afire and cutting down many of the SS men as they sprinted for cover. Thirty yards beyond the church, Harrison's jeep swerved to a halt; his driver was slumped dead over the wheel. Finding the engine knocked out and the Vickers guns jammed, Harrison leaped out with his carbine and kept up a running fire as he made for the second jeep, which had stopped at the edge of the square. Although wounded, he reached the vehicle. Once he was aboard, the jeep roared out of town. In the confusion, 18 French civilians due to be executed for collaboration with Allied "terrorists" escaped into the forests and fields.

Almost as dramatic was the saga of Major Roy Farran, who led 20 jeeps on a marauding expedition that took them across virtually the whole of France. Their harrowing trip began on August 19 at Rennes, in Brittany, where Farran and 60 men of the 2nd SAS landed with orders to penetrate the German lines and make their way cross country to an SAS base 300 miles away in the Forest of Chatillon, north of Dijon. "Within 24 hours of landing," Farran later reported, "the column of jeeps was winding through the forest paths north of Orléans, winkling its way round pockets of Germans to the open country in the enemy rear. So long as we kept to the tangle of country lanes we were fairly safe, for the Germans kept mostly to the metalled highways."

On the first day, the column covered 50 miles without encountering the enemy. For the second leg, Farran decided to split his command into three groups and move them along the same route at 30-minute intervals. At the village of Mailly-le-Chateau, the lead group ran into a storm of machine-gun fire from German positions on the east side of the Yonne River and lost a jeep as they charged through.

On the third day, the lead group lost two more jeeps when it collided with elements of a German corps in the village of Villaines. Worse, there was no time to warn the second group of jeeps, commanded by Farran, who drove around a curve to find the road blocked by a German 75mm gun. Farran's jeep was wrecked, and a number of his men were cut down before the group managed to fight its way clear and flee across country. They were unable to cut back to warn the third group, which in turn stumbled into the ambush and suffered heavy losses.

On the last leg of their journey, Farran's men were fortunate enough to spot a slow-moving German supply train, which they shot up at 15 yards' range and set on fire. Otherwise, the trip had been a disaster. When the column finally limped into the Forest of Chatillon, it had been reduced to seven jeeps and had lost nearly half its men. Yet the survivors had barely settled into their new base before Farran was outlining plans for another attack. He had learned that a German force garrisoned in the Château of Chatillon had dwindled to 150 men, and he decided to attack the château and, if possible, take the Germans prisoner.

The combined strength of the SAS detachment already at the camp and of Farran's detachment was 10 jeeps and 60 men. Farran deployed jeeps at the principal entrances to the town, cut the military telephone wires and began bombarding the château with a three-inch mortar. A quarter of an hour after the action began, a column of 30 German vehicles making its way toward the château was ambushed at a river bridge on the Montbard-Dijon road. Almost before the Germans realized what was happening, SAS machine guns destroyed the first five trucks, two of which were loaded with ammunition. As infantrymen tumbled out of the trucks, Farran and his men laid down a savage fire with machine guns and Bren guns.

The battle went on for three hours, until the Germans' superior numbers gradually began to turn the tide. After the Germans fought their way out of the château and into the center of town, Farran fired two flares to signal withdrawal. But disengaging proved more difficult than expected, and several troopers were lost in the process. Farran and two or three SAS comrades made it only by crawling on their stomachs along the furrows of a plowed field as the Germans raked the field with machine-gun fire.

The following day, fearing a retaliatory attack from the reinforced garrison, the commandos abandoned their camp in the forest and drove farther east to another SAS base in the Vosges. By the time they arrived they had completed the longest jeep journey behind enemy lines by any commando group in the War. They also had the satisfaction of knowing that although their attack had failed to overwhelm the German garrison at Chatillon, it had taken a heavy toll in German lives and matériel.

During the intervals between such daring operations, the commandos spent many hours advising the maquis and instructing them in the use of weapons. "All that long, hot day, I worked with Jacques and his men under the scrubby trees," recalled SAS officer George Millar of a day he spent with maquis near the village of Chaignay, 10 miles north of Dijon. "We sat around in a friendly circle, taking the thick packing grease off Stens, revolvers, automatics, grenades, mines, ammunition, torches, bazookas, rifles, Brens."

Like most of the commandos, Millar had to rely heavily on visual demonstration, since he did not know the French words for such terms as "safety catch," "used cartridge case" and "firing pin." He showed how the weapons worked by repeatedly stripping them down, and he had the maquis practice over and over again such techniques as the forward-crouching stance favored by many commandos to help them fire low. To teach the handling of explosives, Millar demonstrated their assembly step by step—heating the plastic explosive material in boiling water until it was soft and malleable, forming it into perfect 1½-pound cubes, taping the charges together, and fitting them with primers and detonating cord. When the maquis had mastered these arts, he led them on sapping expeditions so they could see how to lay the charges on railway tracks and bridges and how to mask them with khaki adhesive tape.

The maquis, Millar found, were in some need of many sorts of military tutelage. When firing machine guns, for example, their initial tendency was to keep a finger on the trigger until the magazine was empty, instead of firing the gun in bursts. Most of the men Millar worked with at the outset were urban factory workers who had fled when the Germans tried to recruit them as forced labor. Unlike the peasants who would join the Resistance later, they knew almost nothing about the art of living off the land.

Nor were they adept at disguising their presence. When he was led into his first maquis camp, Millar was appalled to find all the access paths worn smooth and the tracks of nailed boots everywhere. He could hear the babble of voices and see and smell cigarette smoke long before he

Special Air Service Captain Derrick Harrison (far left) pauses with his jeep patrol before raiding a German-occupied village 80 miles behind the front lines. An hour after this photograph was taken, his driver was killed. "Had I not stood up to fire," Harrison said, "I would've taken the shots that killed him."

reached the camp. And when he got there, he found that the maquis posted no sentries and maintained no regular listening watch on their midget radios for action messages from London. Their makeshift quarters leaked rain, he noted, and no one had taught them how to build an outdoor latrine.

Within days of their arrival, the commandos usually were able to establish at least minimum security and teach the maquis the rudiments of living in the woods. It was more difficult to restrain the guerrilla fighters' impatience to strike major blows at the enemy. George Millar recalled how one Resistance chief liked to muse about big battles that would drive the Germans out of the country; Millar himself "preferred to turn my attention to derailing the 5:20."

Occasionally, commando warnings against massing in large numbers were ignored, with tragic results. At Vercors, the great plateau and natural fortress southwest of Grenoble where 3,500 maquisards proclaimed a "free republic" in the summer of 1944, advisers from both an Inter-Allied Mission and an OSS Operations Group urged the maquis to disperse and thus avoid a pitched battle with the encircling Germans. The maquis disregarded the advice and were eventually overwhelmed in a murderous battle that cost the lives of 750 Frenchmen.

The maquis and commandos alike depended for their existence on regular airdrops of men and supplies from England. As their operations reached a climax in late summer, airdrops increased almost to a flood. On a single, unexceptional night in August, for example, 42 aircraft took off from Britain with supplies and reinforcements for the commandos. They dropped 150 troops, four jeeps and 700 containers in 22 different landing zones. That same night, 11 gliders with 45 commandos and 11 jeeps landed behind German positions in Brittany.

Commandos responsible for receiving the deliveries often worked around the clock, their days given to raiding and their nights to collecting the dropped supplies. Captain Derrick Harrison was surprised to realize one night as he gathered up canisters of fuel after a drop that he had not slept in four days: "There had been more than enough to keep the days filled," he wrote, "and there had been a drop every night." He was running on pure adrenaline.

Yet for all their frequency, the *parachutages,* as the maquis called them, were highly risky affairs for both the men making the drops and those waiting for them. The bonfires that guided the planes in could just as easily attract German patrols. For security's sake, the drops were rarely scheduled before midnight; usually they took place at 1 or 2 a.m.—which meant that the maquis had only a few hours of darkness in which to gather the supplies and hide them away.

Four strong men were needed to lift the standard containers used in the drops; when these missed the drop zone, as they often did, it was extremely difficult to locate them in the pitch-black forests and carry them out through the undergrowth before dawn. Yet the guerrilla fighters had to try, for a container or a parachute left behind was enough to touch off a thorough German sweep. A sweep usually began with German soldiers forming a circle four kilometers across and then gradually closing in, making escape by road impossible. When the circle got small enough, the Germans set fire to the woods with flamethrowers to flush the quarry and bring the fight to a conclusion.

Statistics showed that more than half the commandos' casualties were suffered either in the initial parachute drop or during the first few minutes on the ground. Because jumps were made at low altitudes it was essential that the static line, which was attached to the airplane and pulled the parachute from its envelope, function perfectly. Reception committees came to dread the loud thud that signaled either a body or a piece of cargo hitting the ground unchecked. Roy Farran remembered as one of his saddest experiences in France hearing such a sound one night and wandering into the reception zone calling the name of the paratrooper he knew was to be dropped. He found the man's body in the morning lying under a tree "as if he were asleep on his arms." His static line had broken.

There was also the ever-present danger that informers in the maquis camps might tip off the Germans to the nonsense phrases that were used as radio signals for a drop: ROMEO HAS BETRAYED JULIET, for example, or MY WALLET IS FULL. Thus alerted, the Germans would bomb and strafe the drop zone, hoping to wipe out the guerrillas waiting below.

On a few occasions, German intelligence learned from informers the night's recognition signal—an agreed-upon letter that reception committees signaled by flashlight in Morse code to low-flying aircraft. Supplied with these code letters, the Germans could lure Allied planes into dropping men and cargo into carefully prepared traps. This occurred in the case of 12 SAS commandos who were dropped near the town of La Ferté Alais, just outside Paris, in July 1944. Nine were seized on landing by the waiting Germans; the others managed to get away.

The captured men were taken to Paris for interrogation by the Gestapo. When the interrogation yielded no information, the Germans dressed the nine in civilian clothes, piled them into a truck and drove them off toward the Allied lines, supposedly to be exchanged for German agents. This seemed too good to be true and—sure enough—when the truck stopped at a wood near Beauvais and an SAS corporal named Vaculik asked one of the Germans in the escort if the commandos were to be shot, he was told that they were.

Vaculik and his companions were lined up in front of two Gestapo officers with submachine pistols, while another agent read their death sentence. Knowing what would happen next, the prisoners broke for the woods when the Gestapo agent stopped reading. Corporal Vaculik got away; another corporal, named Jones, tripped but escaped after the Gestapo men, assuming he was dead, ran past him. The rest were gunned down.

Inevitably there were disputes between commando officers and the maquis—usually over the subtle difference between advising and commanding. Roy Farran found the maquis near his base in the Forest of Chatillon fiercely independent. They wanted only a loose liaison with the commandos and firmly rejected the idea of commando leadership in any of their operations.

Nonetheless, most maquis were reassured by the presence of the commandos and took pride in serving as their comrades-in-arms. U.S. Navy Lieutenant Michael Burke, a member of a Jedburgh team that dropped into the Vosges Mountains, was warmly kissed by welcoming maquis and led off in triumph with his two Jedburgh partners to a camp in the forest. "It was miserably cold that night," Burke recalled, "and there was only one little shed in the woods where we were hiding. All three of us had waterproof sleeping bags, and the maquis didn't have so much as a blanket to spread over them, but they insisted that we sleep inside. It started raining after we turned in, and an hour or so later I heard the door creak open. A shivering Frenchman, soaked to the skin, snuggled down beside us to keep warm." Soon the entire group was jammed inside, making sleep all but impossible. But, said Burke, "we knew those skinny little guys were enjoying their first relaxed night's rest because we were there, and we were glad to be lying beside them."

At the same time, many commando units found themselves forced to curb the extravagant expectations their arrival inspired in the maquis. Derrick Harrison noted that whenever his unit operated far from its drop area in the Yonne valley it encountered isolated maquis bands that refused to believe his jeeps had been parachuted from planes, preferring instead to think they were advance units of the Allied armies. Most of the villages the commandos passed through were under the same misconception. Roy Farran's jeeps, flying Union Jacks, were received with riotous outbursts and a ringing of church bells in premature celebration of liberation.

In the excitement of believing themselves liberated, many villagers incurred the wrath of the Germans, who shot men, women and children in savage reprisal for suspected collaboration with the enemy. In the village of Moussey in eastern France, the Germans interrogated the population on the activities of the 2nd SAS in the area; receiving no satisfactory information, they shipped 210 village men to concentration camps, from which only 70 returned.

Often the commandos themselves were threatened by the attention they received. As Derrick Harrison and his men were trying to slip unobtrusively past German positions near Joigny, they were spotted by villagers. A crowd quickly gathered, hemming in the commandos—and greatly increasing the chances of their being detected by a German patrol. When finally they broke loose and drove on to the next village, the men discovered that word of their arrival had passed by telephone and another crowd awaited them. Knowing the Germans tapped the telephones, the men decided to abandon their itinerary and flee across country.

The commandos lived under extraordinary tension. "Perhaps the worst thing about life behind the lines," Roy Farran recalled, "was the awful feeling of nervousness when hiding in forests. I think it was more the tallness of the trees and the fact that we never saw the sun from one day to another. Every time the leaves rustled or we heard a wild pig running at night, I thought the Germans were creeping up on us. I hoped and prayed the others would not think I was scared."

Partly because their missions were so demanding, not many commandos stayed in France more than a few weeks. Of the 43 SAS operations, the longest was in the Morvan Mountains between Dijon and Nevers, under the command of Lieut. Colonel William Fraser. It began with a drop on the night of June 6, 1944, and continued until September 6. In all, 154 officers and men parachuted into the region, supported by armored jeeps and artillery. Most of their operations were directed against German forces moving from the Côte d'Azur to Normandy, particularly the 9th Panzer Division. In three months, Fraser's men blew up railway lines 22 times, killed or wounded 220 Germans, took 132 prisoners and reported 30 bombing targets to the RAF. The Germans, making one serious attempt to clear them out of the forest, attacked with armored cars and in battalion strength, but Fraser beat them back with brilliant defensive tactics and the aid of a 6-pounder.

By September, with the German armies in full retreat, the commandos' guerrilla functions had almost ended. Now the special forces were urgently needed for another task: to spearhead the fast-rolling Allied armies. One SAS group totaling 700 men was dispatched to northeast Holland, where it operated in the van of the Canadian First Army. It caused so much chaos that the retreating Germans were unable to form a defensive line against the Canadians. In the same area, one and a half squadrons of the 1st SAS—some 180 men—carried out reconnaissance missions for the Canadian 4th Armored Division. Another group of 300 SAS troopers performed the same role for the Polish Armored Division—and later captured German Foreign Minister Joachim von Ribbentrop as he was about to commit suicide in his Hamburg apartment.

On the Jutland Peninsula, Lieut. Colonel Brian Franks combined elements of the 1st and 2nd SAS to form a 430-man strike force that operated with notable daring in front of the Scottish 15th Division, earning the distinction of being the first British unit to enter the German Naval base at Kiel. Such an operation, noted Captain Derrick Harrison, "was not SAS work as we knew it, but it was a job of work." In fact, it was the kind of work that the assault troops of the British 1st and 4th Commando Brigades had been performing since D-Day.

As the Allies drove across the Rhine and the North Ger-

A bomb crater serves as a pen for some of the 850 Germans captured by Commandos at the Rhine River port of Wesel in a surprise attack on the night of March 23, 1945.

man Plain, assault Commandos were at the forefront of the offensive. Their daring was exemplified in the 1st Commando Brigade's crossing of the Rhine at the town of Wesel, where the river was more than 300 yards wide and ran at five knots. Situated on heights, the town was virtually impregnable to frontal attack. But to the west lay a flood plain that was defended only by slit trenches because the Germans had assumed the ground was too soft and too marshy for operations by anything larger than a patrol.

Brigadier Derek Mills-Roberts decided to attempt the unexpected. In a stunning night attack, 1,600 Commandos crossed the fast-flowing river and stormed ashore in brigade strength on the flood plain. They overwhelmed the German trenches and were fighting in the center of Wesel before the Germans could organize their defenses and muster their superior firepower. German troops stumbled out of their cellar billets in a daze to find Commandos in control of the streets and Commando engineers already swinging from girder to girder across the ruined railway bridge to lay a telephone line across the river.

As the Germans fell back from the Rhine, they made skillful use of the natural barriers formed by the rivers crisscrossing the North German Plain. At such points of resistance, the Commandos proved invaluable to the regular Army. At the Weser River they slipped across in darkness and waded through mud and bog up to their waists for three hours to outflank the German defenses and enter the town of Leese from the rear. The surprise was complete. The Commandos sprinted past self-propelled guns facing in the wrong direction and captured an underground rocket factory, complete with technicians and research staff.

At the Aller River, the problem was slightly different. Here the Germans had their backs to the river and were being hard pressed by the 11th Armored Division of the British Second Army. The divisional commander knew that if the German positions crumbled, the enemy troops would flee across the river and blow the bridges as they went. He therefore proposed briefly relaxing the armored pressure while the Commandos slipped behind the German positions and tried to capture the bridges.

Commando scouts discovered that the main-road bridge was too heavily defended to be seized before the Germans could blow it, so they concentrated on the railway bridge a mile downstream. At 11 p.m. two patrols set out, one to overwhelm the sentries on the near bank and the other to swim to the far bank to silence the sentries there. Close behind came No. 3 Commando, moving noiselessly along the river embankment.

The men were unaware that the Germans had picked that same night to retreat and demolish the bridge. As the Commandos approached, there was a thunderous explosion. The closest span of the bridge, which crossed marshy but passable ground, lifted into the air and fell in a mass of twisted metal.

The two patrols reacted almost instantaneously and with great courage. Their men sprinted across the marshy meadow, swarmed up the ruined girders of the bridge and overwhelmed the startled near-bank sentries. Then they raced across the remaining span, suffering several casualties from machine-gun fire. The surviving Commandos dispatched the sentries on the far bank before they, too, could set off explosive charges.

Now that the railroad bridge was secured, the Commandos moved upstream on the far bank, hoping to take the road bridge. They were too late to prevent its being blown by the Germans, but they established a bridgehead and defended it for 48 hours in savage close-quarter fighting. Early on the third day, sappers repaired the bridge enough to allow Allied armor to begin rolling across.

This pattern was repeated all the way to the Elbe—stealthy river crossings by the Commandos at night, followed by circling movements and surprise attacks from the rear. So confident were the Germans in their "unassailable bastions" behind rivers, noted Brigadier Mills-Roberts, that they never learned to anticipate the Commando attacks.

With the crossing of the Elbe in late April, 1945, the war in Western Europe was all but over—and so was the job of the commandos, whether they were functioning as guerrillas or as assault troops. Already units were being withdrawn to England and were looking to the Far East, where special forces engaged against the Japanese had been fighting a far different war.

THE COMMANDOS' COMMANDO

Lord Louis Mountbatten has a smile for a Commando as he makes a final shipboard inspection of a party about to embark on a raid in December 1941.

A WELL-BORN SAILOR WITH A COMMON TOUCH

Wearing his christening robes, the future Lord Louis Mountbatten nestles in the lap of his great-grandmother, Queen Victoria, on July 17, 1900.

The combination of spirit and discipline that distinguished commandos wherever they fought was nowhere more vigorously personified than in the man who, beginning in October 1941, oversaw British Commando undertakings as head of Combined Operations. Lord Louis Mountbatten came of royal stock: His father was a Hessian prince and his mother a granddaughter of Queen Victoria, making him kin to half the crowned heads of Europe. Yet he had an uncommon gift for charming—and leading—ordinary mortals. A 20th Century man blessed with the versatility of an earlier age, he was a daring amateur sportsman, the life of many an elegant dinner party and—within his beloved Royal Navy—a dogged perfectionist and brilliant innovator.

On blood alone, Mountbatten might have claimed high rank and choice assignments. Instead, beginning as a cadet, he built a career on professionalism and hard work—and in the process won the affection of his subordinates and the British public alike.

When war came, Mountbatten at first applied to his command of a destroyer squadron the dash that had brought him peacetime recognition as a sportsman. But the Commandos, once he became their chief, soon found that he had deeper qualities. Often, before the launching of a Commando operation, he minutely inspected the troops about to risk their lives, usually climaxing the visit with an impromptu pep talk. Individually, the men remembered the friendly intensity of his gaze and his grasp of operational details. "I have never been looked at so squarely in the face in my life," recalled one young lieutenant after a Mountbatten inspection, "and he obviously had a great knowledge of the work we were doing. It was an experience of a lifetime."

Lord Louis' connections enabled him to summon top-level support when support was needed; he could and did go straight to the Prime Minister or to his cousin, the King, as the situation required. Such shortcuts did not endear him to some of his peers in the British high command, but they helped him to forge the Commandos into the spearpoint of the eventual Allied reconquest of Europe.

A World War I veteran at 19, First Lieutenant Lord Louis Mountbatten exudes confidence as he stands at the rail of a Royal Navy submarine chaser.

A LIFELONG LOVE FOR THE NAVY

Mountbatten devoted his professional life—and much of his social life as well—to the Royal Navy. Another career, he once said, "never even occurred to me."

He first went to sea as an infant, taken to visit his titled relatives in Germany and Russia; and at five he was sailing on the flagship of the Royal Navy cruiser squadron his German-born father commanded. As a 16-year-old midshipman in World War I, he tasted combat for the first time. And in July 1922, when he married the beautiful Edwina Ashley, granddaughter of an international financier, his shipmates gave him a rousing Naval send-off.

On a picnic in Venice in 1906, young Louis—nicknamed Dickie—wades on the Lido with his father, commander of a Royal Navy squadron in the Mediterranean.

A spanking new Naval cadet, Louis stands outside his parents' home in London in 1913.

First Lieutenant Mountbatten gives his mother and father (just behind, wearing a pale fedora) a tour of his submarine chaser in 1919.

Mountbatten and his bride emerge from an arch of Royal Navy swords after their wedding on July 18, 1922. Below, officers and men from his ship, the Renown, observe the tradition of pulling the bridal car while Londoners throng the curbs. Some newspapers called the event "the wedding of the century."

A DISCIPLINED MAN WITH A ZEST FOR PLAY

His great wealth, athletic good looks and much-publicized fancy for fast cars, motorboats and polo ponies gave Mountbatten a reputation as a playboy. The fact was he took work and play equally seriously, and approached both with the same zest.

His honeymoon in 1922 included a visit to Hollywood where, as a wedding gift, British-born actor Charlie Chaplin made a short film that starred the newly married couple. Mountbatten threw himself into the game of acting *(right)*. But he also recognized film as a potential medium of education, and back at sea he introduced motion pictures for teaching fleet communications to his men.

Lord Louis (left) mimes contrition as Charlie Chaplin offers solace and a Naval aide stands by on a movie set in Hollywood.

Wearing goggles, Mountbatten sits at the wheel of a racing car at the Opel race track in Germany in August 1922. His bride later bought him a powerful car and a 40-knot speedboat that he raced in competitions.

Mountbatten's polo pony bears him onfield for an Army-Navy match in 1933. Teammates said he drilled them "like a Prussian cavalry officer," then replayed their games in slow-motion movies.

Commander Mountbatten (left) pulls an oar during practice with the officers' crew of the destroyer Wishart—fleet champions. An angry loser, he was known to grouse for years over his rare defeats.

The Prince of Wales (center), with Mountbatten at his shoulder, shows off his first tiger in Nepal.

WINNING FRIENDS FOR THE EMPIRE

During the 1920s, Mountbatten made two globe-girdling royal tours of the British Empire as official aide to his cousin and good friend Edward, Prince of Wales and heir to the British throne.

It was a time when national independence movements had begun to stir in the far-flung colonies, especially in India, the pride of the Empire. But the debonair world travelers charmed their hosts at official receptions, glittering balls and elaborate hunting parties, winning friends who would stand by Great Britain when World War II erupted.

Lord Louis and his cousin salute as they drive past a crowd during a visit to the British Crown Colony of Aden in 1921. The innocently worded banner urges Edward to carry a message of fealty to King George V.

Mountbatten stands atop an elephant during the hunting trip in Nepal in 1921. Such excursions strengthened relations with Eastern princes, who supplied the British with troops.

In a lighthearted break from ceremony, the Prince of Wales and Lord Louis dress in the local costume in Japan in 1922. During the visit, Mountbatten discreetly studied Japan's warmaking potential.

A ROYAL MISSION AND WARTIME COMMAND

One of Lord Louis' first missions of World War II was a rather poignant voyage to escort home his cousin Edward, who in 1936 had renounced the British throne for the love of an American divorcée and had been living in exile in France, uncomfortably close to the front lines.

That mission completed, Mountbatten plunged into the fighting. Between 1939 and 1941 he commanded the 5th Destroyer Flotilla and ranged Europe's coasts from Norway to Greece, where his destroyer, the *Kelly,* was sunk beneath him.

Mountbatten's talents and appeal soon vaulted him into even more demanding assignments. At Churchill's urging he became Chief of Combined Operations, coordinating the Commandos' missions with those of the other armed forces. And by 1943 he was Supreme Allied Commander, Southeast Asia, a theater in which commando operations were to lead the drive against the Japanese.

Decked in gold braid that proclaims him an aide-de-camp to the Royal Family, Mountbatten conveys the former Prince of Wales, now the Duke of Windsor, across the Channel from France aboard the destroyer Kelly.

As Supreme Allied Commander in Southeast Asia, Mountbatten reviews the 23rd Indian Division in February of 1944. After the War he became Britain's last Viceroy of India and presided over that nation's attainment of independence.

Vice Admiral Mountbatten briefs Lieut. General Dwight D. Eisenhower in 1942 on the Allied raid on Dieppe, a multinational operation in which a contingent of U.S. Rangers received their baptism of fire.

6

A British major's reconnaissance in a loincloth
Campaigning in a jungle alive with leeches and snakes
Forging a strike force from "jailbirds and racketeers"
Mars Force's thrust to clear the Burma Road
An African regiment with the sting of a tarantula
Probing the swamps with "Lord Louis' Little Navy"
A mission wrecked by a dropped flashlight battery
A Commando lieutenant's heroic last stand

THE JUNGLE LEGIONS

In the spring of 1943, Denis Holmes, a young British major of the 1st Punjab Regiment, shaved off his mustache, put on a loincloth and, carrying a green umbrella against the monsoon rains, set out on a three-month walk behind the Japanese lines in Burma. The unusual mission of Major Holmes was to reconnoiter the land and assess the prospects for British guerrilla action in the Arakan, a coastal province in southern Burma.

Holmes had good luck and encountered no Japanese troops, but he became familiar with another enemy that he described in detail in his journal: It was Burma itself, a shadowy land of uncharted waterways, mangrove swamps and tangled jungle that oppressed him with a sense of loneliness he had rarely known before.

For Western soldiers, Burma was a place of surprising contrasts and unimagined terrors—an unforgiving and alien landscape where the experience gained in other theaters of war often proved to be a misleading guide. In such a setting, Holmes noted dryly in his diary, a man had to make his own plans and devise his own methods. Barefoot and uneasily aware of his conspicuously white arms and legs, Holmes trudged through the rain from village to village, becoming acquainted with the headmen, recruiting villagers as scouts, and assessing the reliability of men who volunteered to serve the British as agents.

Making friends with local fishermen, Holmes persuaded them to take him down the Japanese-held coast in their dugout canoes; he noted details of Japanese fortifications as he went. With the aid of local scouts serving as coolies, he got a precise description of the formidable Japanese fortress at Razabil, with its gun positions tunneled into the hillside. Everywhere he found smoldering resentment of the Japanese, but he also found a pervasive fear. "You will be wishing to go now, sahib, will you not?" the village headman would ask him pointedly at dusk each day, fearful of the reprisals should Holmes be found among them during one of the nighttime raids that were conducted regularly by the Japanese security patrols.

Holmes returned from his lengthy reconnaissance convinced that commando-type operations were essential to any forthcoming offensive in the Arakan. One immediate result was that the Allied Southeast Asia Command decided to strengthen the odd collection of British soldiers, former colonial civil servants and native Burmese who in 1942 had been loosely organized into a unit known as V Force. Partly because Holmes spoke Urdu, a language widely used in Burma, he was given command of V Force and told to whip it into fighting shape. It was a most unmilitary outfit, his former commanding officer warned him, composed of "jailbirds, smugglers, racketeers and all sorts." Holmes took on the challenge with at least a glimmer of understanding—thanks to his three-month hike—of the potential role his unorthodox outfit might play in the retaking of Burma.

V Force was but one of many impromptu outfits born out of the demands of a peculiarly brutal war in that part of Asia. In the Japanese, the Allies were up against a foe who was jungle-wise, tough, tenacious and without mercy. And in the mountains and jungles of Burma, as Holmes and others had discovered, they faced a physical terrain as inhospitable as any in the world. "War can be distorted into disaster more quickly in the jungle than anywhere else," observed Colonel William R. Peers, who fought there with a special detachment of the U.S. Army. "The jungle on your side can spread this disaster to the enemy; with the jungle against you, death explodes in your face."

The Burmese jungle not only covers low-lying areas but climbs the steep mountain ridges, clothing them in giant hardwood trees and enormous creepers that permanently block the light of the sun. Vast areas are given over to bamboo and elephant grass so thick that the only way to get through is to cut a path with a machete. The coastline is fretted with waterways and swamps inhabited by crocodiles and the deadly krite snake. The climate is unhealthy and debilitating. For the most part Burma is hot and humid, with temperatures reaching 115° F. in the shade. But in some regions the temperature may shift more than 20° in an hour, and days that have been hot turn to nights that are bitter cold. During the monsoon season, Burma is one of the wettest places on earth; in some places it rains as much as 15 inches a day.

For commando operations, the terrain was in some ways ideal because of the cover it afforded. But in other ways it was impossibly difficult. Troops operating in the jungle had barely arrived before they were beset by insects and leeches. Some of the leeches were of monstrous size—as long as five inches—and so ubiquitous that they even got into shoes and under bandages. One officer would recall the horror he felt when he examined the foot of one of his men who was limping badly on a long jungle trek. He found that the foot had been virtually eaten away by a hideous, festering leech sore, and that additional sores were spreading up the man's leg. Jungle fighters were assaulted as well by giant red ants, and by an assortment of parasitic, bacterial and viral ills ranging from malaria to a particularly virulent strain of scabies.

Yet in this savage environment the special forces adapted so well that eventually they would boast, with some authority, that they "owned the jungle." The regular Allied forces came to depend on them perhaps more than in any other theater of the War. To troops haunted by the unfamiliar terrors of this alien land, the commando units would become indispensable eyes and ears, assurance against surprise and ambush. Their pervasive presence was "a tremendous boost," recalled Colonel Peers. The regular troops "could feel secure in the knowledge that the guerrillas were far ahead of them, on their flanks and all about them."

The commandos' role was shaped not only by the rigors of the terrain but also by the early history of the fighting in Burma. Early in 1942, the crack Japanese 33rd and 55th Divisions, later reinforced by the 18th and 56th Divisions, had swept through Burma—a self-governing member of the British Commonwealth—in a lightning campaign that stunned and demoralized the Allies. Plentifully equipped with machine guns, trench mortars, mobile artillery and light armor that they used in masterful fashion, the Japanese drove back a scratch force of British, Indian, Burmese and American-led Chinese defenders in a brilliant series of frontal assaults followed by flanking and encircling movements. The Japanese were willing and able to move through the jungle, whereas the Allies stuck largely to the few roads, thus sacrificing the advantages of surprise and mobility.

As a further handicap, the Allied command was badly divided and never could decide on a unified defense. The Americans accused the British of being interested only in protecting India, and the British retorted that the Americans wanted only to keep China in the War. The Chinese vacillated, and Lieut. General Joseph W. "Vinegar Joe" Stilwell, peppery commander of American forces in the area, made no secret of his contempt for China's Generalissimo Chiang Kai-shek.

In the last days of May 1942, the Allied retreat turned into a rout. Battered units of the British and Indian forces limped over the Kalewa-Imphal Road to India—less than half of them got out—while the crumbling Chinese armies withdrew either east toward China or northwest to India via the inhospitable Hukawng Valley. Assessing the enormous loss of men and matériel, General Stilwell said bluntly: "I claim we got a hell of a beating. We got run out of Burma, and it is humiliating as hell. I think we ought to find out what caused it, go back and retake it."

It was not long before Stilwell's call was answered. By the early months of 1943 his British counterpart, General Sir Archibald Wavell, had succeeded in raising and training a number of commando-like units to begin the long and frustrating job of retaking Burma.

One of the first of these units to go into action was a pickup detachment of British, Gurkha and Burmese troops known officially as the 77th Indian Infantry Brigade, and unofficially as the Chindits, a name derived from the fierce sculptured lions that guard Burmese temples. They were recruited and led by Brigadier Orde C. Wingate, an eccentric and brilliant man who often seemed to go out of his way to offend those around him. Wingate seldom bathed, and he sometimes appeared at parties in malodorous fatigues that had seen him through battle. But he was also a brilliant strategist and leader. In Ethiopia in 1941 he had tricked 15,000 Italians into surrendering to him—even though his own force numbered fewer than 1,700.

In Burma, Wingate was to demonstrate his brilliance again, forging a cohesive force out of the disparate men who made up the Chindits. Early in 1943, three thousand Chindits under his command made a three-month-long raid deep into northern Burma, striking at Japanese outposts and wreaking havoc on enemy communications. A year later, Wingate's Chindits, by now 12,000 strong, were back in Burma; they had been air-dropped behind Japanese lines as part of a four-pronged offensive that had been conceived by General Stilwell to drive the Japanese out of the north and open a land route to China. Again the Chindits were effective, but they suffered heavy casualties, which some observers said were the result of their being used more as troops of the line than as commandos. One of the casualties was

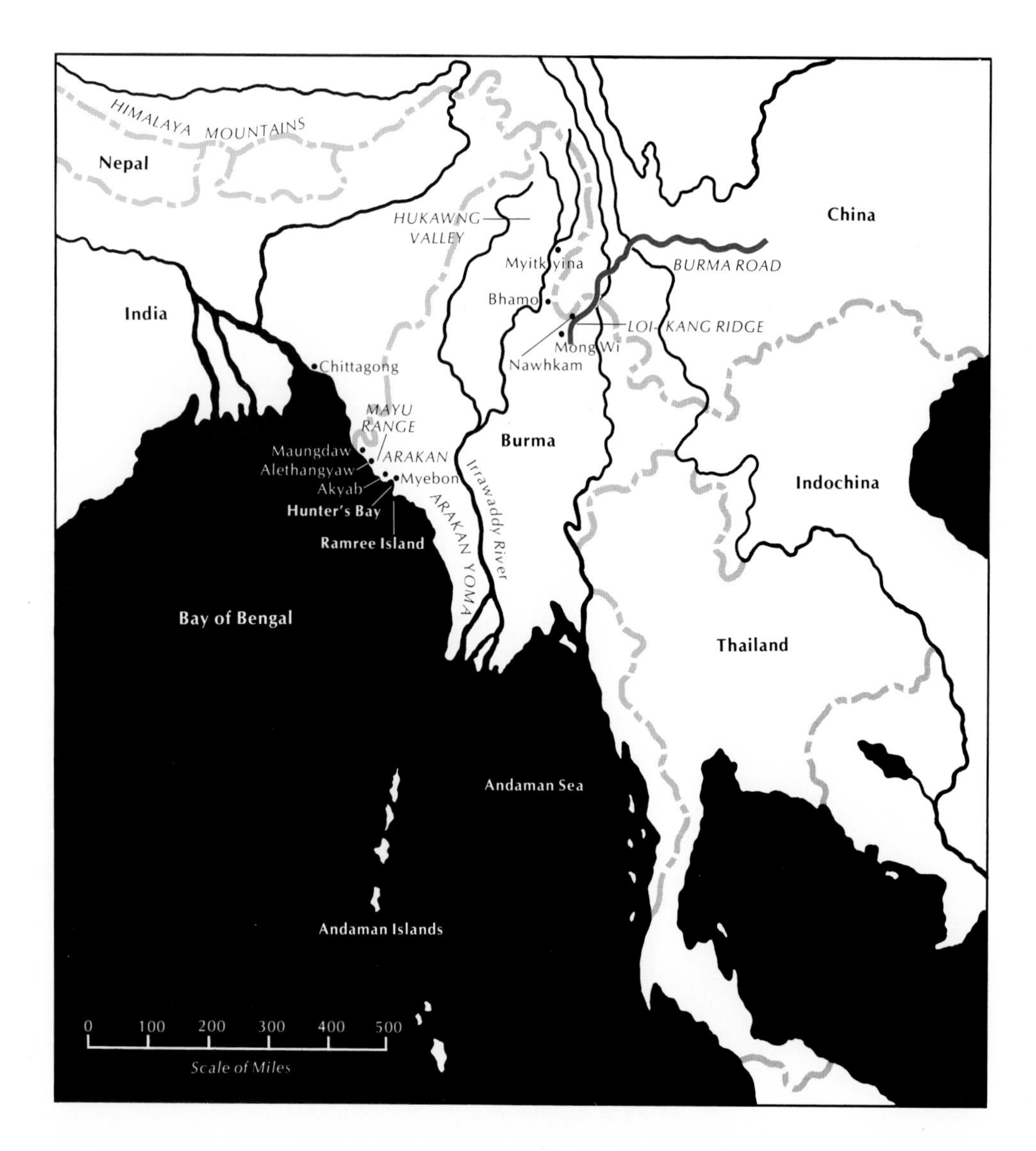

In the Allied campaign to retake Burma, Commandos operated far behind Japanese lines in the northern and central mountains and raided along the west coast. British and American-led Burmese units wrested control of the Burma Road into southern China from the Japanese; Royal Marine Commandos attacked up the streams of the Arakan region, eventually blocking the Japanese retreat.

Brigadier Wingate himself, who was killed in a plane crash.

Much the same fate befell another special unit, Merrill's Marauders, a group of 3,000 American volunteers raised by Brigadier General Frank D. Merrill and trained in India under Wingate's direction. The Maurauders were originally intended to function as a regiment-sized hit-and-run unit that would operate independently and be supplied by airdrop. But Stilwell used them increasingly as an envelopment force that worked in conjunction with the Chinese to try to enclose the Japanese 18th Division in a pincers movement. They performed magnificently; hungry and ridden with sores, and far beyond reach of supplies, they drove themselves to outflank the Japanese again and again, until the Japanese command was compelled to pull back troops from the Chinese front to deal with them. But their casualties were enormous, and critics wondered aloud whether troops so highly trained in commando skills should be used in operations that standard infantry might perform as well.

Perhaps the most unorthodox outfit in Burma was Detachment 101, a daredevil unit of American-led Burmese formed at the behest of General William J. Donovan, Director of the Office of Strategic Services. Detachment 101 was the first American unit trained to operate behind Japanese lines. It came into being with the arrival in India in May 1942 of 21 American recruits, including infantry and Marine officers, engineers and radio technicians. But the majority of Detachment 101 were Kachin tribesmen from the dense jungle along the upper reaches of Burma's Irrawaddy River. These short, rugged men were born fighters, equally at home crossing mountain peaks and following almost invisible tracks through the jungle. The Kachins had an uncanny ability to shadow their foe through the jungle for miles without being seen or heard, and in time the Japanese came to dread them.

From a string of jungle outposts established along a 600-mile front, units of Detachment 101 mounted repeated attacks on Japanese supply lines, blowing up bridges and railway tracks, disrupting communications and providing intelligence for the hard-pressed Allies. Detachment 101's patrols ferreted out Japanese camps and supply installations concealed in the jungle and provided such exact descriptions of local landmarks for pilots of the U.S. Tenth Air Force that the Americans were able to successfully bomb and strafe targets they could not even see. The presence of Detachment 101 patrols in the jungle also lifted the morale of American and British aircrews flying supplies over the "Hump" of the Himalayas from India to China. Now, for the first time, the fliers knew that if they crashed and survived, expert trackers would be coming to try to rescue them. Detachment 101 even had its own air force—a ramshackle assortment of light planes used to supply its men in the field and to bring out the wounded.

During three years of jungle operations, Detachment 101 claimed to have killed a total of 5,447 Japanese, but its importance went beyond its kill rate alone. The constant possibility of guerrilla ambush, at which the Kachins were expert, made the Japanese tense and cautious and ate away at their morale. Allied intelligence officers learned when interviewing captured Japanese soldiers that they rated one Kachin equal to 10 Japanese.

From time to time, detachments of Kachins were lent to other special forces in Burma, including a recently activated long-range penetration group known as the Mars Task Force. The Mars group, under the command of Brigadier General John P. Willey, consisted of two infantry regiments, the 475th and the 124th. Originally a cavalry regiment of the Texas National Guard, the 124th was a colorful outfit. Many of the troopers still wore cut-down riding boots as they hiked through northern Burma.

In November of 1944 the Mars Task Force, supported by Kachin guerrillas, launched a deep penetration strike at Japanese forces and equipment moving along the Burma Road, as part of a general offensive to clear the road for Allied traffic to China. The Mars regiments struck south from Myitkina, following different routes, and then turned east to unite just across the Shweli River. The men traveled light, with only three days of rations and minimal loads of ammunition; after those ran out, the regiments were entirely dependent on airdrops for supplies.

The march was grueling, over narrow trails so steep the men had to rest every minute or so, and even some of the sure-footed pack mules lost their purchase and plunged into ravines. When torrential rains began to fall, the red clay trails became so slippery that the men had to claw their way uphill, discarding cooking utensils, boots and spare fatigues as they went. Crossing the 400-foot-wide Shweli River was a nightmare: Men, mules and two-wheeled carts skidded chaotically down to the water's edge. Once there, the entire column had to make its way across a narrow bamboo bridge that was beginning to be torn apart by the swollen waters of the river.

The miseries of the troops were exacerbated by hunger. Cloud cover prevented airdrops, and food ran out several days before the big transport planes finally managed to get through to drop supplies. The rigors of the march felled some 750 men, many of whom suffered from "march fracture"—a breaking of the arch of the foot from the continued strain of toting field packs up steep trails. One who succumbed was the commanding officer of the 124th regiment, Colonel Thomas J. Heavey, who had to be evacuated from an airstrip hacked out of the scrub near the Shweli River.

The depleted column pressed on, and in a little more than two weeks reached Loi-kang ridge, overlooking the Burma Road. The first Japanese units the task force encountered, in the little hill town of Nawhkam, were taken by surprise and fell back almost without offering a fight.

But surprise is a one-time ally. Control of that sector of the Burma Road depended on possession of the ridge, and once the Japanese had regrouped they fought tenaciously to retain it. Although elements of the Mars Force rapidly occupied the north end of the ridge against only token resistance, they ran into heavy fire as soon as they began moving south. The Japanese on the southern crest had a clear field of fire on the forward positions of the task force and on an alluvial valley below the ridge that Allied transport planes used as a drop zone for supplies. The Japanese were able to lay down such heavy fire against the transports that pilots had difficulty dropping in the area. In a few days the supply situation became critical. Meantime, the Japanese were bringing up reinforcements; among them were first-class troops that a few weeks earlier had fought a desperate battle to hold the

Kachin Rangers on patrol lead their pack ponies down a village road in remote northern Burma. The American-organized guerrillas used elephants and human porters as well as horses to carry their supplies.

Japanese defense line at the Irrawaddy River. Even after being encircled by an Allied force, they had broken out and eluded capture.

For days the battle for control of Loi-kang ridge raged savagely. Units of the Mars Force surged forward in frontal attacks, then fell back in the face of Japanese counterattacks, which were supported by heavy artillery fire. Some of the Allied positions were shelled and attacked for five days without letup, until the men were falling asleep under fire in their foxholes.

Individual acts of heroism abounded. Although bleeding and half-blinded by grenade fragments, and stricken by seeing his own brother cut down, First Lieutenant Jack Knight continued charging Japanese pillboxes with hand grenades until he was himself killed by enemy fire. Private Anthony Whittaker fired three rocket rounds at a pillbox but none of them exploded. Tossing the launcher aside, he rushed the pillbox and knocked it out by slipping grenades through its gun slits. Private Clifton Henderson singlehandedly cleaned out two Japanese machine-gun emplacements. He blasted the first with grenades, then crawled around to the rear door under heavy fire from the second emplacement. Henderson shot down the crew of the first emplacement as the men tried to escape; then he ran inside and turned the machine gun on the second emplacement, silencing it with murderously accurate fire.

The battle for Loi-kang ridge had continued indecisively for two costly weeks when the surviving officers commanding the Mars Force decided on a change in tactics. They sensed that the Japanese on the southern knoll had their attention so fixed on attack from the north that they might be vulnerable to an encircling movement that came up behind them from the south. One night, while elements of the 2nd Battalion staged a diversionary attack from the north, two companies of the 1st Battalion swung around the head of the valley and approached the Japanese positions from the south, taking advantage of a narrow saddle that dipped between two brush-covered knolls. In the morning the two companies attacked, achieving complete surprise and driving the Japanese at last from Loi-kang ridge. Soon Japanese units were falling back all along the line, and within a week Allied trucks were rolling over the Burma Road to China.

Far to the south, in the Arakan, V Force under Major Denis Holmes was fighting a very different kind of war. Here, too, the terrain largely determined the nature of the action. The Arakan is a long, narrow province that slants southwest along a mountain range dividing Burma from India. It then turns south to meet the Bay of Bengal. Wild and mountainous in its northern and central reaches, the Arakan gradually flattens out into a coastal plain that is chopped up into thousands of rice paddies. In many areas, the pattern of the rice fields is broken by serpentine watercourses, or *chaungs,* that overflow with sea water at high tide and become beds of mud when the sea ebbs. Both the Japanese and the Allies found that the plain was virtually impassable to armies, but that smaller units, by relying on local sampans, could traverse it.

Holmes had melded V Force into a remarkably efficient, multiracial unit. He organized levies of Chittagonians—Muslims who originated in the Chittagong district of India and who hated the Japanese with exceptional virulence; they became the most trusted and fearless of V Force scouts. He also brought to V Force the Reconnaissance Regiment of the 81st West African Division. The division, known as the Black Tarantulas, wore a badge that displayed a spider on a yellow field. The 81st was made up of outdoorsmen, strong, enthusiastic raiders, renowned and feared for the skill with which they wielded their long-bladed machetes in close-quarter fighting.

On the attack, the Africans were terrifying. Early on a February morning in 1944, Holmes sent them charging against Japanese gun positions at the village of Damankhali. The sight of the giant figures running out of the dawn mist and the sound of their battle cries sent the Japanese gunners into a blind panic. The Japanese fled and were shot or chopped down. "The Africans were bastards for killing," Holmes noted in his diary—adding that the Tarantulas did not like to take prisoners.

Increasingly, V Force became the eyes and ears of Allied forces in the Arakan. After a raid on the village of Alethangyaw, Holmes brought back papers showing that the Japanese 112th Brigade had been shifted into position to confront the British 7th Division east of the Mayu range. Other V Force scouts reported a supply build-up and the mobilization of Burmese porters in the 112th Brigade's new area of operations. This intelligence strongly suggested a new Japanese offensive.

The offensive came on the 4th of February, when 8,000 Japanese troops encircled the British 7th Division. The division's headquarters was quickly overrun, but because he had been forewarned by V Force, Major General F. W. Messervy, the division commander, was able to set up a defensive position some two miles away. There he announced to his men that they would stand and fight. Aided by airdrops—and by a steady stream of intelligence provided by V Force—Messervy and his division held out for nearly three weeks against wave after wave of Japanese troops. Finally the Japanese withdrew, leaving behind 4,000 dead.

One of V Force's many duties was to supply sampans, or any other kind of water transport it could muster, for the transport of Allied troops through the twisting maze of *chaungs*. Under Holmes's direction, the men assembled and operated a rickety fleet consisting of old wood-fired civilian river steamers, a few motor launches and an assortment of lifeboats. When not running their "navy," the men of V Force gathered intelligence, slipped into the jungle at night to kill unsuspecting Japanese sentries, and guided larger Allied assaults on entrenched Japanese positions.

In all these operations, Holmes remained as personally active as ever, building a reputation for exceptional daring. Once he walked into the village of Lambaguna and coolly mingled with enemy soldiers in the marketplace while a Japanese lieutenant harangued villagers about their responsibilities to the Japanese forces of occupation. Later he led a reconnaissance patrol into the port town of Maungdaw as a crucial preliminary to an anticipated Allied offensive in the Arakan. Having landed nearby by canoe, the patrol probed on foot into the center of town, risking encirclement. They found it deserted.

Hours later, a young lieutenant of the West Yorkshire Regiment was standing outside a command post only three miles from the Japanese lines when he saw a suspicious-looking figure moving toward him through the cold night mist. The man was barefoot and clad only in a dirty loincloth and a ragged khaki shirt. In his hand was a Tommy gun. Crouching, the lieutenant reached for his revolver. Before he had it out of the holster, the figure spoke. "Put it up, man!" he said. "I'm Major Holmes of V Force."

Anxious to meet the advancing regular forces as soon as possible and to report what he had found at Maungdaw, Holmes had abandoned his canoe and walked overland from the deserted port, traveling through territory that was thick with Japanese snipers. After he made his report, the West Yorkshires immediately prepared to move out; they occupied Maungdaw at dawn, turning the town into a supply base, and thereby moved the Allied invasion timetable forward by two weeks.

Closely linked with V Force in these and similar operations was the Small Operations Group, a ragtag collection of mostly British units charged with "providing small parties of uniformed troops trained and equipped to operate against enemy coastal, river and lake areas." Included in the ranks of the Small Operations Group were skilled navigators, ex-

Smiling broadly as he makes a deal, a Kachin Ranger serving with the Mars Task Force in central Burma barters a section of an OSS parachute for a hill dweller's live chicken. Parachutes were much in demand among the Kachins, who made clothing from the material.

pert canoeists, long-distance swimmers, frogmen and sea-reconnaissance scouts trained to swim for miles, using paddleboards, before landing through heavy surf. Together these amphibious operators were known as "Lord Louis' Little Navy" in honor of Lord Louis Mountbatten, who in August of 1943 had become Supreme Allied Commander in Southeast Asia. The venues of the SOG's most daring operations were the sea beaches and the mangrove swamps that fringed the Burma coast.

Beach reconnaissance was hazardous and nerve-racking work. It had to be done swiftly, in complete silence and in the dark. Japanese patrols were on the lookout and at any moment might come softly across the beaches without even flashlights to warn of their approach. Allowing time for canoe transport and swimming ashore, reconnaissance teams rarely got to the beaches before midnight. The men had to be hiding in the jungle or back in their canoes again in scarcely four hours, when the first glimmers of light appeared. Standard departure procedure was for them to swim to some agreed-upon rendezvous, often a large rock rising from the sea, and to signal with shielded flashlights until the canoes came to pick them up.

In dozens of similar operations, beach-reconnaissance teams provided the data on which the eventual amphibious landings of the Arakan campaign were based. Amazingly, they had a low casualty rate, although there were many close calls and some genuine disasters. One Allied team that landed at Ramree Island dropped a single flashlight battery while crossing the beach at night. A fisherman found it the next morning and turned it over to the Japanese; before the reconnaissance team could get off the island, its members were surrounded and gunned down.

One particularly nightmarish mission involved seven canoeists who beached their craft on the shore of Bangtau Bay, in an area of Burma the Japanese had assigned to their ally, Thailand. The canoeists' mission was to scout for possible airfield sites. Four of them tested conditions on the beach while the other three pushed inland through the jungle. They were to rendezvous three nights later. The inland group got to the proposed airfield site after an all-night march, photographed it from the treetops, and took soil samples. On their way back toward the shore they twice had to flatten themselves against the embankment of a road crossing the marshes to avoid Japanese patrols that passed within a few feet of their hiding place. They were spotted by a farmer in a rice field but fled into the jungle and made it back to join the others on the beach, photographing Japanese seaside bunkers on the way.

The men on the beach, however, had been seen by fishermen, and soon Thai police arrived and attacked them. The British soldiers retreated. They then began a desperate two-week flight through the jungle. One after another of the seven were picked off by the pursuing Japanese. Time and again they tried to approach the shore, hoping to rendezvous with their submarine and escape by sea, but by now the beaches were heavily patrolled. One man survived hot pursuit only because he stumbled into a hollow tree, crawled inside it and stayed there all day while the Japanese beat the bushes around him.

Finally only three men remained. They decided to swim to an island half a mile offshore, surprise the crew of a Japanese barge they had seen putting in there, and escape in the barge to islands lying to the west. Emaciated from 17 days of eating nothing but leaves, the three barely survived the swim—and then saw the barge put out to sea before they could reach it. With that hope gone and their strength ebbing, they stumbled into the island's only village and begged for food. The villagers turned them over to Thai Naval officers, who put them in a truck under a tarpaulin and smuggled them out of town past squads of Japanese. They were imprisoned by the Thais for the duration, but they survived.

The risks run by fresh-water patrols on the jungle rivers and in the swamps were no less real than those encountered by the seagoing scouts. As the British in the autumn of 1944 began setting the stage for their drive on Rangoon, the Burmese capital, units of the Small Operations Group were out in the Arakan *chaungs* almost every night, searching for crossing places for the armor and infantry of the XV Corps. Usually they would enter the waterways by motor launch from the sea, muffle the engines, then cautiously probe upstream to within a mile of their objective before they lowered the canoes.

Just finding entry to a *chaung* in the pitch-blackness was a tricky business, and once the men were within the network of uncharted *chaungs* it was all too easy to get lost. There was also constant danger of encountering Japanese patrols concealed along the thickly grown banks or prowling in motorized sampans equipped with searchlights. And any man who slipped overboard to swim, so as not to betray his presence by the soft swish of paddles, was acutely aware that the water was infested with crocodiles and snakes.

One moonless night a Japanese canoe patrolling a narrow *chaung* with thick jungle overhanging each bank collided with two SOG canoes, one after the other. The British canoeists, their faces blackened with grease paint, were taken for natives and were furiously abused in Japanese. Without a word, they slipped away.

On another occasion, four men in a dugout canoe were slipping into a large *chaung* a mile south of Maungdaw when flares suddenly illuminated the sky and Japanese machine guns opened fire. Without hesitation, one of the scouts, a Chittagonian, stood and called in Bengali to the figures on the shore. "We are fishermen," he shouted. "We have been brought in by the tide. We have come to the wrong place." Surprisingly, the bold lie worked. The firing ceased and the flares died away.

Another unit, charged with gathering tidal data obtainable only at dusk, anchored a launch at the mouth of the Myebon River directly beneath a Japanese 75mm battery. The men carried out their mission so coolly that they were never even challenged. Not all of "Lord Louis' Navy" was so fortunate. One group of men who thought they had slipped their canoe successfully past a Japanese patrol one moonless night suddenly were attacked by a motorized sampan and had to paddle desperately through a maze of waterways for two hours before getting clear. As the Japanese became more alert, the British began using motor launches instead of canoes, relying on the launches' speed to help them run through increasingly heavy gantlets of fire.

By the end of 1944 the Japanese were in general retreat from Burma, and the Allied forces began moving into the Arakan. Now large-scale operations would become more important, and so would official Commando formations as opposed to largely improvised units such as V Force. Heavily involved at this stage in the campaign was the British 3rd Commando Brigade, which was made up of the 1st and 5th Commando Battalions, veterans of North Africa and Madagascar, together with two Royal Marine Commando battalions, the 42nd and the 44th. They had been used in Burma before—most notably in a successful landing on the Arakan coast near Alethangyaw that was carried out by the 44th Battalion in March of 1944—but the four units of the brigade had never before operated together. Now they would have the opportunity to do so.

The first mission given the 3rd Commando Brigade was to seize the strategically important port of Akyab, which had dock facilities and an airfield considered essential to the overall Arakan offensive. On January 2, 1945, the largest amphibious force ever seen in Burmese waters assembled for the assault; included in the curious flotilla were old V Force river boats, rice barges and sampans, as well as more conventional naval vessels. The assault craft stormed the

A carbine slung over his field jacket, American Lieut. General Joseph W. Stilwell confers in Burma with his dapper chief, Admiral Lord Louis Mountbatten. Serving as Mountbatten's deputy, the feisty "Vinegar Joe" forged such irregular military outfits as Wingate's Chindits, Merrill's Marauders, OSS Detachment 101 and the Mars Task Force into an international commando army to drive the Japanese from Burma.

beaches at dawn—only to find that the defenders had fled.

It was decidedly an anticlimax, but a good dress rehearsal for the concerted actions that were soon to come. The next 3rd Commando Brigade objective was to cut off the retreat of the Japanese Twenty-eighth Army, which was pouring southward through the Arakan in a desperate attempt to reach the passes over the Arakan mountains before that escape route was blocked by the Allied advance on the east side of the mountains.

The likeliest route open to the Japanese was euphemistically known as the Coast Road; actually it was no more than a rough track that ran along the narrow plain between the sea and the mountains as far as the village of Kangaw, with ramshackle bridges crossing the innumerable *chaungs* along the way. From Kangaw, the road turned inland toward the An Pass and led over the mountains into the interior of Burma. The Small Operations Group was dispatched to confirm that the track was indeed being used. On the morning of January 5, as Motor Launch 439 was slipping cautiously up the Myebon River 10 miles northeast of Akyab, it was suddenly fired upon from the jungle. The patrol had found the Japanese escape route.

The 3rd Commando Brigade now undertook a two-stage operation. Kangaw was the obvious place to cut the road route. Before that could be done, a Japanese force on the nearby Myebon peninsula had to be isolated so that it could not interfere with a Kangaw landing. Accordingly, Brigadier Campbell Hardy, commander of the brigade, ordered his troops to prepare for an amphibious assault on the peninsula. He went on a personal reconnaissance of the Myebon River to determine where his men should land.

Hardy had only recently arrived in the Far East, but he was well known in the Commandos, having taken part in the D-Day landings in Normandy and having been decorated twice. Accompanied by Captain Martin Nott of the Royal Indian Navy, Hardy sailed from Akyab in the sloop *Narbada,* then transferred to a motor launch for the reconnaissance operation up the Myebon.

Chugging slowly up the river, marking a navigable channel with buoys to guide the assault boats, Hardy scanned the jungle banks for possible landing sites. He picked two small beaches, deciding they must be vulnerable to attack because the Japanese had taken the trouble to block them with a line of thick coconut stakes driven into the mud just above the low-water mark.

During the night of January 11, two canoe teams from the Small Operations Group slid into the Myebon River and paddled to one of the beaches designated for the landing. Twenty-five charges with delayed fuses timed to detonate at 6:30 the following morning were fixed to the coconut stakes by shadowy figures working quietly in the darkness. The canoeists were safely back on board the motor launch out at sea when the explosives went off, blowing a gap 25 yards wide in the beach defenses.

Up the river next morning came a motley collection of 50 old vessels, including five tank landing craft that had been allocated to the Southeast Asia theater only after they had been pronounced unserviceable for use in the Mediterranean. The 3rd Commando Brigade was transported in two Royal Indian Navy sloops, four minesweepers and three infantry landing craft.

Twenty minutes before the first assault waves were scheduled to go in, the Royal Air Force screamed overhead with a similarly mixed collection of aircraft—Thunderbolts, Lightnings, Spitfires, Hurricanes and Mitchells—to attack the Japanese defenses.

At 8:30 a.m., high tide, the first landing craft found the gap in the stakes. Under cover of a thick smoke screen laid from the air, No. 42 Commando raced ashore, closely followed by No. 5 Commando. Mines claimed several victims on the beach and one of the assault craft was hit by a shell from a 75mm gun, but most of the first wave reached shore safely and stormed the few Japanese positions still manned after the air bombardment.

The success of the planes in silencing most of the Japanese guns prevented a massacre when the other two Commando units came in to land. The men of Nos. 1 and 44 Commandos were supposed to land on the second beach, but by mistake they followed the first troops in. The tide was receding rapidly as the landing craft came to a halt some 400 yards from the beach in about 12 inches of water. The first group of Commandos jumped out—and immediately sank up to their knees in slime.

"It was murderous," said Quartermaster Sergeant Henry Brown of No. 1 Commando. "There was about three feet of thick, gray mud under the water. You'd get one foot out of the mud and then get stuck with the other. On we plodded, helping each other as best we could. All this time we could hear small-arms fire from the beach, but luckily it was not coming in our direction."

The landing took three hours, and the last floundering men had to be dragged out of the mud with ropes. Lead tanks of the 19th Indian Army Lancers, assigned to support the Commandos, also got stuck. Eventually most of the tanks were landed on the second beach after Gurkha porters attached to the brigade, using only hand tools, had smashed an opening through rocks bordering the beach.

By nightfall the Commandos had secured a bridgehead and made some progress inland, ousting the Japanese from their positions one by one. At dawn the following day they surged on, passing through the village of Myebon. Overcoming stiff opposition, they next captured Kantha, a village lying astride a swampy creek some four miles farther ahead. The tanks, taking advantage of the fact that the Japanese had no long-range antitank guns, overran first one defensive position and then another. One of the tanks clambered up a steep, pagoda-topped hill to crush a Japanese machine-gun post; then suddenly the tank toppled over and somersaulted backward down the hill, coming to rest on its turret. One man's leg was broken but, miraculously, that was the only injury the crew sustained.

Hard on the heels of the advancing Commandos came the 74th Indian Brigade, which eventually took up a defensive position north of the Myebon peninsula. With the Japanese forces on the peninsula thus bottled up, the Commandos began to prepare for a landing at Kangaw. The village was known to be heavily defended against an overland approach from the north or an assault from the Myebon River. But the Small Operations Group had been busy exploring the dark green labyrinth of creeks and swamps south of the village, and the men had discovered three navigable *chaungs* that could be used for an attack. It would mean a detour of nearly 27 miles along tortuous winding creeks in the heart of enemy territory, but the mangrove trees were thick enough to veil the Commandos and give them a reasonable chance of surprise.

The Commandos reembarked on Indian Navy ships from the same beach they had landed on a few days earlier; the ships sailed south and east and anchored for the night of January 21 in Hunter's Bay. On the morning of January 22, the Commandos transferred to landing craft and began the lengthy journey through the hot and stinking mangrove corridors that wound toward Kangaw. One of the *chaungs* was so thickly overgrown that the men had to lower the mast of their landing craft and hack a pathway through the overhanging trees.

The first objective for the Commandos was a wooded ridge rising steeply from the rice paddies west of the village and dominating the area. It was designated Hill 170, and No. 1 Commando, the most experienced unit in the brigade, was given the job of seizing it.

At 1 p.m., after a two-and-one-half-hour journey through the mangrove forest, the leading craft with No. 1 Commando on board nosed into a small beach only 200 yards from Hill 170. Once more, RAF aircraft came over the jungle to plaster the Japanese defenses and lay a smoke screen. The Commandos stormed ashore and overwhelmed the first positions, which were taken completely by surprise—they were, in fact, facing the wrong way.

By nightfall, No. 1 Commando had cleared most of the southern part of the hill and its men were well dug in along the ridge. No. 5 Commando and the brigade headquarters occupied the southern slopes, No. 42 Commando had seized a narrow neck of land connecting the hill with a *chaung,* and No. 44 Commando carried out a successful night attack to capture a lower ridge between Hill 170 and the village of Kangaw.

That same night, the Japanese launched a determined counterattack against the forward positions of No. 1 Commando, hurling grenades as they advanced with reckless courage. It was a confused fight. One Japanese soldier bringing forward a box of fresh ammunition reached the edge of a slit trench; the trench was occupied by Commandos, who shot him. Another group of Japanese burst into a bamboo hut that was occupied by a Commando lance corporal and his squad, who were later said to have dispatched their unwelcome visitors by strangling them. The attack was finally beaten back at midnight; one Commando had been killed and 11 wounded. At daybreak, nine Japanese bodies were counted around the Commando position.

At 10 o'clock that morning, elements of No. 1 Commando, supported by artillery, took over the northern part of the hill, strengthening their hold considerably. During the day, the men of No. 44 Commando were heavily shelled by 75mm guns at close range and then were charged by screaming Japanese troops. Before the attack was repulsed, the British had lost 16 men killed and 45 wounded.

During the next few days, the Allies consolidated their overall hold on the bridgehead, moving up supplies and reinforcements, including Sherman tanks, while the Commandos sat tight on Hill 170, enduring almost ceaseless bombardment by artillery. Colonel Peter Young recalled watching a line of Indian soldiers bringing up supplies and witnessing a particular act of gallantry: "When some shells came down a man was hit and the rest scattered, all save for one gallant soul who knelt down beside the wounded man and there amidst the shells patched up his wounds. It was all done in a cool and matter-of-fact way," Young said, "but in that flat exposed paddy it called for an iron nerve to behave as he did."

On January 24, the 51st Indian Brigade landed at the bridgehead and attacked the village of Kangaw. After severe fighting, they managed at last to cut the so-called Coast Road. For a few days there was a welcome lull, but it was followed by one of the most ferocious battles of the Arakan campaign. At 5:45 a.m. on January 31, the Japanese, trying to drive the British off Hill 170 and regain the village, opened up the heaviest artillery bombardment so far against the northernmost positions, held by No. 4 Troop of No. 1 Commando. The bombardment was followed immediately by a massive infantry assault. The two dozen men of No. 4 Troop watched from their slit trenches as hundreds of Japanese soldiers crawled up the hill toward them.

Packed aboard assault craft, men of the British 3rd Commando Brigade move upstream for a surprise attack on Kangaw during the Arakan campaign in Burma in January 1945. The Commandos hit the village from its swampy and lightly defended southern side, cutting the Japanese escape route along Burma's southeast coast.

To the rear of No. 4 Troop, a suicide squad of Japanese assault engineers who were armed with pole charges broke into the tank position in an attempt to put the three Shermans there out of commission. A platoon of Bombay Grenadiers who had been assigned to protect the tanks grappled with the Japanese. Nevertheless, the Japanese succeeded in destroying one tank and damaging a second beyond immediate repair. The third tank escaped, crashing down the far side of Hill 170 and straight over a slit trench that was occupied by two startled Commandos, who survived only by ducking at the last moment.

Meanwhile, No. 4 Troop had come under heavy mortar and machine-gun fire. One of its section commanders, Lieutenant George Knowland—who had recently been commissioned after distinguished service as a sergeant with the Commandos in Sicily—moved coolly from trench to trench, oblivious of the danger, offering his men a few final words of encouragement.

When the attack started in earnest, Commandos higher up the hill were astonished to see Knowland running about in the open, throwing belts of ammunition into the trenches, occasionally lobbing a grenade at the enemy or firing a burst from his rifle. After one of his forward light machine-gun crews was wounded, he sent back for replacements and ran up to man the gun himself until help arrived. The Japanese were hiding in a depression only about 10 yards from the trench, so Knowland stood up to get a better shot and fired from the hip while medical orderlies tried to help the wounded men in the trench. Two Commandos moving up to take over the machine gun were hit before they could get to the position; Knowland kept firing until three more replacements arrived.

As another wave of Japanese infantry closed on his position, Knowland sent the crew of a 2-inch mortar to replace casualties in a forward trench, then he picked up the mortar and stood in the open, firing with the base of the weapon resting against a tree. His first shell killed six Japanese. When he ran out of shells, he raced back through a hail of grenades, mortar and machine-gun fire to get more.

Knowland's incredible luck soon deserted him, though his courage did not. With the Japanese surging forward, he had no time to get more ammunition; so he picked up his rifle and emptied the magazine in the direction of the enemy, then grabbed a Tommy gun from one of his wounded men. While defiantly firing this weapon, he was hit and killed. Fourteen of his men were casualties, six of his forward emplacements had been overrun, but his heroic stand had saved the day. The Japanese never got farther than No. 4 Troop's position. Knowland was posthumously awarded the Victoria Cross.

Fighting continued until dusk. The Japanese had determined to retake Hill 170 whatever the cost. If they could win back its commanding slopes, they would have a chance of destroying the Allied bridgehead, which it overlooked, and of cutting off the Indian brigade in Kangaw. Despite help from the remaining Sherman tanks, counterattacks by Commandos on the hill failed to dislodge the Japanese from the six forward positions they had seized.

The pause ended the following morning, when Japanese infantry resumed the attack with unabated ferocity. The Japanese set up three machine-gun posts on spurs around the northern slope of the hill and kept up a steady fire on the Commando trenches. No. 6 Troop of No. 1 Commando launched a counterattack to try to dislodge one of the machine guns, but lost half its men in the attempt.

Wave upon wave of Japanese soldiers carrying rifles with

long, thin bayonets forged up the hill; wave upon wave was beaten back. The Commandos fired their machine guns until the barrels overheated. Casualties were replaced immediately; at one gun 12 men were hit, one after the other. "It came to a point," said young Private L. J. Greenslade, "where a man who was climbing up the hill with ammunition or supplies was the next minute being brought down on a stretcher."

But the Commandos' casualties were nothing compared to those of the Japanese, whose bodies now littered the lower slopes of the hill. "It was horrible," said Colonel Ken Trevor, who as commanding officer of No. 1 Commando had directed the battle throughout from a forward slit trench. "There were piles and piles and piles of dead bodies in front of us." At twilight on February 1, RAF Thunderbolts attacked the Japanese positions; then the battle subsided once more with the tropical darkness.

Next morning, the Japanese were gone. "When it was light enough," said Peter Young, "I went forward to look at the ground where No. 4 Troop had fought. I could hardly move a step without treading on a dead Jap. There were nearly 300 of them. Almost the first of our own dead I saw was Knowland. He lay on his back, one knee slightly raised, with a peaceful smiling look on his face, his head uncovered. Farther down the hill, 20 paces from our forward trenches, two of our men lay side by side as if they had together made a private counterattack. I saw one soldier dead in his slit trench with three Japs. They were dead too."

The carnage was unlike anything the Commandos in Burma had seen before or wished to see again. An astonishing 340 bodies were counted in an area approximately 100 yards square around No. 4 Troop's trenches. Accounts vary, but according to some estimates as many as 2,000 Japanese soldiers died in the attempt to retake Hill 170; they were buried by bulldozers. A total of 45 Commandos had been killed and 90 had been wounded.

A special order of the day was issued by Lieut. General Philip Christison, commander of the XV Corps, to which the 3rd Commando Brigade was attached. The Commandos' "indifference to personal danger and resourceful determination in adversity have been an inspiration to all their comrades," he said. Critics who had sometimes complained that commandos were doing the work of infantry in the Burma campaign had nothing to complain about here: The Kangaw assault had combined surprise, tactical daring, and a tenacity that confounded the Japanese. It was, said General Christison to his troops, "the decisive battle of the Arakan campaign."

The success of the Kangaw assault also served as vindication, if more were needed, of the validity of the commando idea. No forces during the whole of World War II had been greeted with greater initial skepticism nor placed under more intense pressure to prove their worth in the field. From Norway to France to the Sahara they did so—imaginatively and often heroically. In Burma, Major Denis Holmes had watched with satisfaction as the attitude of regular Army officers working with his V Force irregulars changed from hostility to tolerance and finally to dependence and trust. In Europe, British Commandos liked to repeat as their most valued accolade General Sir Bernard L. Montgomery's dry remark that Commandos he had observed were "real proper chaps"—high recognition from that demanding and often cantankerous regular Army man. Beyond question, the special forces had proved the value of individual initiative and daring in an increasingly mechanized war.

OBJECTIVE: BOUGAINVILLE

Using a captured Japanese field gun and its ammunition, U.S. Marine Raiders fire at snipers hidden in the jungle of the Pacific island of Bougainville.

AN ISLAND MISSION FOR MARINE RAIDERS

Marine Raiders, many wearing jungle camouflage, clamber from their transport into a landing barge off Bougainville on November 1, 1943.

Shortly after Pearl Harbor, President Roosevelt—impressed by the British Commandos—encouraged the U.S. Marine Corps to establish special units designated Marine Raiders. They were to carry out independent amphibious raids and guerrilla missions, and to collaborate with other Marine units as the spearhead of larger operations. During the first year of the Pacific war, on the long, island-hopping road to Tokyo, they raided deep behind Japanese lines on Guadalcanal and staged a surprise assault on Makin Island. Then, in November 1943, some 2,000 men of the 2nd and 3rd Marine Raider Battalions were assigned to the vanguard of a division-strength Marine invasion of Bougainville, the largest and northernmost of the Solomon Islands.

The Japanese had fortified Bougainville with five air bases and 40,000 troops. Outnumbered, the Americans chose their invasion point with an eye to surprise: Cape Torokina, on the remote southwestern coast—a place bordered by steep, narrow beaches pounded by the surf of the Solomon Sea and cut off from the rest of Bougainville by mountains, swamp and jungle.

Surprise was evident when the Marines struck on November 1. The Japanese had only a few hundred men and a single 75mm gun at Cape Torokina. "Because we thought the poor topographical features would hamper enemy operations," a Japanese colonel later conceded, "we did not anticipate a landing here and were not adequately prepared."

Nevertheless, Japanese infantry, protected by pillboxes hidden in the dense jungle that fringed the shore, peppered the Raiders' landing craft with rifle fire as they approached the beach in the vanguard of the Marine assault. "As the gate of our barge clanged down, we ran out as nervous as bulls entering the bull ring," wrote William Chickering, a correspondent for *Time* and *Life* who made the landing.

The 2nd Raider Battalion quickly captured trenches dug 30 yards from the beach, and the 3rd Battalion required a day to mop up a Japanese garrison entrenched on an islet just offshore. Then the Marine Raiders started inland on a new—and more difficult—mission.

Ignoring the dead Japanese sprawled before them, Raiders dig in at Cape Torokina. One correspondent summed up the landing as "dramatic but bloody."

A DEADLY CONTEST OF HIDE-AND-SEEK

Once the pillboxes had been cleared and the division had dug in, the Marine Raiders headed up a barely discernible jungle path. Their mission: to capture the junction of two trails, named Piva and Numa Numa, that linked Japanese air bases and served as the primary overland approach to Cape Torokina. By taking the trail junction, the Raiders would sever the Japanese line of supply and reinforcement.

The junction was less than three miles inland, but it would take the Marine Raiders seven hard days to get there. Their advance through the thick undergrowth was slowed by Japanese snipers, who seemed able to melt away into the jungle.

Adapting to the situation, the Raiders tried some unusual tactics to bring the Japanese out of hiding. Sometimes they sent a light tank or armored vehicle well ahead of them. Such a target often proved irresistible, even maddening; in one instance a Japanese soldier broke cover and, bayonet fixed, charged a tank—which crushed him under its treads. When the muck was too deep or the jungle too dense for armor, the Raiders used specially trained scout dogs to sniff out the Japanese.

About 300 yards from the junction, both sides finally were forced into the open and into what one American officer called "a toe-to-toe slugging match, the Raiders and Japanese screaming at one another." After two days of fighting at close quarters, the Japanese retreated and the junction fell.

Framed by the doorway of one of 25 ironwood- and coconut-log pillboxes captured at Torokina, a Marine Raider searches for surviving Japanese soldiers.

Carrying full packs, Raiders hike single file up a narrow footpath. The Japanese, said an American sergeant, "brought out a whole bag of tricks"—among them pretending to surrender, then opening fire.

A point man signals waiting Marine Raiders that the route ahead of them is clear. To make sure, the Marines often sprayed the trees indiscriminately with automatic-weapons fire.

Kneeling in a water-filled foxhole, Raiders await a counterattack. The dead Japanese soldier lying at their right was a victim of the Raider tactic of withholding return fire until the enemy reached point-blank range.

A patrol advances, using Doberman pinschers and German shepherds. "Not only did the dogs smell out hidden Japanese," an officer wrote, "but their presence gave confidence."

A Raider private named Lansley sprints past a disabled American light tank to join waiting Marines. The Japanese had used the body of a dead Marine (lower left) as bait. Lansley responded by singlehandedly attacking a Japanese machine-gun nest and killing eight Japanese.

In a trench, a medic (upper right) comforts one wounded Marine while another receives plasma.

Raiders take a wary break. As one man said, the jungle could be "an unhealthy place to rest."

Relieved by other troops after they have captured the main trail junction in their sector of Bougainville, U.S. Marine Raiders trudge on toward their next

assignment. In January of 1944 the Raiders were disbanded as a specially designated outfit and the men were dispersed among other Marine battalions.

BIBLIOGRAPHY

Alsop, Stewart, and Thomas Braden, *Sub Rosa: The O.S.S. and American Espionage*. Reynal & Hitchcock, 1946.
Altieri, James, *The Spearheaders*. Bobbs-Merrill, 1960.
Arena, Nino, *Aquile Senza Ali: I Paracadutisti Italiani nella Seconda Guerra Mondiale*. Milan: U. Mursia & Co., 1972.
Aron, Robert, *De Gaulle Before Paris*. London: Putnam, 1962.
Bartz, Karl, *The Downfall of the German Soviet Service*. London: William Kimber, 1956.
Beaumont, Roger, *Military Elites*. Bobbs-Merrill, 1974.
Bekker, Cajus, *The Luftwaffe War Diaries*. Transl. and ed. by Frank Ziegler. Ballantine Books, 1966.
Belgian Ministry of National Defense, History Section, *The Battle of Fort Eben-Emael, 10 and 11 May 1940 (The 7th Infantry Division on the Albert Canal*, Part 8). Transl. by U.S. Army, Historical Division, European Command, no date.
The Best from Yank, the Army Weekly. World Publishing, 1948.
"Bougainville." *Life*, November 29, 1943.
Brockdorff, Werner, *Geheimkommandos des Zweiten Weltkrieges*. Munich: Welsermühl, 1967.
Brown, Anthony Cave, *Bodyguard of Lies*. Harper & Row, 1975.
Buckley, Christopher, *Norway: The Commandos: Dieppe*. London: Her Majesty's Stationery Office, 1951.
Butler, Rupert, *Hand of Steel*. London: Hamlyn Paperbacks, 1980.
Clark, Alan, *Barbarossa: The Russian-German Conflict, 1941-1945*. William Morrow, 1965.
Clarke, Dudley, *Seven Assignments*. London: Jonathan Cape, 1948.
Colby, William, and Peter Forbath, *Honorable Men: My Life in the CIA*. Simon and Schuster, 1978.
Collins, James L., Jr., ed., *The Marshall Cavendish Illustrated Encyclopedia of World War II*. Marshall Cavendish Corporation, 1972.
Cook, Graeme, *Commandos in Action*. Taplinger Publishing, 1974.
Cowles, Virginia, *The Phantom Major*. London: Collins, 1958.
Crichton-Stuart, Michael, *G Patrol*. London: William Kimber, 1958.
De Jong, Louis, *The German Fifth Column in the Second World War*. Transl. by C. M. Geyl. University of Chicago Press, 1956.
Durnford-Slater, John, *Commando*. London: William Kimber, 1953.
Edwards, Roger, *German Airborne Troops, 1936-1945*. Doubleday, 1974.
Ellis, John, *The Social History of the Machine Gun*. Pantheon, 1976.
Farran, Roy, *Winged Dagger*. London: Collins, 1948.
Fergusson, Bernard, *The Watery Maze*. London: Collins, 1961.
Foley, C., *Commando Extraordinary*. London: Longmans Green, 1954.
Foot, M. R. D.:
Resistance. London: Eyre Methuen, 1976.
SOE in France. London: Her Majesty's Stationery Office, 1966.
Ford, Corey, *Donovan of the OSS*. London: Robert Hale, 1971.
Frank, Benis M., and Henry I. Shaw Jr., *Victory and Occupation: History of U.S. Marine Corps Operations in World War II*. Historical Branch, G-3 Division, Headquarters, U.S. Marine Corps, 1968.
Frost, John, *A Drop Too Many*. London: Cassell, 1980.
Gardner, Hugh H., *Guerrilla and Counterguerrilla Warfare in Greece, 1941-1945*. Office of the Chief of Military History, Department of the Army, 1962.
Gilchrist, Donald, *Castle Commando*. London: Oliver & Boyd, 1960.
Halsey, William F., and J. Bryan III, *Admiral Halsey's Story*. McGraw-Hill, 1947.
Harrison, D. I., *These Men Are Dangerous*. London: Cassell, 1957.
Heilbrunn, Otto, *Warfare in the Enemy's Rear*. Praeger, 1963.
Hislop, John, *Anything but a Soldier*. London: Michael Joseph, 1965.
Hoffmann, Peter, *The History of the German Resistance, 1933-1945*. Transl. by Richard Barry. The MIT Press, 1977.
Hogg, Ian V.:
The Complete Illustrated Encyclopedia of the World's Firearms. A & W Publishing, 1978.
The Complete Machine Gun: 1885 to the Present. London: Phoebus, 1979.
Höhne, Heinz, *Canaris*. Doubleday, 1979.
Hough, Richard:
Mountbatten. Random House, 1981.
Mountbatten: 80 Years in Pictures. Viking Press, 1979.
Howe, George F., *United States Army in World War II, Mediterranean Theater of Operations. Northwest Africa: Seizing the Initiative in the West*. Office of the Chief of Military History, Department of the Army, 1957.
James, Malcolm, *Born of the Desert*. London: Collins, 1945.
Keyes, Elizabeth, *Geoffrey Keyes of the Rommel Raid*. London: George Newnes, 1956.
Kirby, S. Woodburn, *The War against Japan*:
Vol. 3, *The Decisive Battles*. London: Her Majesty's Stationery Office, 1962.
Vol. 4, *The Reconquest of Burma*. London: Her Majesty's Stationery Office, 1965.
Kriegsheim, Herbert, *Getarnt, Getäuscht und Doch Getreu: Die Geheimnisvollen Brandenburger*. Berlin (West): Bernard & Graefe, 1959.
Ladd, James, *Commandos and Rangers of World War II*. St. Martin's Press, 1978.
Landsborough, Gordon, *Tobruk Commando*. London: Cassell, 1956.
Lassen, Suzanne, *Anders Lassen VC*. London: Muller, 1965.
Lepotier, Adolphe August Marie, *Raiders from the Sea*. Transl. by Mervin Savill. London: William Kimber, 1954.
Leverkeuhn, Paul, *German Military Intelligence*. Praeger, 1954.
Lloyd Owen, David, *The Desert My Dwelling Place*. London: Cassell, 1957.
Lockhart, Bruce, *The Marines Were There*. London: Putnam, 1950.
Lodwick, John, *The Filibusters*. London: Cassell, 1947.
Lovat, Lord, *March Past*. London: Weidenfeld & Nicolson, 1978.
Lucas Phillips, C. E.:
Cockleshell Heroes. London: Wyman & Sons, 1957.
The Greatest Raid of All. London: Heinemann, 1958.
The Raiders of Arakan. London: Heinemann, 1971.
MacArthur, Douglas, *Reports of General MacArthur: The Campaigns of MacArthur in the Pacific*, Vol. 1. U.S. Government Printing Office, 1966.
McIntyre, Peter, *Peter McIntyre: War Artist*. Wellington, New Zealand: A. H. & A. W. Reed, 1981.
Macksey, Kenneth, *The Partisans of Europe in World War II*. London: Hart-Davis, 1975.
Maclean, Fitzroy, *Eastern Approaches*. London: Jonathan Cape, 1949.
Mason, David, *Raid on St. Nazaire*. Ballantine, 1970.
Maund, L. E. H., *Assault from the Sea*. London: Methuen, 1974.
Millar, George, *The Bruneval Raid*. Doubleday, 1975.
Mills-Roberts, Derek, *Clash by Night: A Commando Chronicle*. London: William Kimber, 1956.
Mrazek, James E., *The Fall of Eben Emael: Prelude to Dunkerque*. McKay, 1970.
Parrish, Thomas, ed., *The Simon and Schuster Encyclopedia of World War II*. Simon and Schuster, 1978.
Peers, William, *Behind the Burma Road: The Story of America's Most Successful Guerrilla Force*. Little, Brown, 1963.
Peniakoff, Vladimir, *Popski's Private Army*. Crowell, 1950.
Petrow, Richard, *The Bitter Years: The Invasion and Occupation of Denmark and Norway, April 1940-May 1945*. Morrow Quill Paperbacks, 1974.
Playfair, I. S. O., *The Mediterranean and Middle East*:
Vol. 2, *The Germans Come to the Help of Their Ally*. London: Her Majesty's Stationery Office, 1956.
Vol. 3, *British Fortunes Reach Their Lowest Ebb*. London: Her Majesty's Stationery Office, 1960.
Vol. 4, *The Destruction of the Axis Forces in Africa*. London: Her Majesty's Stationery Office, 1966.
Ramsay, Winston G., ed., "Eben-Emael." *After the Battle* magazine, No. 5. London: Battle of Britain Prints, 1974.
Roskill, S. W., *The War at Sea, 1939-1945*:
Vol. 3, Pt. 1, *The Offensive, 1st June 1943-31st May 1944*. London: Her Majesty's Stationery Office, 1960.
Vol. 3, Pt. 2, *The Offensive, 1st June 1944-14th August 1945*. London: Her Majesty's Stationery Office, 1961.
Saunders, Hilary St. George, *The Green Beret*. London: Michael Joseph, 1949.
Shaw, Henry I., Jr., and Douglas T. Kane, *Isolation of Rabaul (History of U.S. Marine Corps Operations in World War II*, Vol. 2). Historical Branch, G-3 Division, Headquarters, U.S. Marine Corps, 1963.
Shaw, William B. K., *The Long Range Desert Group*. London: Collins, 1945.
Shirer, William L., *The Rise and Fall of the Third Reich*. Simon and Schuster, 1960.
Skorzeny, Otto, *Skorzeny's Secret Missions*. E. P. Dutton, 1951.
Spaeter, Helmuth, *Die Brandenburger: Eine Deutsche Kommandotruppe*. Munich: Walter Angerer, 1978.
Strutton, Bill, and Michael Pearson, *The Secret Invaders*. London: Hodder & Stoughton, 1958.
Swinson, Arthur, *Desert Strike Force*. Ballantine, 1971.
Terraine, John, *The Life and Times of Lord Mountbatten*. Holt, Rinehart & Winston, 1980.
Toland, John, *Adolf Hitler*. Doubleday, 1976.
Truscott, Lucian K., *Command Missions: A Personal Story*. Dutton, 1954.
Updegraph, Charles L., Jr., *U.S. Marine Corps Special Units of World War II*. History and Museums Division, Headquarters, U.S. Marine Corps, 1972.
Warner, Philip, *The Special Air Service*. London: William Kimber, 1972.
Whiting, Charles, *Skorzeny*. Ballantine, 1972.
Yank—the GI Story of the War. Duell, Sloane & Pearce, 1947.
Young, Peter:
Commando. Ballantine, 1969.
Storm from the Sea. London: William Kimber, 1958.

PICTURE CREDITS

Credits from left to right are separated by semicolons, from top to bottom by dashes.

COVER and page 1: Imperial War Museum, London.

THE STORMING OF EBEN EMAEL—6-8: Ullstein Bilderdienst, Berlin (West). 9: Presse-Seeger, Albstadt, Federal Republic of Germany. 10, 11: Bundesarchiv, Koblenz. 12, 13: Bundesarchiv, Koblenz—Imperial War Museum, courtesy *After the Battle* magazine, London; Süddeutscher Verlag Bilderdienst, Munich. 14, 15: Jiri Jiru, courtesy Musée Royal de l'Armée et d'Histoire Militaire, Brussels; Imperial War Museum, courtesy *After the Battle* magazine, London (2). 16: Imperial War Museum, courtesy *After the Battle* magazine, London—Bundesarchiv, Koblenz. 17: Jiri Jiru, courtesy Musée Royal de l'Armée et d'Histoire Militaire, Brussels—Bundesarchiv, Koblenz. 18, 19: Bildarchiv Preussischer Kulturbesitz, Berlin (West).

A NEW BREED OF SOLDIER—22: Map by Tarijy Elsab. 23: Keystone Press, London. 24: Imperial War Museum, London. 26, 27: Art by John Batchelor, London. 28: Brigadier Peter Young, England. 29: Imperial War Museum, London. 32, 33: Painting by R. Eurich, courtesy Imperial War Museum, London (LD 3475). 34: Imperial War Museum, London. 36: U.S. Army. 37: Derek Bayes, courtesy The Commando Association, London. 39: Bibliothek für Zeitgeschichte, Stuttgart. 40: Brigadier C. E. Lucas Phillips, Surrey, England.

A FIERY PROVING GROUND—42-49: Imperial War Museum, London. 50, 51: Pathé News, Inc., except top right, Imperial War Museum, London. 52, 53: Popperfoto, London; Pathé News, Inc. (2)—Imperial War Museum, London. 54-57: Imperial War Museum, London.

FORGING A KILLER FORCE—58, 59: Keystone Press, London. 60: U.S. Army. 61: Documentation Française, courtesy Archives Tallandier, Paris. 62: Imperial War Museum, London—Keystone Press, London. 63: Derek Bayes, courtesy The Commando Association, London—U.S. Army (2). 64: Imperial War Museum, courtesy Archives Tallandier, Paris—U.S. Army. 65: Imperial War Museum, London, except bottom right, UPI. 66: Imperial War Museum, London. 67: U.S. Army—Imperial War Museum, London. 68: Imperial War Museum, London. 69: Imperial War Museum, London—Documentation Française, courtesy Archives Tallandier, Paris. 70: U.S. Army—Imperial War Museum, London. 71: Keystone Press, London—Wide World. 72, 73: Imperial War Museum, London.

RAIDERS OF THE SAHARA—76, 77: Map by Tarijy Elsab. 80-83: Imperial War Museum, London. 86: Major General D. L. Lloyd Owen, courtesy Imperial War Museum, London. 88, 89: R. P. Lawson, England. 90: U.S. Army.

ROVERS IN A SEA OF SAND—92, 93: Major General D. L. Lloyd Owen, courtesy Imperial War Museum, London. 94, 95: Imperial War Museum, London. 96, 97: Left and top right: Imperial War Museum, London. 98, 99: R. P. Lawson, England; Imperial War Museum, London (2). 100, 101: Major General D. L. Lloyd Owen, courtesy Imperial War Museum, London; Imperial War Museum, London; Major General D. L. Lloyd Owen, courtesy Imperial War Museum, London—R. P. Lawson, England. 102, 103: Imperial War Museum, London.

A WORLD OF HARSH BEAUTY—104, 105: Ray Cranbourne, from *Peter McIntyre: War Artist* by Peter McIntyre, published by A. H. & A. W. Reed Ltd., Wellington, New Zealand, 1981. 106: New Zealand Army. 107-111: Ray Cranbourne from *Peter McIntyre: War Artist* by Peter McIntyre, published by A. H. & A. W. Reed Ltd., Wellington, New Zealand, 1981.

THE WATERBORNE IRREGULARS—114: H. G. Hasler, Lochgilphead, Argyll, Scotland. 115: Map by Tarijy Elsab. 116: H. G. Hasler, Lochgilphead, Argyll, Scotland. 117: Adapted from a drawing by H. G. Hasler from *Cockleshell Heroes* by C. E. Lucas Phillips, published by William Heinemann Ltd., London, 1956. 120: C. Clabby, Plymouth, England; from *Cockleshell Heroes* by C. E. Lucas Phillips, published by William Heinemann Ltd., London, 1956; I. Mackinnon, Glasgow, Scotland; from *Cockleshell Heroes* by C. E. Lucas Phillips, published by William Heinemann Ltd., London, 1956—from *Cockleshell Heroes* by C. E. Lucas Phillips, published by William Heinemann Ltd., London, 1956 (2); H. G. Hasler, Lochgilphead, Argyll, Scotland; W. E. Sparks, Canvey Island, Essex, England. 124: Adapted from a drawing by James Ladd. 126: Imperial War Museum, London.

MASTERS OF DECEPTION—130: Map by Tarijy Elsab. 131: Bundesarchiv, Koblenz. 132: Ullstein Bilderdienst, Berlin (West). 133: David Kahn Collection. 135, 137: From *Getarnt, Getäuscht und Doch Getreu: Die Geheimnisvollen Brandenburger* by Herbert Kriegsheim, published by Bernard & Graefe, Berlin (West), 1959. 139: Bundesarchiv, Koblenz. 140: Imperial War Museum, London.

ITALY'S INNOVATIVE ARSENAL—142-147: Courtesy Nino Arena, Rome. 148: Courtesy Nino Arena, Rome—Ufficio Storico, Stato Maggiore Marina, Rome (2). 149: Courtesy Nino Arena, Rome. 150, 151: Courtesy Nino Arena, Rome; Ufficio Storico, Stato Maggiore Esercito, Rome.

PHANTOMS IN ARMS—154: Map by Tarijy Elsab. 155: Derek Bayes, courtesy The Commando Association, London. 157: Photo Lapi-Viollet, Paris. 158, 159: from *SOE in France* by M. R. D. Foot, HMSO, London, 1966, reproduced with the permission of the Controller of Her Majesty's Stationery Office. 161: D. I. Harrison, London. 164: Imperial War Museum, London.

THE COMMANDOS' COMMANDO—166, 167: Imperial War Museum, London. 168-170: Broadlands Archives, England. 171: The Press Association Ltd., London—BBC Hulton Picture Library, London. 172: Broadlands Archives, England. 173: Keystone Press, London—Broadlands Archives, England. 174, 175: Broadlands Archives, England, except center, UPI. 176, 177: Broadlands Archives, England, except inset, UPI.

THE JUNGLE LEGIONS—180: Map by Tarijy Elsab. 182-186: U.S. Army. 188: Brigadier Peter Young, England.

OBJECTIVE: BOUGAINVILLE—192, 193—U.S. Marine Corps. 194: Wide World. 195, 196: William C. Shrout for *Life*. 197-199: U.S. Marine Corps. 200, 201: U.S. Marine Corps, except top right, U.S. Marine Corps, courtesy UPI. 202, 203: U.S. Marine Corps.

ACKNOWLEDGMENTS

For help given in the preparation of this book, the editors wish to express their gratitude to Walter Angerer, Munich; Marie-Claire Anthonioz, Musée de l'Ordre de la Libération, Paris; Nino Arena, Rome; Brigadier R. A. Bagnold, OBE, FRS, Kent, England; Armande Bourgoin, Paris; Colonel Oreste Bovio, Ufficio Storico, Stato Maggiore Esercito, Rome; Henry Brown, MBE, General Secretary, Commando Association, London; Maurice Chauvet, Paris; William E. Colby, Washington, D.C.; Colonel Maurice Courdesses, Fondation Général Leclerc, Saint-Germain-en-Laye, France; Jacques Delarue, Paris; Guy de Pierpont, Liège, Belgium; Deutsches Institut für Filmkinde, Wiesbaden, West Germany; Dutch Commando Corps, Roosendaal, Netherlands; P. G. Eekman, Vlissinger, Netherlands; Jack Elliot, The Smithsonian Institution, Washington, D.C.; F. O. Finzel, Oberkirchen, West Germany; Colonel Roger Flamand, Bligny-sur-Ouche, France; Ulrich Frodien, Süddeutscher Verlag, Bilderdienst, Munich; General Carlo Gay (Ret.), Caserta, Italy; Donald Gilchrist, Ayr, Scotland; Gérard Guicheteau, Paris; H. G. Hasler, Argyll, Scotland; E. C. Hine, Imperial War Museum, London; Ian V. Hogg, Worcestershire, England; Gunnery Sergeant William K. Judge, USMC, Chief, DAVA Still Photographic Depository, Marine Corps Historical Center, Washington, D.C.; Heidi Klein, Bildarchiv Preussischer Kulturbesitz, Berlin (West); Dr. Roland Klemig, Bildarchiv Preussischer Kulturbesitz, Berlin (West); James Ladd, Nottinghamshire, England; Colonel Ian Lapraik, DSO, OBE, MC, TD, Buckinghamshire, England; Dr. R. P. Lawson, Calne, England; Claude Lévy, Institut d'Histoire du Temps Présent, Paris; Brigadier General Jan Linzel, Military Attaché, Embassy of the Netherlands, Jakarta, Indonesia; Major General David Lloyd Owen, CB, DSO, OBE, MC, Norwich, England; Brigadier C. E. Lucas Phillips, OBE, MC, Surrey, England; Général Jacques Massu, Neuilly-sur-Seine, France; Peter Masters, Art Director, General Services Administration, Washington, D.C.; Peter McIntyre, Wellington, New Zealand; Françoise Mercier, Institut d'Histoire du Temps Présent, Paris; Serge Michel, "La Rahla," Paris; Elizabeth Moore, *Illustrated London News*, London; Colonel James E. Mrazek, USA (Ret.), Bethesda, Maryland; Daphne M. Mundinger, Paris; Meinrad Nilges, Bundesarchiv, Koblenz, West Germany; P. W. Pavey, Imperial War Museum, London; Brigadier G. L. Prendergast, Inverness-shire, Scotland; Hannes Quaschinsky, ADN-Zentralbild, Berlin, DDR; Marianne Ranson, Institut d'Histoire du Temps Présent, Paris; C. De Reiter, Elst, Netherlands; Vladimir Remeš, Prague; Jacqueline Sarazac, Serres-Castets, France; Axel Schulz, Ullstein Bilderdienst, Berlin (West); Carlo Segers, Brussels; Kenneth L. Smith-Christmas, Registrar/Curator, United States Marine Corps Museum, Washington, D.C.; W. E. Sparks, Canvey Island, England; David Stirling, DSO, OBE, London; Regina Strather, DAVA Still Photographic Depository, Marine Corps Historical Center, Washington, D.C.; Wolfgang Streubel, Ullstein Bilderdienst, Berlin (West); Lieut. Colonel Michel Terlinden, Brussels; Brigadier Kenneth Trevor, CBE, DSO, Chester, England; J. Tuynman, Vlissinger, Netherlands; Helmut Wenzel, Celle, West Germany; M. J. Willis, Imperial War Museum, London.

The index for this book was prepared by Nicholas J. Anthony.

INDEX

Numerals in italics indicate an illustration of the subject mentioned.

G

H

I

J

K

L

M